Elizabethan Narrative Poems

THE ARDEN SHAKESPEARE STATE OF PLAY SERIES

General Editors: Lena Cowen Orlin and Ann Thompson

Macbeth: The State of Play, edited by Ann Thompson
Othello: The State of Play, edited by Lena Cowen Orlin
The Revenger's Tragedy: The State of Play, edited by Gretchen E. Minton
The Sonnets: The State of Play, edited by Hannah Crawforth, Elizabeth Scott-Baumann and Clare Whitehead
Titus Andronicus: The State of Play, edited by Farah Karim-Cooper

Elizabethan Narrative Poems

The State of Play

Edited by
Lynn Enterline

THE ARDEN SHAKESPEARE
LONDON • NEW YORK • OXFORD • NEW DELHI • SYDNEY

THE ARDEN SHAKESPEARE
Bloomsbury Publishing Plc
50 Bedford Square, London, WC1B 3DP, UK
1385 Broadway, New York, NY 10018, USA
29 Earlsfort Terrace, Dublin 2, Ireland

BLOOMSBURY, THE ARDEN SHAKESPEARE and the Arden Shakespeare logo
are trademarks of Bloomsbury Publishing Plc

First published in Great Britain 2019
This paperback edition published in 2021

Copyright © Lynn Enterline and contributors, 2019

Lynn Enterline and contributors have asserted their rights under the Copyright,
Designs and Patents Act, 1988, to be identified as the authors of this work.

Cover image © Shutterstock

All rights reserved. No part of this publication may be reproduced or transmitted
in any form or by any means, electronic or mechanical, including photocopying,
recording, or any information storage or retrieval system, without prior permission
in writing from the publishers.

Bloomsbury Publishing Plc does not have any control over, or responsibility for, any
third-party websites referred to or in this book. All internet addresses given in this
book were correct at the time of going to press. The author and publisher regret any
inconvenience caused if addresses have changed or sites have ceased to
exist, but can accept no responsibility for any such changes.

A catalogue record for this book is available from the British Library.

Library of Congress Control Number: 2019941515.

ISBN:	HB:	978-1-3500-7336-4
	PB:	978-1-3501-9763-3
	ePDF:	978-1-3500-7338-8
	eBook:	978-1-3500-7337-1

Series: Arden Shakespeare The State of Play

Typeset by RefineCatch Limited, Bungay, Suffolk

To find out more about our authors and books visit www.bloomsbury.com
and sign up for our newsletters

CONTENTS

Series preface vii
Notes on contributors viii

Introduction: On 'schoolmen's cunning notes' 1
Lynn Enterline

Part One   Reckoning with rhetoric

1 'Reck'ning' with Shakespeare's Orpheus in *The Rape of Lucrece* 21
Jenny C. Mann

2 Poetry at the limits of rhetoric in Shakespeare's *The Rape of Lucrece* 45
Rachel Eisendrath

Part Two   Debating *mimesis*

3 Epic Oenone, pastoral Paris: Undoing the Virgilian *rota* in Thomas Heywood's *Oenone and Paris* 71
Joseph M. Ortiz

4 'Arte with her contending, doth aspire T'excell the naturall': Contending for representation in the Elizabethan epyllion 95
Andrew Fleck

5 Learning to read with *Lucrece*   119
   Catherine Nicholson

Part Three   Epyllia, masculinity and sexuality

6 From discontent to disdain: Thomas Lodge's *Scillaes Metamorphosis* and the Inns of Court   143
   Jessica Winston

7 Love will tear us apart: Campion's *Umbra* and Shakespeare's *Venus and Adonis*   167
   John S. Garrison

8 Love loves: *Venus and Adonis*, *Venus and Anchises*   189
   Stephen Guy-Bray

Part Four   Classicism and mercantile capital

9 Crossing the Hellespont: The erotics of the everyday in Marlowe's *Hero and Leander*   207
   Jane Raisch

10 'Unthriftie waste': Epyllia, idleness and general economy   237
   Barbara Correll

Appendix   257
Index   258

SERIES PREFACE

The Arden Shakespeare
State of Play
Series Editors: Lena Cowen Orlin and Ann Thompson

This series represents a collaboration between King's College London and Georgetown University. King's is the home of the London Shakespeare Centre and Georgetown is the home of the Shakespeare Association of America (SAA). Each volume in the series is an expedition to discover the 'state of play' with respect to specific works by Shakespeare. Our method is to convene a seminar at the annual convention of the SAA and see what it is that preoccupies scholars now. SAA seminars are enrolled through an open registration process that brings together academics from all stages of their careers. Participants prepare short papers that are circulated in advance and then discussed when the seminar convenes on conference weekend. From the papers submitted, the seminar leader selects a group for inclusion in a collection that aims to include fresh work by emerging voices and established scholars both. The general editors are grateful for the further collaboration of Bloomsbury Publishing, and especially our commissioning editors Margaret Bartley and Mark Dudgeon.

NOTES ON CONTRIBUTORS

Barbara Correll is Associate Professor of English at Cornell University. She has a PhD in Comparative Literature from the University of Wisconsin and is the author of *The End of Conduct: Grobianus and the Renaissance Text of the Subject* (1996) and co-editor of *Disgust in Early Modern English Literature* (2016). She has published essays on Shakespeare, Donne, Marlowe, Erasmus, and others.

Rachel Eisendrath is Assistant Professor of English and Chair of the Medieval and Renaissance Studies Program at Barnard College, Columbia University. She is the author of *Poetry in a World of Things: Aesthetics and Empiricism in Renaissance Ekphrasis* (2018).

Lynn Enterline is Nancy Perot Professor of English Literature at Vanderbilt University, where she specializes in early modern literature, classical antecedents, gender studies and literary and rhetorical theory, ancient to modern. She received a BA from Oxford in Classics and a PhD in English from Cornell University. Her most recent monograph is *Shakespeare's Schoolroom: Rhetoric, Sexuality, Emotion* (2012) and she is currently working on a new book, *Epic Discontent: On the Critical Potential of Passionate Character*.

Andrew Fleck is Associate Professor of English at the University of Texas at El Paso where he teaches early modern British literature. He has published articles on sixteenth-century poetry, prose and drama in *Modern Philology*, *Studies in Philology*, *SEL* and *JMEMS*.

John S. Garrison is Associate Professor of English at Grinnell College, where he teaches courses on early modern literature and culture. He holds a BA in English from the University of California, Berkeley, and a PhD in English from the University of California, Davis. He is the author of *Friendship and Queer Theory in the Renaissance* (2014), *Glass* (Bloomsbury, 2015) and *Shakespeare and the Afterlife* (2018).

Stephen Guy-Bray is Professor of English at the University of British Columbia. He specializes in Renaissance poetry and queer theory and is author, co-author and editor of several books in those fields; the most recent is *The Age of Thomas Nashe: Text, Bodies, and Trespasses of Authorship in Early Modern England* (2013). His monograph, *Shakespeare and Queer Representation*, is forthcoming.

Jenny C. Mann is Associate Professor of English at Cornell University. She received her BA from Yale University and her PhD from Northwestern University. She is the author of *Outlaw Rhetoric: Figuring Vernacular Eloquence in Shakespeare's England* (2012). She is currently at work on a new project titled *The Trial of Orpheus: Renaissance Poetics and the History of Knowledge* and is also co-editing a special issue of *Philological Quarterly* titled 'Imagining Early Modern Scientific Forms'.

Catherine Nicholson is Associate Professor of English at Yale University, where she teaches and writes about Renaissance literature, including essays on Shakespeare, Marlowe, Spenser, sixteenth-century rhetorical handbooks and the art of common-placing. She is the author of *Uncommon Tongues: Eloquence and Eccentricity in the English Renaissance* (2014) and is currently working on a second book project, *Spenser's Readers*, which uses Spenser's famously difficult poem as the focal point of an experiment in reading with and against reception history.

Joseph M. Ortiz is Associate Professor of English at the University of Texas, El Paso. He received his BA from Yale University and his PhD from Princeton University. He is the author of *Broken Harmony: Shakespeare and the Politics of Music* (2011).

Jane Raisch is Lecturer in Renaissance and Early Modern Literature at the University of York with a doctorate in Comparative Literature from the University of California, Berkeley. Her research focuses on early modern English Hellenism, the histories of fiction and scholarship and early print culture. She recently published an article on the reception of Lucian in Thomas More's *Utopia* in *English Literary History*.

Jessica Winston is Professor of English at Idaho State University, where she specializes in sixteenth-century drama and poetry. She is the author of *Lawyers at Play: Literature, Law, and Politics at the Early Modern Inns of Court, 1558–1581* (2016), which was awarded the 2017 Joseph L. Andrews Legal Literature Award from the American Association of Law Libraries. She is also co-editor of *Elizabethan Seneca: Three Tragedies* (2012). Her new projects focus on closet drama and Tudor drama in performance.

Introduction

On 'schoolmen's cunning notes'

Lynn Enterline

This volume traces dynamic conversations that took place in narrative verse in London between 1589 and the early 1600s, when Shakespeare and a coterie of similarly educated dramatists, poets and lawyers composed and published erotic minor epics in response to one another. Elizabethan epyllia have been described as the day's literary avant-garde; as experimental, competitive, rhetorically and poetically self-conscious, metamorphic and suffused with subversive eroticism. At once learned and provocative, these poems draw largely on Ovidian material but also on the poetry of Virgil and Musaeus. They unfold in mythic, imagined worlds far removed from urban London – and far from England, for that matter. But despite the apparent remove, minor epics allowed classically educated poets to engage in wide-ranging investigations of sixteenth-century expectations for proper masculine conduct – whether institutional, economic, national, poetic, emotional or sexual. Investigating the complexities of this literary conversation, the following essays extend the ongoing, vigorous reassessment of humanism's unintended consequences.[1] And they do so, moreover, by drawing attention to the diverse and often sceptical forms that early modern classicism could take in the hands of those educated according to the 'new' Latin pedagogy that bore within it traces of Tudor England's educational institutions: grammar schools, universities and the Inns of Court.

Shakespeare's Ovidian narrative poems expose the ways that contemporary pedagogy might not achieve its stated goals, veer off in unforeseen directions, or unleash startling reflections on the relationships between poets and their teachers. Where Lucrece rails against the forensic techniques taught in 'skill-contending schools' as inadequate to her 'case' (1018), and rebukes Tarquin by asking, 'wilt thou be the school where Lust shall learn?' (617), his Venus recalls the obtuse *praeceptor amoris* from Ovid's *Ars amatoria*, bringing a poem deemed scandalous into public view while satirizing humanist pedagogues: Venus conducts a failed 'lesson' in desire based on imitation ('O, learn to love; the lesson is but plain / And once made perfect, never lost again').[2] Venus' copious rhetorical manoeuvres eventually goad Adonis into declaring himself an 'orator too green' to refute her 'theme' of love, which he disdains, though he tries to argue his case nonetheless (806; 770).[3] Neither poem could have been written had their author not attended one of those 'skill-contending schools', and both presume a similarly educated audience. Though Lucrece dismisses the verbal facility necessary to both grammar school and legal training as 'idle', 'unprofitable', and 'weak' –

> Out, idle words . . .
> Debate where leisure serves with dull debaters;
> To trembling clients be you mediators:
> For me, I force not argument a straw,
> Since that my case is past the help of law
>
> (1016–22)

– Shakespeare was hardly alone among minor epic poets to cast a critical eye on the declared benefits of humanist pedagogical methods.

For example, when Thomas Lodge, member of Lincoln's Inn, launched the vogue for epyllia by publishing *Scillaes Metamorphosis* (1589), he put the idea of pedagogy at the heart of his poem. Opening on the banks of the river Isis in Oxford, where he had once studied (MA Trinity College, 1581), Lodge invents a god who rebukes the heartsick narrator for not having attended properly to his lessons. 'Thy books have schoold thee from this fond repent', Glaucus chides, because the narrator's woe indicates that he has failed to absorb what 'schoolmen's cunning notes' reveal about the vicissitudes of desire (4.3; 7.1).[4] In *Salmacis and Hermaphroditus* (1602), Francis Beaumont, member of the Inner Temple, adopts a narrator who is similarly dubious about the efficacy of the forensic skills inculcated by a legal education. Not long into a poem made up of 'wanton lines' about 'wanton speeches' from the 'beauteous Nymph', Salmacis (1; 73l; 692), the narrator takes Jove on a detour to the court of Astrea, goddess of justice. There, the narrator tells us, 'the dewe of justice ... did seldome fall, / And when it dropt, the drops were very small' (163–4). Jove himself must pay a fee to find Astrea – and is eventually robbed completely – while moving through an early modern version of *Bleak House*: Astrea's hall is 'Full of darke angles and of hidden ways / Crooked Maenanders, infinite delays' (177–8).

And in *Hero and Leander* (1598), Marlowe's ostentatiously digressive narrator ends the first book with an aetiological detour to explain why the classical 'Learning' exhibited in his epyllion is less than useful (465). Indeed, it brings penury: 'guile keeps learning down', and 'he and Povertie' will 'always kiss' (482, 470). Marlowe also converts the humanist commonplace of verbal *copia* ('wealth or fullness of speech') into a cascading series of images for jewellery, gems, gold and treasure only to take Leander to the bottom of the sea where the only 'use' for such wealth is to be turned into the 'ground' for erotic 'sport':

> [T]he ground
> Was strewd with pearle, and in low corrall groves,
> Sweet singing Meremaids, sported with their loves
> On heapes of heavvie gold, and tooke great pleasure
> To spurn in carelesse sort the shipwracke treasure.
>
> (2.160–4)

His pointed feminine rhyme, pleasure/treasure, counters educators' claims for *copia*'s moral and social benefits.[5] In response to humanist faith that knowledge of ancient rhetoric contributed to personal advancement and improved the commonwealth, Elizabethan epyllia indulge in excess, superfluous ornament, indirection and digression – the narrative stuff of squandered time and useless pleasure.

The essays here bring a variety of current critical methodologies and questions to bear on *Venus and Adonis* (1593), *The Rape of Lucrece* (1594) and the many Ovidian erotic narratives with which Shakespeare engaged – or that engaged, in turn, with his. Readers will find entire essays devoted to his two minor epics, others that take a comparative approach, moving between poems by Shakespeare and those by other contemporary authors, and still others that focus largely on non-Shakespearean texts. Rather than proceed by author or chronology, this book offers four sections that draw attention to the chief, interlocking problems with which these writers were all preoccupied. (For ease of reference, an appendix provides a chronological list of epyllia discussed in the collection.) Taken as a whole, these essays demonstrate how classical rhetorical training in general and Ovid's *Metamorphoses* in particular gave early modern writers a highly developed, shared set of ancient myths, tropes, figures and generic conventions within which to interrogate contemporary poetic norms as well as received categories of social distinction. They rely upon the important work of James Ellis and William Weaver on what the institutional contexts of the Inns of Court and grammar schools reveal about the connection between a rhetorical education and definitions of masculinity in the period.⁶ But several scholars in this volume draw conclusions about humanism's impact on Tudor masculinity that differ from Ellis and Weaver, as well as from one another – evidence of the lively state of debate in early modern studies about the intertwined histories of sexuality and emotion. Ellis and Weaver approach epyllia by focusing on stories about young men in transition from puberty to adult life; and Ellis develops a genealogical argument that 'the epyllion invents, through its reinterpretation of Ovidian mythical narratives, a new version of heterosexuality' based on a 'fraternal and contractual model'.⁷ But several of these essays lean more toward Georgia Brown's view that 'the epyllion ... acknowledges a fluidity between male and female desires', 'between male and female identities', and creates 'parallels between the tactics employed by authors of those literary texts, and those conventionally ascribed to women' in a culture organized around father-power.⁸ This collection does not propose a solution to these interpretive differences; rather, it engages in what will no doubt remain a spirited debate.

Sharing a general understanding that epyllia are indebted to (and often reflect upon) humanist curricula and the discursive habits imparted in its educational institutions, each author in this volume explores how far minor epics also subject widespread humanist aspirations and assumptions to scrutiny and critique. Among them: the virtual equivalence between poetry and rhetoric (*dulce et utile*); the personal and social benefits of *imitatio* based on reverence for ancient precedent; the utility of classical learning for the English commonwealth; definitions of proper masculine conduct (economic, national, military, institutional, poetic, emotional and sexual); and the presumed hierarchy of value between elite classical and popular vernacular culture. In particular, so-called 'minor epics' put pressure on the imperial epic's vision of martial and civic masculinity, often distancing themselves from what one scholar calls the 'cultural high ground' granted Virgil's *Aeneid* in the humanist curriculum.⁹ In other words, the following essays examine the ways that epyllia challenge conventional categories of social distinction based on classical authority and precedent, paternal primacy, and the purported moral and social efficacy of eloquence. Classicizing yet challenging, epyllia mobilize ancient narratives, rhetorical figures and generic codes to estrange sixteenth-century norms by proposing virtual worlds with alternative modes of representing, thinking, feeling, loving, spending time and bearing witness. Beyond interrogating classicism's direct social usefulness, moreover, Tudor minor epics engage in thought experiments about ancient and early modern rhetorical and poetic theory, asking readers to consider the aesthetic (as well as ethical) consequences of training in ancient rhetoric and England's debt to the Greco-Roman past. If there is any genre that invites an interpretive perspective that Joel Altman calls a 'rhetorical anthropology', it is the Elizabethan epyllion.[10]

Epyllion, minor epic, Ovidian erotic narrative, Elizabethan narrative poetry: I've used these names and phrases interchangeably. The variety of terms borrowed or invented to categorize the poems in question gives a sense of their allure as well as their difficulty. Critics rarely are satisfied with any one of these labels. Yet they persist because each seems to grasp some crucial aspect of this brief, contentious, yet popular literary vogue. What counts as an Elizabethan 'epyllion' is far from settled and will likely remain so. Anthologies differ about which poems are in and which out; and critics who take up the genre still feel it necessary to list which epyllia make up the body of poems under study.[11] The question of genre remains as complex and unsettled now as when Clark Hulse observed, in 1981, how closely epyllia resemble historical 'complaint' poems.[12] The boundaries of the genre remain porous: in its intriguing affinities with other poetic modes, the minor epic operates as a 'mixed' genre that draws whatever 'identity' it has by way of its engagement with, as well as difference from, other literary and rhetorical forms.[13] Given that Ovid's stories about change, hybridity, category crisis and liminal transition inspire these poems, the non-identity of the 'genre' attests to its Ovidian origins and commitments.

The epyllion allowed many of the major Elizabethan poets to experiment with the social and poetic parameters of appropriate masculine conduct. But they are, at the same time, expansive and fluid enough to engage actively with the increasingly popular poetry of ventriloquized female complaint. Shakespeare's Venus and Lucrece, Lodge's Scilla and her sympathizing nymphs, Heywood's Oenone, John Weever's Melliflora (*Faunus and Melliflora*, 1600) and Beaumont's Salmacis all struggle with the theory and practice of ancient rhetoric. Even Marlowe's Hero, who has far less to say than Leander, knows an 'Orator' when she hears one: 'Who taught thee Rhetoricke to deceive a maid?' (340, 338). Such characters remind us that minor epics, while written by men who have acquired the cultural capital of 'the father tongue', nonetheless remain closely attentive to female desires and grievances.[14] Indeed, the narrators who adopt 'female' voices in these poems tend to stress their protagonists' knowledge of rhetoric and its liabilities, forge distinct alliances with them, or suggest that such characters might be surrogate figures for either poets or readers.

For example, Shakespeare's Venus adopts the stance of a Petrarchan lyric poet, in which case her failure to persuade and unrequited woe come with the literary territory. His Lucrece is the only character in the poem to use paper and ink; and in her complaint, she tries to lend a 'tongue' to Hecuba and Philomela just as the narrator lends one to her (1465). Heywood's Oenone combines the programmatic dimension of Ariadne's lament in Ovid's *Heroides* with that of the *Metamorphoses*' Orpheus: she weeps at the water's edge, begging 'rocks' and 'streams' to become animate and asking the surrounding animals to 'howle, & lament' with her (128–30).[15] Weever's Melliflora, mistakenly thinking Faunus has been killed by a boar, cuts 'dolefull Sestines, mourning epitaphs' into trees (721). And Melliflora's skills in erotic *suasoria* are arguably better than Faunus'.[16] Where Faunus falters on initial approach – 'Mistrusting each word which his wit had done . . . He tore his papers, cast away his pen . . . the more he studied, the worse it grew' (190–8) – Melliflora is the first to deliver an effective invitation to meet

(220–35). For her part, Beaumont's Salmacis displays a working knowledge of contemporary literary history when she woos Hermaphroditus, entreating him by closely imitating Shakespeare's Venus. Salmacis compares him to Pygmalion's statue, calling him 'A flinty heart within a snowy breast', inviting readers to remember Venus's 'flint-hearted boy' who 'burns with bashful shame' (*Venus*, 95, 49). Like Adonis before him, Beaumont's Hermaphroditus 'knew not what love was, yet love did shame him, / Making him blush, and yet his blush became him' (*Salmacis*, 661–2). And imitating Shakespeare's language of entangled eyes, Beaumont invents a new erotic drama: Hermaphroditus nearly succumbs to her, but stops when he sees himself reflected in Salmacis's eyes. And so the nymph rebukes him, like Venus before her, for being another Narcissus, 'the peevish elfe, / Lov'd of all others' but who 'needs would love himself' (705–6). And as Rachel Eisendrath analyses, even in *Lucrece* – a poem whose plot revolves around the violent assertion of sexual difference and hierarchy – the narrator erodes that distinction: Tarquin defaces 'his' own best part – 'his' soul – which the narrator unexpectedly genders as female by giving her, 'his' soul, a voice. We read that 'his soul's fair temple is defaced ... *She* says *her* subjects with foul insurrection / Have battered down *her* consecrated wall' (719–23, emphasis mine). His female soul protests that Tarquin's city, like Lucrece's, has been sacked.

The essays here do not seek to solve the problem of genre or provide a new taxonomy. Rather, they examine the questions that arise from the experimental, shape-shifting ethos of sixteenth-century epyllia. The volume sketches a kind of Venn diagram exploring areas of overlap and contest between epyllia and other prominent Elizabethan genres: epic, pastoral, drama, love lyric, complaint and satire. Like the narrative poems they analyse, these essays interrogate received early modern distinctions and challenge our own. As Joseph Ortiz argues about *Oenone and Paris* (1594), Heywood saw in the epyllion a way to experiment with generic differences inherited from the Roman past as well as the poetic and social values humanists associated with them. On his account, Heywood shifts between Virgilian epic, minor epic and pastoral to probe the perceived hierarchy of genres on which the idea of pursuing a poetic career by imitating Virgil's was based. Barbara Correll similarly interprets the difference between Marlowe and Spenser on the epyllion's proclivity for pleasure and 'unthrifty waste' by moving across genres – *Hero and Leander*, *The Faerie Queene* and *Antony and Cleopatra* – to demonstrate that Shakespeare's tragedy draws elements from the epyllion into itself in order to disrupt 'Roman values' even as it stages them, thus offering an alternative vision to Plutarch's moralizing about Antony's 'idle pastimes' and extravagant time wasting.

I emphasized the epyllion's non-identity – or better yet, its tendency to work differentially by defining itself in tension with and against other forms – because the following essays tease out this problem in various ways. Most obviously, as Jane Raisch describes, the epyllion is a form that in Tudor England and the ancient world flags the poem in question as 'not epic'. Raisch, Andrew Fleck, Joseph Ortiz and Stephen Guy-Bray show that Marlowe, Beaumont, Heywood and Phineas Fletcher revisit inherited mythological scenes only to critique epic conventions and values – whether in relation to literary history, contemporary London's mercantile culture, or classically derived definitions of socially legible masculine behaviour and poetic decorum. In a similar vein, Rachel Eisendrath and Jenny Mann adopt different interpretive angles on *Lucrece* to demonstrate that while the poem loudly announces its debt to rhetorical training, practice and theory, Shakespeare nonetheless carves out a place in the narrative for poetry as something that is 'not rhetoric'.

There is yet one more way in which the current 'state of play' in criticism of the epyllion displaces an identity category: Shakespeare. It is as true now as in 2007 that Shakespeare's epyllia are 'the most neglected items in [his] canon', despite their evident popularity among early modern readers and their crucial role in establishing his literary reputation.[17] But it is also true that with the recent exceptions cited here, critics generally approach his narrative poems in isolation from other minor epics with which they were engaged. That evacuation from contemporary literary experiment and debate is something this volume hopes to help change. Readers will encounter material signs of the problem in the textual evidence cited in the following pages: where many editions render Shakespeare's epyllia in modern spelling, none of the other poems in this collection (with the exception of Marlowe's) have received such treatment. And in Marlowe's case, the modern editions often alter the original in significant ways: introducing 'sestiads', which were Chapman's invention; and aggressively reorganizing the final lines in ways that underline a teleological model for the sexual encounter that the original text leaves far more ambiguous.[18] We have therefore chosen to remain true to the non-Shakespearean texts as they are currently available to us, preserving the spelling dissimilarities because they offer a revealing index of the literary conversation as well as the differences in the way minor epic poets have been treated.

Some essays here focus on Shakespeare's poems alone, but they do so in light of both ancient and contemporary discourses about rhetoric and poetry. Others put his epyllia into conversation with a variety of contemporary narrative poems in the vernacular – some expected (Marlowe's *Hero and Leander*, Spenser's *Fairie Queene*) and some less so (*Muiopotmos* [1590], Lodge's *Glaucus and Scylla*, Heywood's *Oenone and Paris*, Beaumont's *Salmacis and Hermaphroditus*, Phineas Fletcher's *Venus and Anchises: Brittain's Ida* [1628] and Thomas Nashe's *Lenten Stuff* [1599], among others). And in the case of *Umbra* (1595/1619), the neo-Latin poem by Thomas Campion (a Cambridge student and member of Gray's Inn), John Garrison asks us to rethink the classical/vernacular divide that was far more tenuous in their moment than our own.

In Part One, 'Reckoning with rhetoric', Mann and Eisendrath reinvigorate Ovid's scepticism about identity categories by focusing on what Lucrece's voice contributes to the genre's reflections on the tension between oratory and poetry. For

Mann, the myth of Orpheus embedded in ancient and early modern writing about rhetoric's nearly palpable physical force becomes, in Shakespeare's hands, a story with which to critique this vision, to propose an 'alternate mythos of *poesis*' by moving attention from verbal power to Orpheus's (Ovidian) verbal failure, from rhetoric's presumed social benefits to thinking about language as an 'ungovernable force' that nonetheless links genders in mutual bodily and emotional suffering (p. 38). For Eisendrath, glimpses of commiseration from a distance in *Lucrece* propose a withdrawal from rhetoric's end game: action in the world. She attends to subtle meta-critical moments that gesture towards another world of silence, inner contemplation and fellow feeling without pragmatic efficacy – and in this retreat from symbolic action, anticipate the non-purposive arena of the aesthetic we associate with a post-Kantian world (p. 63).

Part Two, 'Debating *mimesis*', investigates the unexpected ways epyllia take up ancient and contemporary debates about the poetics and practice of imitation. For Ortiz, Heywood's *Oenone and Paris* imitates a host of earlier texts to think through genre – particularly epic – in the aftermath of the 1590 *Fairie Queene* and in relation to the arc of a poetic career. Fleck moves across several epyllia (including *Venus and Adonis*) to underline its agonistic ethos, pointing out how often these poets draw on ancient as well as early modern stories about the competition between verbal and visual arts (*paragone*). On his account, epyllia draw stories of artistic rivalry into themselves in order to vie with both ancient and contemporary competitors and to advance an aggressive case for the superiority of verbal art. Catherine Nicholson's essay ends this section on minor epic theorizing about imitation by turning attention to acts of reading in *Lucrece*, demonstrating that the narrator invites readers to think carefully about the 'ethics and efficacy of readerly mimesis' (p. 121). Exploring scenes that expose the personal and social risks of literary and educational *imitatio*, she argues (*pace* humanist pedagogues) that 'learning how to limit or refuse the influence of a text on one's thoughts, feelings and actions is one of the poem's central lessons' (p. 137).

The essays in Part Three, 'Epyllia, masculinity and sexuality', push in different directions from what Jessica Winston describes as the 'models of male development and civic selfhood' that have been proposed to account for Elizabethan epyllia. Winston reads Lodge's *Glaucus and Scilla* in the context of his concern with 'Gentlemen of the Innes of Court and Chauncerie', arguing that Lodge sets out to 'inculcate' in its readers 'a disposition or attitude to the world . . . that could help members of the Inns to resist the potentially harmful allurements' of London. But by the poem's end, the narrator promotes 'a model figure who is *not* part' of his community, who responds to his world with disdain, pursuing an independent and 'socially isolated' existence with 'no future' (p. 162). Garrison reads Campion's *Umbra* alongside *Venus and Adonis* to illuminate Campion's labile depictions of gender and sexuality – particularly in relation to literary history (Latin as well as English) – in a poem whose choice of language gives the author latitude to depict same-sex erotics without euphemism. Morpheus, the god of sleep, pursues his seduction by entering a beautiful boy's dreams and cross-dressing in multiple female disguises, each of which are drawn from classical and early modern poetry. For Garrison, *Umbra* equates reading poetry with sexual awakening. And it narrates a disturbing metamorphic story about sexual violation that eventually drives the young man mad with disappointment upon waking, but at the same time introduces readers to new erotic possibilities alien to normative social expectations. Guy-Bray compares *Venus and Adonis* to Fletcher's *Venus and Anchises*, entertaining the possibility that Shakespeare's protagonist is asexual – that Adonis, as he puts it, 'turns his back on the ceaseless becoming of human life, one salient form of which is pedagogy' (p. 195). He follows the equivalence between sexuality and pedagogy into Fletcher's epyllion, where both narrator and protagonist receive erotic instruction. But by contrast to the teleology of the humanist curriculum, this poem about the sexual education of Anchises, Aeneas's father, refuses any association with Virgilian epic. On his account, by deflecting attention from the story of 'the history of entire peoples' and 'beginnings of a new empire' that was so influential in Tudor England, Fletcher suggests that the minor epic is a form 'that can only lead to more art' (p. 202). Both Garrison's and Guy-Bray's essays underscore how often epyllia, however devoted to *eros*, swerve away from biological reproduction to the useless realm of poetic beauty.

Part Four, 'Classicism and mercantile capital', turns to epyllia that use the genre's provocative celebration of unproductive pleasures to think about the urban, mercantile realities of sixteenth-century London. Raisch outlines the connections that Marlowe (and Jonson and Thomas Nashe after him) makes between London and the Hellespont in Musaeus's story of Hero and Leander. A Hellenistic poet from fifth-century Alexandria, Musaeus leaves the epic world of myth and heroic action behind to focus, instead, on every day metropolitan life. The 'new fictional life of antiquity' to which Marlowe responds in Musaeus' poem is not 'animated by the whims of the gods' or 'the call of heroic duty', but by a focus on youthful sexuality that 'unfolds amidst the boundaries of familiar structures and daily routines' (p. 227). That Marlowe picks up on and develops Musaeus' investment in urban life rather than epic gods leads her to argue that the true inheritor of Marlowe's vision is Thomas Nashe, who in *Lenten Stuff* epitomizes the story of Hero and Leander in a mock encomium to a red herring set on the docks of contemporary Yarmouth. Where Raisch leans backward, outlining how Marlowe adapts a story about city life from the cosmopolitan, Hellenistic world, Correll leans forward to George Bataille's theory of a general economy. She illuminates the critical potential of that theory, and of the epyllion's engagement with 'waste and idleness', for current economic criticism. Focusing on idleness and excess in Marlowe, Spenser and Shakespeare, Correll shows that these texts entertain, delight in (or perhaps cannot avoid), the kind of 'unconditional expenditure' that Bataille proposes to counter the dominant narrative of a 'restricted economy' in most economic theory. 'If a part of wealth', Bataille writes, 'is doomed to destruction or at least to unproductive use without any possible profit, it is logical, even inescapable, to surrender commodities without return'.[19] For Correll, the correspondence between the epyllion's devotion to 'unthriftie waste' and Bataille's notion of unconditional expenditure reveals a literature that challenges modern economic readings that presume a teleological model for sixteenth-century 'proto-capitalism'. These texts, she finds, offer a 'creative rebuff' that entertains alternative economic arrangements and corresponding social and affective structures that might have emerged (and might still) (p. 252).

The opening lines of *The Merchant of Venice* conjure a mental picture, very nearly an ekphrasis, of 'dangerous rocks' that 'touch' the side of Antonio's vessel only to 'scatter all' his 'spices on the stream' and 'enrobe the roaring waters' with his 'silks' (1.1.35). The extended vision reminds us that Shakespeare shares the resonant figure of the shipwreck with Marlowe, a figure that brings the idea of riches doomed to destruction without profit – 'even now worth this, / And now worth nothing' – before the eyes (1.1.36–7). Marlowe's scene of 'shipwracke treasure' turns the humanist ideal of *copia* into a gorgeous, time-wasting vision of rhetorical, sexual and economic expenditure without return. As such, the 'ground ... strewd with pearle' and 'sweet singing Meremaids ... on heapes of heavvie gold' register the epyllion's pugnacious dalliance with all kinds of non-productive, endless excess. Anticipating the non-purposive world of aesthetics while estranging intertwined teleologies about profitable exchange and socially useful sexual conduct, Tudor epyllia offer rich, and not entirely wasteful, food for thought.

Notes

1   For such reassessments see, *inter alia*: Leonard Barkan, *Transuming Passion: Ganymede and the Erotics of Humanism* (Stanford: Stanford University Press, 1991); Georgia Brown,

Redefining Elizabethan Literature (Cambridge: Cambridge University Press, 2004); Colin Burrow, *Shakespeare and Classical Antiquity* (Oxford: Oxford University Press, 2013); Jeff Dolven, *Scenes of Instruction in Renaissance Romance* (Chicago: University of Chicago Press, 2007); James Ellis, *Sexuality and Citizenship: Metamorphosis in Elizabethan Erotic Verse* (Toronto: University of Toronto Press, 2003); Lynn Enterline, *The Rhetoric of the Body from Ovid to Shakespeare* and *Shakespeare's Schoolroom: Rhetoric, Discipline, Emotion*; Elizabeth Hanson, 'Fellow Students: Hamlet, Horatio and the Early Modern University', *Shakespeare Quarterly* 62 (2011): 205–29; Richard Halpern, *The Poetics of Primitive Accumulation: English Renaissance Culture and the Genealogy of Capital* (Ithaca: Cornell University Press, 1991); Alan Stewart, *Close Readers: Humanism and Sodomy in Early Modern England* (Princeton: Princeton University Press, 2014).

2 All citations to Shakespeare's epyllia are from *Shakespeare's Poems*, eds Katherine Duncan-Jones and H.R. Woudhuysen (London: Bloomsbury Press, 2007). For Ovid's *praeceptor amoris* as a model for Shakespeare's Venus, see M.L. Stapleton, 'Venus as *Praeceptor*: The *Ars Amatoria* in *Venus and Adonis*', in *Venus and Adonis: Critical Essays*, ed. Philip C. Kolin (New York: Routledge, 1997), 309–22.

3 For further analysis of Shakespeare's response to contemporary pedagogy in both poems, see *Shakespeare's Schoolroom*.

4 Unless otherwise indicated, all citations to non-Shakespearean epyllia in this volume are from Elizabeth Story Donno, ed., *Elizabethan Minor Epics* (New York: Columbia University Press, 1963).

5 For a full discussion of Marlowe's critique of *copia*'s social efficacy and anticipation of the aesthetic as end-less sexuality and rhetoric, see my 'Elizabethan Minor Epics', in *The Oxford History of Classical Reception in English*, vol. 2, eds Patrick Cheney and Philip Hardie (Oxford: Oxford University Press, 2016), 253–72. Georgia Brown is similarly struck by the poem's interest in 'leisurely expansion and time-wasting', which she also sees as 'a specifically aesthetic space' ('Marlowe's Poems and Classicism', in *The Cambridge Companion to Christopher Marlowe*, ed. Patrick Cheney [Cambridge: Cambridge University Press, 2004], 117).

6 See *Sexuality and Citizenship* and William Weaver, *Untutored Lines: The Making of the English Epyllion* (Edinburgh: Edinburgh University Press, 2012).
7 *Sexuality and Citizenship*, 4.
8 *Redefining*, 108. That I concur with Brown's view will be evident from my 'Drama, Pedagogy, and the Female Complaint: Or, What's Troy Got to Do with It?', in *Swiss Papers in English Language and Literature*, vol. 31, eds Elizabeth Dutton and James McBain (Tubingen: Gunter Narr Verlag, 2015).
9 Margaret Tudeau-Clayton, 'What is My Nation? Language, Verse, and Politics in Tudor Translations of Virgil's *Aeneid*', in *The Oxford Handbook of Tudor Literature, 1485–1603*, eds Mike Pincombe and Cathy Shrank (Oxford: Oxford University Press, 2009).
10 See Joel Altman, *The Improbability of Othello: Rhetorical Anthropology and Shakespearean Selfhood* (Chicago: University of Chicago Press, 2010).
11 Donno's collection differs from Nigel Smith's *Elizabethan Narrative Verse* (Cambridge, MA: Harvard University Press, 1963).
12 Clark Hulse, *Metamorphic Verse: The Elizabethan Minor Epic* (Princeton: Princeton University Press, 1981), 17–18. His study remains the definitive account of the epyllion's experimental work with other genres.
13 Ibid., 17.
14 See John Kerrigan, *Motives of Woe: Shakespeare and 'Female Complaint', A Critical Anthology* (Oxford: Oxford University Press, 1991).
15 For a full account of the affinities Lodge creates between his narrator's poetic skill, Scilla's lament and the echoing chorus of nymphs, see 'Elizabethan Minor Epics', 265–9.
16 See Brown, who argues that *Faunus and Melliflora* 'produce[s] both a transvestite form of authorship, and a paradox of gender, which flaunts both masculine and feminine characteristics' (*Redefining*, 155).
17 Duncan-Jones, in *Shakespeare's Poems*, 4.

18 For a revealing discussion of the tensions among Marlowe's poetics of digression and delay, editorial intervention and the ideological pressure of sexual teleology, see Judith Haber, *Desire and Dramatic Form in Early Modern England* (Cambridge: Cambridge University Press, 2009), chapter 3.

19 Georges Bataille, *The Accursed Share: an Essay on General Economy*, vol. 1 (New York: Zone Books, 1991), 26.

PART ONE

Reckoning with rhetoric

1

'Reck'ning' with Shakespeare's Orpheus in *The Rape of Lucrece*

Jenny C. Mann

Rhetoric so ensnares men's minds and so sweetly lures them with her chains that at one moment she can move them to pity, at another she can drive them to hatred, at another she can fire them with warlike passion, and at another lift them up to contempt of death itself.

JOHN MILTON, *Third Prolusion* (ca.1628/9)

Shakespeare's *The Rape of Lucrece* is obsessed with rhetoric: the poem concatenates a series of culturally powerful myths about verbal eloquence's ability to motivate aesthetic accomplishment, political transformation and subject formation. Rhetoric constitutes both the topic and mode of *Lucrece*; notorious for its elaborately ornamented verbal surface, the poem also draws on the meta-technical language and the mythic motifs that characterize early modern theories of eloquence. But in making these motifs the subject of its own song, the poem transforms standard humanist conceptions of rhetorical eloquence and its cultural, social and bodily effects. The transformation of rhetoric emerges in a scattered series of allusions to the figure of Orpheus, the mythic orator-poet who 'plays' in the background of the poem, shaping its vision of the force of verbal eloquence to alter the world (553). This fragmented Orphic motif comprises an alternate mythos of *poesis*, one that diverges from conventional depictions of verbal eloquence. Taken together, these allusions dramatize Shakespeare's transformation of classical rhetoric into a medium for English poetry.

According to Horace's depiction of poetic eloquence, Orpheus' ability to 'move' recalcitrant audiences signifies the power of artful language to transform the barbarous into the civilized, and by the late Middle Ages the myth of Orpheus was widely construed as an allegory of the *artes humanes*. Humanists fasten onto the idea of Orpheus as a civilizer who brings order to barbaric cultures, thereby adopting Orpheus as a cultural hero for the early modern man of letters. To quote one of the more familiar English examples, George Puttenham's *Arte of English Poesie* (1589) explains, 'Orpheus assembled the wild beasts to come in herds to hearken to his music and by that means made them tame, implying thereby how by his discreet and wholesome lessons uttered in harmony and with melodious instruments, he brought the rude and savage people to a more civil and orderly life'. Yet despite the ubiquity and power of the mythography of Orpheus-as-civilizer, Shakespeare's allusions to Orpheus tend not to ratify this vision. Rather, his works reference other aspects of the ancient myth, including the motif of dismemberment, the failure of artful language to wield any power, the difficulty of distinguishing the civilized from the barbarous, and the conflict between poetic eloquence and right action. Shakespeare's allusions to Orpheus thus allow scepticism about the force and effects of eloquence to invade the depiction of Orphic song.

Such scepticism about the beneficial social effects of eloquence also renders his Orpheus deeply Ovidian.

Throughout its long history, the art of rhetoric presents itself as capable of channelling physical violence into verbal debate, and thereby turning savagery into civic order. In addition to Orpheus, the iconic Renaissance figure for this conversion is the emblem of Hercules Gallicus, who draws listeners to him by the force of a chain fastened between his tongue and his audience's ears. Renaissance humanists often mobilized the rape of Lucretia and its aftermath to attest to these very fictions of eloquence: Brutus parades Lucretia's violated body throughout Rome, and, as narrated in 'The Argument' to Shakespeare's poem, his 'bitter invective against the tyranny of the King' so *moves* the people 'that, with one consent and a general acclamation, the Tarquins were all exiled, and the state government changed from kings to consuls'. The literal and rhetorical display of Lucrece's violated body overthrows a tyrannical government without requiring the force of arms. However, the poem that follows the prose Argument unfolds a series of devastating challenges to the link between rhetoric and beneficial civic transformation. In so doing, it yokes rhetoric and brutality, constructing Lucrece as a character who is violently 'enchained' to rhetoric's fictions, subject to Collatine's dangerous 'Reck'ning' (cognate to OE 'chain' or 'fetter') and the rape and public display that follow hard on its heels (934, 19). By taking both the force and media of eloquence as its subject (made visible in the figure of the chain), Shakespeare's *Lucrece* moves overtly against the mythic fictions that the art of rhetoric tells about itself in the Renaissance. In so doing, the poem turns Orpheus into a figure for the disquieting combination of empowerment and vulnerability that results from the transformation of rhetorical eloquence into a poetic medium. My essay will first detail the significance of the Orpheus myth and the figure of the chain for early modern conceptions of eloquence before examining how the poem mobilizes these figures to conjure a vision of poetic transmission that renders the poet profoundly vulnerable to external forces.

The force of rhetoric

Renaissance rhetoric insistently depicts its own linguistic operations in terms of *force* (that is power, physical strength, vigour). This requires some manoeuvring, since for classical and Renaissance moralizers, talking is *not* action, and talking to excess amounts to a culturally noxious *otium*, or idleness, the antithesis of desirable Roman *virtus*, or manly valour. Defenders of rhetoric as civically valuable must counter this charge, and thus Thomas Wilson begins his English *Art of Rhetoric* by narrating a classical anecdote that attests to the superior strength of rhetorical eloquence over and above that of brute physical force:

> When Pyrrhus, king of Epirotes, made battle against the Romans, and could neither by force of arms nor yet any policy win certain strongholds, he used commonly to send one Cineas (a noble orator and sometimes scholar to Demosthenes) to persuade with the captains and the people that were in them that they should yield up the said hold or towns without fight or resistance. And so it came to pass that through the pithy eloquence of this noble orator, divers strong castles and fortresses were peaceably given up into the hands of Pyrrhus, which he should have found very hard and tedious to win by the sword. And this thing was not Pyrrhus himself ashamed in his common talk, to the praise of the said orator, openly to confess, alleging that Cineas through the eloquence of his tongue won more cities unto him than ever himself should else have been able by force to subdue.[1]

Rhetoric provides victory without bloodshed. The anecdote depicts the persuasions of eloquence as mightier than the physical 'force of arms', and in so doing, it also redefines the very idea of 'force', claiming its strength and vigour on behalf of effective speech rather than armed action. Wilson subsequently declares that 'such force hath the tongue, and such is the power of eloquence and reason, that most men are forced even to yield in that which most standeth against their will'.[2] The reiteration of the term 'force' in this short sentence reminds us that the violence of the invading army has been converted into the 'power of eloquence', attesting to Roland Barthes' general observation that rhetoric comes into being when violent disputes over property rights are channelled into verbal debate.[3] The conversion of physical violence into verbal deliberation comprises rhetoric's so-called civilizing function.

Orpheus is the mythic figure par excellence for the conversion of physical violence into forceful speech, as well as one of the most infamous examples of the failure of such a conversion. Orpheus first appears in the poetry of early Greece as a poet-shaman whose song works a kind of magic on its audience, thus providing a mythic embodiment of the power of oral poetry to hold its hearers spellbound in 'pleasure' or 'delight' [*terpsis, hēdonē*], as Homer terms it.[4] Ancient literature offers divergent responses to the apparent magic of Orphic eloquence: Euripides and Aeschylus associate the pleasure of Orpheus' song with the power of art and civilization, while Plato regards Orpheus' verbal magic with great suspicion.[5] Roman versions of the Orpheus myth, including that contained in Virgil's *Georgics* and Ovid's *Metamorphoses*, tend to emphasize Orpheus' role as lover of Eurydice, outlining the standard version of the myth for Renaissance audiences. After a snake fatally bites Eurydice, Orpheus descends into the underworld in order to win her back. He uses the power of his song to persuade the gods of Hades to release his bride, only to lose her a second time when he disobeys their command not to gaze back as they depart the underworld. In his grief Orpheus renounces all women, promising to love only boys, and his mournful song draws trees, beasts and stones to follow him. Yet despite his song's power to tame the natural world, Orpheus is torn apart by a howling band of Bacchae in revenge for his disdain of women. Dismemberment, however, does not quiet his voice, and Orpheus' severed head and lyre continue to sing as they float down the Hebrus to the island of Lesbos, where Apollo protects the head from the bite of a snake and gives it the power of prophecy. Like the earliest tales of the Orphic myth, these versions emphasize the magical force of artful language; but Virgil and Ovid also highlight the impotence of Orpheus' song, as he fails to bring Eurydice fully out of the underworld and is eventually torn to pieces. In the *Metamorphoses*, Orpheus is killed, as Joseph Ortiz explains, because he cannot 'move' the Bacchantes (*in illo tempore primum / inrita dicentem nec quicquam voce moventem* [XI.39–40]) and thus cannot move the actual stones being thrown at him.[6] He dies when hit on the 'mouth', leaving his blood stains 'on the rocks, unheard' (*tum denique saxa / non exauditi rubuerunt sanguine vatis* [18–19]).

Greek treatments of the Orpheus myth depict him as a shaman-theologian while Roman versions emphasize his love for Eurydice; however, all classical versions of the tale endow Orpheus' song with the power to charm animals, trees and stones. The precise nature of Orpheus' enchanting song is variously interpreted: Horace identifies it with the art of poetry while Cicero views it as a type of political oratory. Francis Bacon will later claim it is a version of natural and moral philosophy. However, whatever the nature of his song, Orpheus incarnates a civilizing force in the majority of classical and Christian interpretations of the myth.[7] The primary source for this inflection of the Orphic myth is Horace's *Ars Poetica*, which declares that 'Orpheus, the priest and interpreter of the gods, deterred the savage race of men from slaughters and inhuman diet; hence said to tame tigers and furious lions: Amphion too, the builder of the Theban wall, was said to give the stones motion with the sound of his lyre, and to lead them whithersoever he would, by engaging persuasion'.[8] The myth of the orator/poet-as-civilizer provides one of the enabling fictions of Renaissance humanism, and it is narrated over and over again in sixteenth-century texts.[9] English retellings of

Horace attest to the 'force' of rhetorical or poetic eloquence, as in William Webbe's *Discourse of English Poetrie* (1589), which argues that both eloquence and poetry 'being framed in such sweete measure of sentences and pleasant harmonie ... drawing as it were by force the hearers eares euen whether soeuer it lysteth ... And here hence is sayde that men were first withdrawne from a wylde and sauage kinde of life to ciuillity and gentleness and the right knowledge of humanity by the force of this measurable or tunable speaking'.[10] The 'force' of Orphic eloquence, according to these defences of English art, derives from its 'sweete measure of sentences and pleasant harmonie', which have a coercive effect belied by their alluring 'frames'. Verbal force launches audiences into motion, a motion figured by Webbe's image of artful language drawing 'the hearers eares' wherever it pleases (or 'lysteth', a term that means both attentive hearing and an appetite or desire [*OED*]).

As these references can only begin to indicate, the language of force saturates descriptions of rhetoric in the Renaissance, often going hand-in-hand with allusions to Orphic song. And as in Webbe's *Discourse*, sixteenth-century descriptions of *poesis* adopt this very terminology and mythic frame in order to make identical claims about the forceful effects of poesy. The earliest poets, according to Philip Sidney's *Defense of Poesy* (ca.1579), 'draw with their charming sweetness the wild untamed wits to an admiration of knowledge. So, as Amphion was said to move stones with his poetry to build Thebes, and Orpheus to be listened to by beasts, indeed, stony and beastly people ...'[11] In mobilizing the Orphic myth of forceful eloquence in order to defend their own artistic practice, Renaissance poets are particularly alive to the contrast between the sweet sounds of eloquence and its vaunted power to subdue savage and unruly audiences. Sidney's *Defense* and Puttenham's *Arte* both use the Greek rhetorical term *energeia* to refer to the physical efficacy of poetic eloquence, what Sidney calls its 'forcibleness' and Puttenham calls its 'strong and virtuous operation'.[12] When alluding to eloquent language's 'forcibleness', Sidney and Puttenham turn the encounter between the poet-rhetor's words and the bodies of his audience into a physical one, and the conduit of that encounter is what Sidney calls 'the material point of poesy'.[13] Poetic allusions to linguistic eloquence often describe artfully figured language more particularly as a piercing and ravishing power, an overwhelming and unwilled penetration of the body. For example, Joshua Poole's catalogue of poetical synonyms for 'eloquence' in *The English Parnassus* (1657), collected from the works of diverse English poets, begins by describing it as 'Heart-stealing, soul-moving, soul-raping'.[14] Sidney's *Defense* similarly describes poetry as 'heart-ravishing knowledge', and these allusions to rape and ravishment indicate that the forcibleness of eloquence is tinged with violence and often understood as a sexualized penetration of the body.[15] The poet, according to Sidney, creates an image that can 'strike, pierce, [and] possess the sight of the soul'.[16] As these passages suggest, rhetoric's discourse of force stresses the physical, material action of artful language – and does so as bodily penetration and inscription.[17] And here, again, Orpheus is the exemplar: as Francis Clement writes in *The petie schole* (1587), 'Orpheus his tongue surmounted all other ... it delited, and allured: it moued, and rauished: it pearsed, and pleased'.[18]

According to the claims put forward by the art of rhetoric and mobilized by early modern theories of poesy, verbal eloquence wields a palpable force that moves, ravishes, pierces, and pleases its audiences. Nevertheless, though it is resolutely material and often sexualized, the force of eloquence works at a distance. That is, the object of eloquence is moved and 'drawn' without being physically touched by the orator-poet. The operations of such an action-at-a-distance are emblematized by another myth cherished by the early modern arts of eloquence: that of the Hercules Gallicus. The Gallic Hercules draws audiences by the force of a chain fastened between his tongue and his listeners' ears, and this image is a popular icon of eloquence in the sixteenth century. The figure is first described in Lucian's *Hercules*, a second-century text that was first published in the fifteenth century, but Andrea Alciati's sixteenth-century collection of emblems provides the primary source for subsequent images of the Hercules Gallicus.[19] These images picture Hercules with his traditional accoutrements (lion skin, club and bow); however, he leads the crowd not with weapons, but via a chain that connects his mouth to their ears. In the first edition of Alciati's collection, the following tag accompanies the image: '*Eloquentia fortitudine praestantior*' ('Eloquence is more efficacious than force').[20] The myth of Hercules Gallicus thus converts Hercules' famed physical strength into a different kind of power, a specifically rhetorical power that operates at a distance. In so doing, it reclaims the concept of heroic, physical 'force' from deeds of arms and transfers them to acts of speech.

Though the image of the Gallic Hercules as an icon of eloquence was not as pervasive in England as in France, it appears in two important sixteenth-century English rhetorics: Wilson's *Art of Rhetoric* and Puttenham's *Art of English Poesy*. Each of these texts celebrates the force of eloquence, describing it as possessing considerable physical reality, yet still distinct from the outright threat of actual physical violence. For example, immediately after he first asserts eloquence's civilizing power, Wilson conjures the image of Hercules and his linked chain:

> Such force hath the tongue, and such is the power of eloquence and reason, that most men are forced even to yield in that which most standeth against their will. And therefore the poets do feign that Hercules, being a man of great wisdom, had all men linked together by the ears in a chain to draw them and lead them even as he lusted. For his wit was so great, his tongue so eloquent, and his experience such, that no one man was able to withstand his reason, but everyone was rather driven to do that which he would, and to will that which he did, agreeing to his advice both in order and work in all that ever they were able.[21]

Though Wilson disclaims physical violence, the language of force pervades his 'feigned' description of eloquence, as men are 'driven' to follow the will of the quasi-divine orator. The links of the chain allow Hercules to 'lead them even as he lusted', a phrase that identifies the will of the orator with the operations of sexual desire. Yet although Wilson allows some negative connotations of rhetorical force to creep into his descriptions of the activity of eloquence, he resolutely insists that this force tends towards socially productive order. However, unlike Wilson, Puttenham's *Art of English Poesy* does not insist that the piercing action of eloquence necessarily produces good Christian order. Moreover, Puttenham's rhetorical poetics is quite comfortable with the apparent violence rhetorical eloquence can wreak upon the body, declaring outright that persuasions are both 'violent and forcible'.[22] It is in demonstration of this claim that Puttenham describes the image of Hercules Gallicus. The image ends a complicated series of interlocked anecdotes meant to demonstrate the potential violence of the 'force of persuasion'.[23] At the culmination of his tale, Puttenham proffers a new figure for the provocative force of eloquence, the chain of Hercules:

> I find this opinion confirmed by a pretty device or emblem that Lucian allegeth he saw in the portrait of Hercules within the city of Marseilles in Provence, where they had figured a lusty old man with a long chain tied by one end at his tongue, by the other end at the people's ears, who stood afar off and seemed to be drawn to him by the force of that chain fastened to his tongue, as who would say, by force of his persuasions.[24]

In Puttenham's text, the power of Hercules to 'lead them even as he lusted' has become the power of a 'lusty old man' who can draw people to him even standing 'afar off'. And once again, the image of Hercules Gallicus represents the moment of contact between language and the body as the culmination of a linked chain.

The image of the chain of eloquence thus enables a series of profitable conversions that work in concert to establish the power of eloquence and make it available to English poets. In order to demonstrate and defend the force of eloquence to their readers, these rhetorical manuals mobilize a variety of mythic tales and emblems, including those featuring Orpheus and the Hercules Gallicus. These allusions mark the culmination of a series of prior conversions and translations. Lucian's tale of the Gallic Hercules narrates the conversion of physical power into rhetorical power, while the image of his chain converts the idea of rhetorical force and its social effects into a tangible figure of physical connection. And when the English manuals reference Lucian's Hercules, the descriptions of the emblem continue to shuttle from text to image and back again – the texts describe an emblem, an image which has already converted the language of Hercules' speech into the figure of the chain – allowing the chain to be simultaneously both iconographic and figurative.[25] Allusions to Hercules' chain within sixteenth-century treatments of rhetoric also convert a scene of face-to-face exchange to one of writing (ancient rhetoric assumed the primacy of speech as the substance of the art while early modern rhetoric took writing as its primary practice).[26] These chiastic transformations from force to figure and back again enable both the production of eloquent speech (which operates through powerfully persuasive figurative constructions) and the construction of an early modern art dedicated to transmitting this capability (which requires that certain phenomena become objects and media of artistic activity). Meanwhile, the image of the chain makes these conversions visible, while also figuring eloquence's mode of operation as a flexible sequence of ligaments strong enough to place others in bondage.

The rhetoric of *Lucrece*

The figure of Orpheus and the image of eloquence as a chain flicker in the background of *The Rape of Lucrece*, as the poem endeavours to expose the proximity of linguistic force and physical violence within the rhetorical tradition. Its action famously begins with a contest of epideictic oratory, as Collatine speaks publicly in 'praise' of his wife's peerless beauty, 'Reck'ning his fortune at such high-proud rate / That kings might be espoused to more fame, / But king nor peer to such a peerless dame' (19–21). The poet describes Collatine's eloquence as 'unwise' because it 'Unlock[s] the treasure of his happy state' (10, 16). The pointed deployment of the verb 'reckon' identifies Collatine's accounting of his wife's worth as a set of rhetorical calculations that also comprise a 'fetter' or 'chain'.[27] The subsequent allusion to unlocked treasure further identifies Lucrece with the dominant image for rhetorical eloquence in the sixteenth century, what Erasmus terms *copia*: the storehouse of riches from which the orator takes the material of his speech.[28] Lucrece's chaste beauty is her husband's 'treasure', as well as the subject matter, or discursive riches that constitute the persuasiveness of his rhetoric. (And after the rape, Lucrece's 'pure Chastity is rifled of her store' as she herself becomes 'the guiltless casket' of stolen 'treasure' [692; 1056–1057].) Within the poem Lucrece's body is simultaneously the object of praise, the constituent force of persuasion itself (her 'beauty pleadeth' and 'itself doth of itself persuade' [268, 29]), and the subject of the violence that ensues from these persuasions. She is also the most eloquent orator featured in the poem.[29] In this way, her character becomes a means of 'reckoning' with the ways in which the force and media of eloquence become violently, but also, somehow, *beautifully*, entangled with one another (an entanglement evident immediately prior to the rape, when 'Her hair, like golden threads, played with her breath' [400]).

In presenting the rape of Lucrece as a direct consequence of Collatine's epideictic rhetoric, Shakespeare's poem takes rhetoric's most cherished fantasy – that it converts physical violence into verbal debate and thereby civilizes men – only to dramatize its inversion: verbal 'force' motivates and indeed becomes self-identical with the physical 'force' of the rapist (182). The narrator openly chides Collatine for his reckless eloquence, but far too late, as Tarquin is already racing towards Lucrece 'From the besieged ARDEA all in post' in the opening line of the poem (1). The rest of the poem exemplifies *copia* in action, perhaps even run amok, as Shakespeare expands seventy-three lines of Livy into nearly 2,000 lines of poetry. In keeping with this principle of expansion, the poetry itself is characterized by an excessive ornamental style, dense with figures and elaborate conceits. Shakespeare's version of the story returns obsessively to scenes of persuasion, worrying over the successes and failures of eloquence to motivate action and civilize men. Lucrece is the focal point of these reflections: she unsuccessfully pleads with her rapist to spare her, and then successfully persuades her husband and his compatriots to avenge her. In the intervening time she laments her predicament while holding 'disputation' with the figures in a tapestry depicting the Fall of Troy (1101). Her character both attests to the discursive practices of England's rhetorical culture (which trains writers to speak in the voice of Ovidian characters) and also interrogates the ideology that props up that culture (which claims that rhetorical eloquence is a civilizing force that deflects physical violence).[30] After all, the outcome of her beauty's 'persuasions' is Tarquin's conviction that 'As from this cold flint I enforced this fire, / So LUCRECE must I force to my desire' (181–2).

Rhetoric thus provides the means whereby Shakespeare expands his classical source into eloquent poetry of his own, and also becomes the primary thematic focus of the narrative. Perhaps more subtly, the poem also profits from the mythic motifs and meta-technical language common to the art of rhetoric. Nancy Vickers notes that 'colour' – a synonym for rhetorical ornament – appears more often in *Lucrece* than in any other Shakespearean text.[31] Similarly, the incidence of the word 'force' and its cognates in the poem is matched only by Shakespeare's history plays. *Lucrece* expresses its reflections on the force of persuasion in images of writing and inscription, as Lucrece imagines her violation graven, charactered, quoted, and stamped on her body and that of her husband (755, 807, 812, 829). Because 'Poor women's faces are their own faults' books', Lucrece's face becomes 'that map which deep impression bears / Of hard misfortune, carved in it with tears' (1253; 1712–13). The poem thus, in Samuel Arkin's words, gives 'heightened attention to the literal and figurative carving of poetic trope and image'.[32] And it is Lucrece's body that becomes the essential medium of figurative force's violence.

Late twentieth-century scholarship, particularly feminist scholarship, has paid careful attention to the rhetoric of *Lucrece*. The elaborate digressions and glossy rhetorical surface once derided as an aesthetic failure now strike many as essential to the poem's ethical and political positions.[33] Vickers puts it best when she writes that in its obsession with rhetoric, *Lucrece* 'reveals the rhetorical strategies that descriptive occasions generate, and underlines the potential consequences of being female matter for male oratory'.[34] Not only does the poem stipulate Collatine's epideictic rhetoric as the effective cause of the rape (and thus the poem, as Joel Fineman emphasizes), but it also yokes a particular set of metaphors (of military invasion, for example) as engines of Tarquin's violence. Thus, as Katherine Maus recommends in the title of an influential essay, addressing the violence in the poem requires 'taking tropes seriously'.[35] But despite the new consensus that the elaborate artifice of *Lucrece* is essential to its ethical postures, enabling the poem to direct our attention to the ways in which aesthetics and politics become intertwined, there is considerable disagreement about the extent to which the poem (and the subjectivity of the poet) are complicit with the patriarchal violence that it describes. The poem primes us to worry over this problem: *Lucrece*, as Lynn Enterline emphasizes, insists on the convergence between writing the poem and carrying out the acts of violence narrated in it.[36] For some readers, the exposure of the violent consequences of descriptive rhetoric for the female body does not undo the system it exposes; rather, it simply provides the vehicle for Shakespeare's own dominance as a poet.[37] Without entirely disputing this interpretation, more recent scholarship has modulated the identification of Shakespeare's art with patriarchal violence, arguing that the poem also creates a space for an alternate ethics of affective persuasion and engagement that does not require violence against the female body.[38] As we will see, the poem offers up the figure of Orpheus as a means of thinking through the charged alignment of violence, vulnerability and artistic production in Lucrece's story. Allusions to Orpheus make visible the most politically and ethically troubling interpretive cruxes of the poem.

The poem stresses Lucrece's considerable eloquence, but she still cannot deflect the violence both provoked and embodied by her husband's oratory and her own beauty. At the moment she fails to persuade Tarquin to call off his assault, the poet tells us that she 'Pleads in a wilderness where are no laws ... And moody PLUTO winks while ORPHEUS plays' (544, 553). Orpheus' appearance at the very moment that verbal eloquence fails to achieve its desired ends (perhaps because its palpable force is *already present* in the onrushing sexual violence) is characteristic of Shakespeare, who frequently alludes to Orpheus at moments of subjection and vulnerability. In dramatizing the violence that rhetoric wreaks on Lucrece's body and mind, and likening her vulnerability to futile Orphic song, the poem suggests that the aspiring poet is likewise subject to the inscribing force of rhetoric. Indeed, the dispersed network of allusions to Orpheus within the Shakespearean corpus imply that when trying to move others with words, the poet himself becomes the impressionable medium or instrument of eloquence rather than simply its font. For example, in *The Two Gentlemen of Verona*, the aptly named Proteus advises that 'Orpheus' lute was strung with poets' sinews / Whose golden touch could soften steel and stones' (3.2.77–8). Here, Orpheus both strums the lyre and comprises the body of the instrument being played ('strung with poets' sinews'); he is author and medium of his own song. Shakespeare's Orpheus intimates that becoming the conduit of a powerful eloquence does not shore up the strength of the poet, but rather renders the poet vulnerable to impression by a superior force. The passage further indicates that the moment that words *fail* to persuade is precisely the moment that they become Orphic poetry. Enterline puts it even more precisely when she writes that such allusions transform the failed plea into a 'virtual poetic ontology'.[39] In this way, as Michael C. Clody has persuasively argued, Orpheus is the emblem for an alternate idea of poetic agency that hovers at the fringes of the poem, one that briefly counters the politicized authority of rhetoric with an alternate poetics of cancellation. According to Clody's argument, by identifying Lucrece's mourning with the song of Orpheus, the poem undermines the familiar fantasy of poetic immortality preserved in verse with a vision of cancellation that entails the striking out, tearing and cutting apart of the poem and its author.[40]

The subsequent appearances of Orpheus in *Lucrece* stitch together the force and media of eloquence, helping to secure a new vision of Orphic song as that which fails to civilize the beastly and deflect physical violence. After the rape, Lucrece laments that 'Opportunity' has 'Cancelled my fortunes, and *enchained* me / To endless date of never-ending woes' (932–5, my emphasis). She briefly fantasizes that she can transfer her vulnerability back to Tarquin himself, pleading with Time to

> Stone him with hardened hearts harder than stones,
> And let mild women to him lose their mildness,
> Wilder to him than tigers in their wildness.
>
> (978–80)

She later disparages such curses as 'idle words', 'Unprofitable sounds, weak arbitrators!' (1016–17). Such arguments are 'vain', that is, light, empty, without any significant force or power (1023; *OED*). Even later in the night after she has failed to prevent her own assault, a failure the poet likens to Orpheus' botched attempt to bring Eurydice out of the underworld, Lucrece momentarily wishes she could transform herself into a kind of Orphic lyre. She promises 'as frets upon an instrument', to 'tune our heart-strings to true languishment' (1140–1). As she describes her body as the instrument, or medium, of eloquence, she speaks once again in the voice of an Ovidian character, calling:

> Come, PHILOMEL, that sing'st of ravishment,
> Make thy sad grove in my dishevelled hair.
> As the dank earth weeps at thy languishment,
> So I at each sad strain will strain a tear,
> And with deep groans the diapason bear;
> > For burden-wise, I'll hum on TARQUIN still,
> > While thou on TEREUS descants better skill.
>
> ...
>
> And for, poor bird, thou sing'st not in the day,
> As shaming any eye should thee behold,
> Some dark deep desert seated from the way,
> That knows not parching heat nor freezing cold,
> Will we find out, and there we will unfold
> > To creatures stern sad tunes to change their kinds:
> > Since men prove beasts, let beasts bear gentle minds.
>
> (1128–34, 1142–8)

First Lucrece turns herself into a harmonious instrument, which can 'bear' the 'diapason', or resonant concord, to Philomel's 'sad strain'. She will pierce her own woes so as to 'tune' her 'heartstrings' to Philomel's song of 'true languishment'. Then at the conclusion to the passage, she imagines journeying to the woods, where she will attempt to turn beasts 'gentle', thus evoking Orpheus once again as a figure for the song that comes in the aftermath of a rhetorical violence.[41] But as the passage reveals, the most palpable effects of such a song are in the transformation of the singer herself. Such a transformation enables the composition of Shakespeare's poem, which requires that the poet become 'ensnared' in rhetoric's chains, both source and medium of his own eloquence.

Conclusion: Shakespeare's Orpheus

Though early modern writers and contemporary scholars habitually treat rhetoric and poetics as synonymous in the late sixteenth century, *Lucrece* dilates on the consequential distinctions between oratory and poetry. It does so via allusions to Orpheus, whose persona is dispersed in fragments across the larger tapestry of the poem. This diffuse Orphic motif constructs an alternate mythos of *poesis*, one that diverges from conventional depictions of verbal eloquence as a force that empowers the robust male speaker. The scattered Orphic moments in *Lucrece* question the vaunted force of eloquence to empower the orator and move audiences where it will. *Lucrece* thus dramatizes the conversion of classical rhetoric into English poetry. Renaissance re-tellings of the Orpheus story conceive of eloquent language not merely as a representation of the world, but as a mode of action *in* the world.[42] Sixteenth-century rhetorical training promises to teach English writers to shape and control the force of an all-powerful eloquence, becoming Orphic civilizers of their own burgeoning commonwealth. But in Shakespeare's works, rather than an agent of civic order, Orpheus becomes instead a figure for the hyperbolic, transformative, ungovernable power of eloquence. Moreover, in *Lucrece* we see linguistic eloquence lose its power to 'move' beastly men, as in the more familiar parts of the Orpheus story. Orphic song does not seem to empower the English poet in any clear way – as it does in the allusions to Orpheus in handbooks of rhetoric – but rather renders the poet vulnerable to a force that eludes his control, turning his own body into a medium of poetic impressions. To put it another way, once we detach Orpheus' story from a civilizing trajectory, as Shakespeare does in *Lucrece* and elsewhere, a sense of the disturbing magic of Orphic song re-enters our conceptualizations of eloquence. This, to my mind, is a crucial outcome of the conversion of rhetoric into poetry embodied by *The Rape of Lucrece*. As I stated in an aside in the introduction, such scepticism about the beneficial effects of eloquence renders Shakespeare's Orpheus profoundly Ovidian in nature: Orpheus exits the earthly world in the *Metamorphoses* not in triumph, but with his limbs 'scattered', his severed head floating down the gentle current of the river Hebrus, compulsively tuning itself to the harmonies of the world around it: 'The lyre made mournful sounds, and the lifeless tongue murmured / In Mournful harmony, and the banks echoed / The strains of mourning' [*flebile nescio quid queritur lyra, flebile lingua / murmur exanimis, respondent flexible ripae*]' (IX.48, 52–4). So too does Lucrece's 'bleeding body' *move* 'thorough Rome', an impressionable medium that serves 'to publish TARQUIN's foul offense' (1851–2).

Notes

1 Thomas Wilson, *The Art of Rhetoric (1560)*, ed. Peter E. Medine (University Park, PA: Pennsylvania State University Press, 1994), 35.

2 Ibid., 42.

3 Roland Barthes, 'The Old Rhetoric: An Aide-Memoire', *The Semiotic Challenge*, trans. Richard Howard (Berkeley: University of California Press, 1994), 16.

4 Charles Segal, *Orpheus: The Myth of the Poet* (Baltimore: Johns Hopkins University Press, 1989), 15.

5 Ibid.

6 Joseph Ortiz, *Broken Harmony: Shakespeare and the Politics of Music* (Ithaca: Cornell University Press, 2011), 39.

7 Patricia Vicari, 'Spargamos: Orpheus Among the Christians', in *Orpheus: The Metamorphoses of a Myth*, ed. John Warden (Toronto: University of Toronto Press, 1982), 63–84.

8 *The Works of Horace*, eds C. Smart and Theodore Alois Buckley (New York: Harper & Brothers, 1863), 391–401. As Rebhorn and Whigham explain in their introduction to *The Art of English Poesy by George Puttenham: A Critical Edition*, the myth of the orator/poet-as-civilizer also occurs in Cicero, *De inventione* 1.2.2–3 and Quintilian, *Institutio Oratoria*, 2.16.9 (Ithaca: Cornell University Press, 2007), 96.

9 Rebhorn traces Renaissance versions of the myth of the orator-civilizer to passages in texts written by Isocrates, Cicero, Horace and Quintilian. Italian, French, Spanish and English writers who circulated this myth include Francesco Petrarch, Coluccio

Salutati, Andrea Brenta, Joan de Guzman, Guillaume Du Vair, Raphael Regius, Thomas Wilson, George Puttenham and M. Le Grand. See *The Emperor of Men's Minds: Literature and the Renaissance Discourse of Rhetoric* (Ithaca: Cornell Unviersity Press, 1995), 24–8.

10 William Webbe, *A Discourse of English Poetrie*, *Elizabethan Critical Essays*, Vol. I, ed. G. Gregory Smith (Oxford: Oxford University Press, 1904), 231.

11 In *Sir Philip Sidney: The Major Works*, ed. Katherine Duncan-Jones (Oxford: Oxford University Press, 2002), 213. The repeated use of 'draw' in these examples underscores the beastliness of the orator-poet's audiences, who are likened to beasts of labour put to the plow of the poet's devices (*OED*). Future citations of Sidney are to this edition.

12 Sidney, 246; Puttenham, 227. See also Margreta de Grazia, 'Words as Things', *Shakespeare Studies* 28 (2000): 231–5. In both Sidney and Puttenham, Orpheus attests to the priority of poesy before all other arts of knowledge, as well as its singular force (Puttenham, 6).

13 Sidney, 246.

14 *The English Parnassus, 1657* (Menston, England: The Scolar Press Ltd., 1972), 171.

15 For a careful account of the sexualized language used by Renaissance rhetoricians, see Rebhorn, *The Emperor of Men's Minds*, 158–70.

16 Sidney, 214, 222.

17 Rhetoric could thus be thought of, in Coppélia Kahn's terms, as one of the 'patriarchal structures that authorize rape' ('The Rape in Shakespeare's *Lucrece*', *Shakespeare Studies* 9 [1976]: 144). Stephanie Jed demonstrated how humanist philology inscribed the rape of Lucrece in its very practice, revealing how reproducing this story constitutes a founding gesture of the entire humanist enterprise (*Chaste Thinking: The Rape of Lucretia and the Birth of Humanism* [Bloomington, IN: Indiana University Press, 1989]).

18 Francis Clement, *The Petie Schole with an English Orthographie* (London: 1587), 45.

19 Erasmus and Guillaume Budé translated Lucian's text into Latin in the early sixteenth century, which gave the figure wide exposure in European culture, particularly in France, where Hercules Gallicus symbolized the union of eloquence and political power. The Gallic Hercules was illustrated in mythological collections and emblem books, insuring the widespread circulation of this idiosyncratic image of Hercules as an orator-civilizer who controls his people not through violence but through eloquence. See *The Emperor of Men's Minds*, 66–79. See also Robert E. Hallowell, 'Ronsard and the Gallic Hercules Myth', *Studies in the Renaissance* 9 (1962): 242–55. Alciati's *Emblemata* was first printed in Latin in 1531 and was reissued and translated many times in the coming century (Rebhorn, 67).

20 Rebhorn's translation, 67.

21 Wilson, 42.

22 Puttenham, 226.

23 Ibid., 225.

24 Puttenham, 225–6.

25 This is perhaps an iteration of the tendency for Renaissance rhetoric and poetics to conflate the force of *energeia* with the visualized power of *enargeia*. See Joseph Campana, 'On Not Defending Poetry: Spenser, Suffering, and the Energy of Affect', *PMLA* 120.1 (January 2005): 33–48.

26 While I haven't been able to address this process in great detail here, the conversion of speech to writing is key to the larger history I want to tell about the place of eloquence in an early modern map of knowledge. As John Guillory explains, 'by the later seventeenth century the sense of communication as speech or discourse was selected out as the primary sense, which ceased thereafter to imply the scene of immediate contact or presence and came contrarily to be associated with an action often involving distance in time and space'. Such a shift could explain why the chain of Hercules is so crucial in sixteenth-century rhetoric: it allows the art to claim that even when rhetoric acts at a distance (as in writing), it still produces a physically proximate contact between orator and audience. This claim is, apparently, no longer uniformly persuasive at the end of the seventeenth century. See Guillory, 'Genesis

of the Media Concept', *Critical Inquiry* 36.2 (Winter 2010): 321–62, 332.

27 *OED*. Such calculations also inscribe the rape of Lucretia in narrative of legal and political change. As Stephane Jed writes, 'In Livy's narrative, the passage from Lucretia's chastity to Tarquin's violation of this chastity to Brutus' castigation of the Romans for their tears forms a lexical chain which embodies a logic of chaste thinking: the rape of Lucretia is transformed into an injury against the honor of her male survivors by virtue of this chain; and Brutus takes over from Lucretia the function of preserving chastity by castigating the Romans for their tears' (*Chaste Thinking*, 11). Jed emphasizes that the 'chain effect' continues within Livy's text and in the tradition that celebrates the narrative.

28 See Terence Cave, *The Cornucopian Text* (Oxford: Oxford University Press, 1979).

29 See William Weaver, '"O teach me how to make mine own excuse": Forensic Performance in Lucrece', *Shakespeare Quarterly* (2009): 421–9.

30 Lynn Enterline shows how school training in *ethopoeia* prompted Elizabethan students to impersonate Ovidian characters. These were 'formal exercises in personification', and shaped the formation of schoolboy character and emotion via detours through Ovidian poetry (*Shakespeare's Schoolroom*, 92–4; 124–39).

31 Nancy Vickers, '"The blazon of sweet beauty's best": Shakespeare's Lucrece', in *Shakespeare and the Question of Theory*, eds Patricia Parker and Geoffrey Hartman (New York: Methuen, 1985), 95–115, 107.

32 Samuel Arkin, '"That map which deep impression bears": *Lucrece* and the Anatomy of Shakespeare's Sympathy', *Shakespeare Quarterly* 64.3 (Fall 2013): 349–71, 356.

33 As Joel Fineman summarizes, the poem has an 'extravagant rhetorical manner', 'brittle artificiality of diction', and an 'over-conceited style'. 'Shakespeare's Will: The Temporality of Rape', *Representations* 20 (August 1987): 25–76, 32. This relatively new perspective on the integration of political and aesthetic questions has been enabled in large part by the work of

feminist literary criticism; as Lynn A. Higgins and Brenda R. Silver write, such work has established that 'the politics and aesthetics of rape are one'. See 'Introduction: Rereading Rape', *Rape and Representation* (New York: Columbia University Press, 1991), 1.

34 Vickers, 96.

35 Katherine Eisaman Maus, 'Taking Tropes Seriously: Language and Violence in Shakespeare's *Rape of Lucrece*', *Shakespeare Quarterly* 37 (Spring 1986).

36 *The Rhetoric of the Body*, 155. As Fineman writes, 'precisely because the poem ... makes thematic and incriminating issue out of "oratory", the poem's own rhetoricity is once again performatively implicated in the rape that it reports, as though the poem itself, *because* it speaks rhetorically, were speaking to its reader's "ear" so as to "taint" its reader's "heart"' (35–6).

37 For Vickers, for example, *Lucrece* is the creation of a rhetorical tradition that enables the verbalization of the male gaze. To draw on Coppélia Kahn's formulation, this debate revolves around the question of 'who or what speaks in the character we call Lucrece'? ('Lucrece: The Sexual Politics of Subjectivity', in *Rape and Representation*, 142). To what extent can the poet elude inscription into the constructs of power that subject Lucrece to the laws of chastity? It is difficult for modern readers to settle the question, in part because, as Melissa Sanchez emphasizes, the poem 'depicts agency in such confused and paradoxical terms' (*Erotic Subjects: The Sexuality of Politics in Early Modern English Literature* [Oxford: Oxford University Press, 2011], 89).

38 See Arkin as well as Michael C. Clody, 'Orpheus, Unseen: *Lucrece*'s Cancellation Fantasy', *Philological Quarterly* 3 92.4 (2013): 449–69.

39 *The Rhetoric of the Body*, 172. In rendering this conclusion, which entails reading Shakespeare in concert with Petrarch's *Rime sparse*, Enterline provides a powerful insight into how Shakespeare refashions the myth of Orpheus in his own poetry: Shakespeare uses the plot of the rape 'to stress the figural and formal problems of the failed words themselves. And by staging this failed plea, [both Petrarch and Shakespeare] stress that such failure has profound consequences for the inner condition of the

speaker who utters his or her words of address in vain . . . Both the beauty of the words themselves and the subjective condition of "exile" emerge as a kind of after-effect of language's failure to bring about the changes of which it speaks . . . Because Tarquin refuses Lucrece's demand for pity, her voice reminds the narrator of Orpheus'.

40 Clody, 'Orpheus, Unseen'.
41 Book IV of Virgil's *Georgics* also compares Orpheus' song to the grieving of a nightingale.
42 See Lynn Enterline, 'Afterword: Touching Rhetoric', in *Sensible Flesh: On Touch in Early Modern Culture*, ed. Elizabeth Harvey (Philadelphia: University of Pennsylvania Press, 2003), 221.

2

Poetry at the limits of rhetoric in Shakespeare's *The Rape of Lucrece*

Rachel Eisendrath

The extensive role of rhetorical theory in Shakespeare's 1594 narrative poem, *The Rape of Lucrece*, now attracts critical interest as powerfully as it once alienated and distanced literary scholars of a previous generation. Writing in 1932, Douglas Bush characterized the poem's density of rhetoric as 'baffling', apparently disappointed that this poem, which told an ancient tale of rape, seemed to express 'a clever brain', but no 'quickened pulse'. For him, the poem suffocates the excitement of its story by swathing it in layer upon layer of the most artificial verbal 'tissue of ingenuities', with antitheses and other 'incessant conceits'.[1] Interest in the poem eventually re-emerged from a number of scholarly quarters,[2] including those involved in the larger project of tracing the intertwinement of early modern law and literature and of excavating the categories of forensic rhetoric buried in the history of late-sixteenth- and seventeenth-century English literature.[3] The drama of the schoolroom, where rhetorical categories such as opportunity and circumstance were beaten into poets like

Shakespeare, seemed to manifest with new urgency in the vexed speeches of Lucrece and Tarquin, who again and again seem to be speaking in front of assemblies or in courtrooms, even when they are only deliberating within themselves.[4]

As a result of this important scholarly work, a new question can now arise: what then makes this poem *different* from a set of schoolboy exercises in rhetoric? In asking this question, I do not intend to undermine the role of rhetoric in this poem; rather, I understand the poem as so saturated with rhetoric that it provides a kind of test case for beginning to delineate the subtle limits of rhetoric in poetry. If the poem seems to be immersed in rhetoric and rhetorical theory, it also again and again recoils from rhetoric's commitment to instrumentalizing modes of thought. Rhetoric, as Aristotle said, is practical; it is concerned with negotiating alternative possibilities and coming to a decision for the sake of action.[5] In reading and rereading this very difficult poem, where the characters are constantly trying to persuade one another in order to achieve desired ends, I am repeatedly struck by a peculiar sensation: that, even as the poem emphasizes (perhaps to the point of semi-parodic excess) the rhetorical basis of its thinking and of its use of language, some part of the poem is also watching from behind its own overly gilded lines. Another mentality, that is, appears at work behind the poem's elaborate rhetorical surface.

In this essay, I'll start by examining a series of largely overlooked images which provide a basis for this elusive sensation and which are not fully explicable according to rhetorical ends. I'll then trace the significance of these images by exploring how Shakespeare develops a unique poetics by testing the limits of rhetorical persuasion.

Fellow-feeling at a remove

The first image is a peculiarly elusive one. After the rape, Lucrece imagines putting on trial a series of personified figures (Night, Opportunity, and Time) and finds each of them guilty in turn for the crime she has suffered. This imagined courtroom trial has been important to recent critics in showing the poem's extensive debt to rhetorical theory, especially to the categories of forensic rhetoric. Lorna Hutson, for example, has masterfully elucidated the passage's detailed use of *occasio*,[6] and William Weaver of *narratio* and *confirmatio*.[7]

Yet in testifying against the personification of night, Lucrece articulates a peculiar image that does not quite make sense in rhetorical terms. In fact, it may even be anti-rhetorical:

> Were TARQUIN Night, as he is but Night's child,
> The silver-shining queen he would distain;
> Her twinkling handmaids too, by him defiled,
> Through Night's black bosom should not peep again.
> So should I have co-partners in my pain;
>   And fellowship in woe doth woe assuage.
>
> (785–90)

Lucrece suggests that if her rapist were the night, he would have raped the moon as well as all the stars, 'her twinkling handmaids'. It is as though nothing in this world can escape Tarquin's despoiling touch. The image of stars is, perhaps, the superlative of our imaginations, the *ne-plus-ultra*. Stars often represent the beauty of the world that lies just out of reach: when Marlowe's Faustus sees Helen, for instance, he says, 'O, thou art fairer than the evening air, / Clad in the beauty of a thousand stars'.[8] In *The Rape of Lucrece*, the image of raped stars evokes a sense of loss and defilement that lies beyond all bounds. As devastating as is this image, though, it offers Lucrece a temporary sense of company: the stars would become, she says, 'co-partners in my pain', assuaging her woe through their 'fellowship'.

But the sense of company she imagines is of a special kind. Lucrece describes the stars, once raped, going dark and withdrawing from her view. 'Through Night's black bosom', she says, they 'should not peep again'. Here's an audience that is imagined retracting from her, that is incapable of providing any kind of help. This image of raped stars going dark and disappearing from view evokes the strangest possible sense of company: one that preserves Lucrece's isolation.

It may be significant that this audience is imagined as female, given that rhetoric typically operates in homosocial contexts, whether one thinks of schoolrooms or courtrooms. It is a male audience that the poem imagines for its own initial speeches, when Collatine acts as 'publisher' (33) of his wife's beauty by praising it in front of other men in the war camp. In contrast, lyric poetry has – it is not remarked enough – a long tradition of imagining a female audience. Dante addressed his lyric sequence to women. In *La Vita Nuova*, he explains that the first poet started writing love poems in the vernacular because he wanted to be understood by a woman who did not know Latin (25). One canzone (19) specifically addresses 'ladies who know by insight what love is' (*donne ch' avete intelletto d'amore*), and the narrator draws to a close his mournful sequence by, in one of the last songs (31), calling upon the song itself to seek the company of 'ladies and young maidens'.[9] He does not seem to be asking these women for anything (these are not poems of seduction); rather, he merely calls upon women in the collective as an audience who might pity his woe from a distance. This appeal to women for pity influences the later tradition. Petrarch, for example, in his *Rime sparse* calls upon women who might 'grieve for me' (268, l. 59).[10] This tradition of a female audience for lyric also helps shape what might be considered lyrical moments in Shakespeare's plays. Ophelia, after singing her (vernacular) folk songs, exits by famously calling out to women in the plural, 'Goodnight, ladies, goodnight. Sweet ladies, goodnight, goodnight' (4.5.72–3) – even though she has been talking to a group of men (there being present only one woman, Gertrude).[11] In *Othello*, similarly, when Desdemona sings her 'Willow Song', she does so to a female audience, Emilia; moreover, she tells us that she, in turn, heard the song from her mother's maid, Barbary. And when Emilia is dying, she sings this same song specifically to her dead mistress. These singers are not persuading their audiences to do something. In fact, the impossibility of anyone's assistance seems part of the point in all these cases. A different logic seems at work from that in rhetoric.

And the image of the raped stars, as surprising as it may be, is not unique in Shakespeare's *Lucrece*. There are other images that, scattered throughout this epyllion, curiously resemble this one, at least in key aspects. To take another example: in the ekphrasis of the picture representing the fall of Troy, which Lucrece examines after the rape, Shakespeare describes a part of the picture that, like the image of raped stars, also entails a kind of reciprocity in grief, this time among men, curiously experienced across a distance:

> And from the towers of TROY there would appear
> The very eyes of men through loop-holes thrust,
> Gazing upon the GREEKS with little lust.
> > Such sweet observance in this work was had
> > That one might see those far-off eyes look sad.
>
> (1382–6)

In these stanzas, which evoke the verisimilitude that is traditional in an ekphrasis, Shakespeare asks us to imagine something non-traditional: that we can see into the little openings in the side of the towers. The view is so precise that, moreover, we can observe the eyes of men peering back from within. In these eyes, furthermore, we can see at work a complex mix of emotions – the eyes may be 'thrust' through the loop-holes, suggesting eagerness, but they look with 'little lust'. Shakespeare develops further this withdrawn quality: 'one might see those far-off eyes look sad.' The soldiers' eyes are withdrawn in two senses: not only in terms of distance because they are 'far-off' but also emotionally because they 'look sad'.

We find in this passage a combination of a few unusual elements that recalls the raped stars. In both cases, characters look back from a distance at Lucrece from within an image or representation. These figures in some ways mirror the situation of the one looking (the stars have also been raped; the soldiers also look sad). Furthermore, these characters – being only representations or images – are incapable of providing any direct assistance. What they seem to offer is a distant mirror, an *idea* of sympathy or fellow feeling.

To the collection of these two unusual images, we can add a third, through which the significance of a distanced sympathy comes to fruition. As Lucrece continues to look at the picture showing the fall of Troy, she eventually finds what she's looking for, which is 'a face where all distress is stelled', that is, the face of Hecuba:

> To this well-painted piece is LUCRECE come,
> To find a face where all distress is stelled.
> Many she sees where cares have carved some,
> But none where all distress and dolour dwelled
> Till she despairing HECUBA beheld,
>   Staring on PRIAM's wounds with her old eyes,
>   Which bleeding under PYRRHUS' proud foot lies.
>
> In her the painter had anatomized
> Time's ruin, beauty's wrack, and grim care's reign.
> Her cheeks with chaps and wrinkles were disguised;
> Of what she was no semblance did remain.
> Her blue blood changed to black in every vein,
>   Wanting the spring that those shrunk pipes had fed,
>   Showed life imprisoned in a body dead.
>
> On this sad shadow LUCRECE spends her eyes,
> And shapes her sorrow to the beldam's woes,
> Who nothing wants to answer her but cries
> And bitter words to ban her cruel foes:
> The painter was no god to lend her those,
>   And therefore LUCRECE swears he did her wrong
>   To give her so much grief and not a tongue.
>
> 'Poor instrument' quoth she, 'without a sound,
> I'll tune thy woes with my lamenting tongue'.
>
> (1443–65)

Again we find an image that offers a distanced reflection of Lucrece. Hecuba, who is described as a kind of historical ruin, mirrors Lucrece's lamentable, thing-like condition, as I have analysed elsewhere.[12] Notice how the line 'she despairing HECUBA beheld' is constructed so that, as Colin Burrow points out, 'despairing' can apply to either woman, linking or *pairing* them.[13] Furthermore, Hecuba is a representation (i.e., is not immediately present even in the world of the poem), and therefore cannot of course offer any practical help.

It could be argued that Lucrece's empathetic response to the image of Hecuba fits theories of rhetorical composition. Lucrece promises to speak for her, to 'tune thy woes with my lamenting tongue'. In this way, Lucrece attempts to spur her own feelings through the use of images, following the directions of Quintilian's *Institutes of Oratory*, which was heavily used in the English schoolroom. He explains that the only way that an orator can elicit the feelings he wants from his audience is to first elicit them from himself: 'The chief requisite, then, for moving the feelings of others, is, as far as I can judge, that we ourselves be moved'.[14] To do that effectively, the orator must not only adjust his external show of emotion (his words and looks) but, before that, also his internal state of mind. Quintilian offers strategies for the orator to excite his own emotions. The orator might, for example, try to visualize clearly for himself the events that he is describing. But he cannot pretend merely to witness these events – he must try to pretend that he is directly affected by them. Quintilian reiterates this point more than once:

> we must endeavour to believe, and to feel convinced, that the evils of which we complain have actually happened to ourselves. We must imagine ourselves to be those very persons for whom we lament as having suffered grievous, undeserved, and pitiable treatment; we must not plead their cause as that of another, but must endeavor to feel for a time their sufferings; and thus we shall say for them what we should in similar circumstances say for ourselves.[15]

Thus, there is no faking the external signs of feeling; the orator, not unlike a modern-day method actor, must summon the internal conditions that will allow him really to feel those emotions for himself, inwardly.

However, in considering the evident parallels of this scene with the dictates of rhetorical theory, what becomes noticeable is that Lucrece's situation is really so *unlike* that of an orator. An orator is trying to find a way to evoke the experience that he is describing by imagining that it impacted him directly – by imagining, for example, that he were the victim of the crime that he is trying to prosecute. What makes Lucrece's situation different, of course, is that she actually *is* the victim of the crime. Why then does Lucrece need to imagine herself as the victim? Something more peculiar starts to emerge: it is almost as though, in order to be able to feel what is in fact her own reality, she needs to imagine a version of her situation via that of a semi-fictional character. What the image of Hecuba provides, in other words, is a deflected relationship with herself – as though this self were not immediately available to her. A parallel situation, also involving the image of Hecuba, plays out in *Hamlet*, where the prince finds in the Player's representation of Hecuba's grief the passion that he should be able to summon for himself.[16]

And there's another important difference from oratory. It may seem as if Lucrece goes to the picture of Troy to generate further woe for the sake of rhetorical *inventio*. (Indeed, the narrator suggests as much when describing her 'pausing for means to mourn some newer way', 1365.) We learn later, however, that she seems to have gone to the picture for the opposite reason – not to increase her feeling, but to assuage it.

> Being from the feeling of her own grief brought
> By deep surmise of others' detriment,
> Losing her woes in shows of discontent.
>   It easeth some, though none it ever cured,
>   To think their dolour others have endured.

(1578–82)

Lucrece's 'deep surmise', or profound looking at a surface, seems to mitigate her experience of woe and to offer her some (albeit limited) measure of relief.

The picture of Troy's fall brings Lucrece both closer to and further from the feeling of her own grief into an experience that is shared. She feels that her experience is shared through looking at the *representation* of another person, through '*shows* of discontent', through '*painted* images', through '*think[ing of]* their dolour'. Like the idea of raped stars which withdraw from view or fearful eyes looking through the peepholes in the tower, Hecuba provides an image of fellow-feeling that is also distanced. The communion and sense of company all these images offer are not direct, not immediate, not actually proximate, but deflected through what is no more than the idea of company.

Lucrece, I suggest, is a surrogate for us readers – our mirror in the text.[17] Just as we do, Lucrece studies representations of other people in order to discover a collective sense of human fellowship. These figures cannot help her in any practical way. And yet, through projecting herself into these images, she seems to find a renewed relationship with her own experience and an amelioration of her suffering in the world.

Poetic contemplation

Marc Fumaroli, whose 1980 *L'âge de l'éloquence* has played a key role in reviving scholarly interest in the history of rhetoric, resists conflating poetry (or literature in general) with rhetoric. No one is more aware than he of the many ways that the histories of rhetorical theory and poetics are intertwined. Just as rhetoric, according to Cicero, is designed to serve a tripartite purpose of teaching, pleasing and moving,[18] so too, according to Renaissance poetic theorists like Julius Scaliger and Sir Philip Sidney, does poetry. Poetry has long borrowed from the delineation of tropes and figures that rhetoricians have articulated; and rhetoric has long looked to poetry for examples of these tropes and figures. In addition, in regard to English literature, we now know how deeply literary and legal cultures were intertwined both in the grammar school classroom and in the Inns of Court.[19] Yet however embedded in one another, rhetoric and poetry can imply 'situations of discourse' that are, Fumaroli asserts, 'radically different'.[20] Rhetoric emphasizes speech that has been adapted to a given context,[21] one in which people are trying to come to a decision, to form an opinion, to act. The aim is pragmatic: to persuade listeners. However, the goals of a written poem are much harder to define: 'This same eloquence, set down in writing, detached from its original context, is retired from the sphere of action. It becomes the object of an experience that is completely altered – that of reading, a *contemplative* activity of which the repercussions in the realm of action are much more distant, if not completely elusive'.[22] Unable to respond directly to any immediate audience (recall that Socrates accused the written word of 'rolling around all over the place',[23] repeating the same thing over and over again indiscriminately), a poem seems to withdraw into a more internal relation with readers. Augustine, a former teacher of rhetoric, describes his spiritual teacher, Ambrose, reading silently to himself – a new orientation to words is suggested by the saint's internal relation to the text.[24]

In discussing the shift to text and to silent reading in regard to Edmund Spenser's *The Faerie Queene*, Harry Berger, Jr argues that texts that represent speeches can turn against the 'rhetorical transaction' they represent and, in doing so, throw oratorical values into question.[25] 'As I see it, the major change these shifts involve is the disruption of the normative scheme that dominates the theory and practice of oratory from classical to humanist rhetoric, the scheme in which tropological means serve the transactional ends of persuasion, indoctrination, instruction, and control'.[26] In other words, the written text can deploy the tropological aspects of rhetoric to distance its readers from the transactional ends of rhetoric. If the perfect orator, according to Cicero, produces speech that compels agreement, that is able to swing the judge round to hardness or gentleness of heart, 'as though by some machinery [*aut tanquam machinatione aliqua*]',[27] literature can critique this very transaction. Hamlet, for example, complains that Rosencrantz and Guildenstern 'play upon me' (3.2.356) as though he were a kind of machine or instrument, but also articulates the existence of another part of himself, what he calls his 'heart's core' (3.2.69) that stands apart from such manipulations – or so he hopes.

What ultimately matters for Fumaroli is not whether words are spoken or written, public or private, but whether they serve the demands of the active or contemplative life. While it is true that the contemplative life and active life overlap (contemplation being a kind of action), the fundamental difference is one of ends versus means. According to this line of thinking, the satisfactions poetic contemplation provides lies in itself, that is, in the act of contemplation. This point derives, as Fumaroli emphasizes, from Aristotle's idea in the *Nicomachean Ethics* that 'from study we derive nothing beyond the activity of studying'.[28] Practical virtues, which are crucial, have an end outside of themselves: they are a means intended to produce the conditions (peace and prosperity) that make contemplation possible. That this kind of contemplative enjoyment could be linked with the study of the arts is made explicit in the *Politics* (1338a), where Aristotle talks about why music is deemed an important part of an education: not because it constitutes a useful or necessary kind of help in business, but because it is an inherently pleasurable kind of intellectual activity. This intellectual contemplation is worthwhile, he asserts, because even though our intellects may constitute only a very small part of ourselves, this part is, he claims, the best part: 'One might even regard it as each man's true self'.[29]

It is a relatively familiar point that early humanists, unlike some ancient theorists like Aristotle, did not tend to make the distinction between rhetoric and poetry we have been exploring. A Quattrocento humanist like Leonardo Bruni, for example, advocated the study of literature as a means of training readers in faculties of prudence and judgement, as well as in eloquence.

Giovanni Pontano similarly situates poetry as an art dedicated to prudence, by which men will be 'incited to virtue'.[30] However, as Victoria Kahn has shown, in the later Renaissance the awareness arose that literature, where 'dialogue turns in on itself', might not lend itself so seamlessly to practical considerations.[31] Poets seemed to be creating texts that referred more to themselves than to the outside world. For example, although his lifelong friend Fulke Greville would claim that Sidney only wrote to inspire right action ('his end was not writing, even while he wrote'[32]), Sidney himself was not entirely consistent on this point. In one 1578 letter, for example, Sidney questions the idea that the best kind of study is that which can be turned most readily to practical purpose:

> let us see if we are not endowing our showy errors with a lovely yet painted face. For while the mind is thus as it were drawn out of itself, it cannot turn its keenness upon itself, inwardly to contemplate itself – a work with which nothing men can be energetically busy at can compare.[33]

Here, at least, the kind of activity that Sidney most values is the activity of contemplation – an activity by which, as Aristotle recommends, the mind is drawn inward toward self-reflection.

An independent poetics seemed to be emerging, and with it a critical perspective on rhetoric. Tensions emerged, in Jeff Dolven's terms, between the schoolmaster and the poet.[34] In plays ranging from *The Taming of the Shrew* to *Love's Labour's Lost*, Shakespeare lampoons his own grammar-school rhetorical training. In numerous scenes, the schoolmaster appears to be some species of buffoon, whether one that is bloodlessly pedantic or lasciviously slavering. In other cases, such as in Portia's mercy speech in the *Merchant of Venice*, Shakespeare suggests the potential hypocrisy of rhetoric.

And yet, in exploring Shakespeare's extensive debt to rhetoric, it is easy to lose sight of his critical perspective on it. In his 2014 *Forensic Shakespeare*, for example, Quentin Skinner acknowledges Shakespeare's interest in the limits of rhetoric,[35] but devotes the vast majority of the book to showing how Shakespeare follows the precepts of ancient and Renaissance rhetorical theory (especially the rules governing *inventio*) 'with a remarkable degree of tenacity and exactitude'.[36] Organizing his study according to the parts of a forensic speech (*prohoemium*, *narratio*, *probatio*, etc.), Skinner culls and elucidates the relevant ancient and Renaissance precepts for constructing forensic arguments, as found in Cicero or Quintilian or Erasmus, and then analyses various passages of Shakespeare to show how they illustrate these rules. Here, for instance, is how Skinner sets up an analysis of a passage of *Lucrece*:

> There are three different ways in which you may be able to argue that you did not act *cum consulto* [intentionally], and hence that you deserve to be excused. As the [pseudo-Ciceronian] *Ad Herennium* puts it, you can plead that you acted out of necessity, or out of ignorance, or that the crime occurred by chance. Cicero adds that, if you enter a plea of *necessitudo*, you will need to assert 'the accused can be defended on the grounds that what they did was done in consequence of some external force'. This is the defence that Lucrece proceeds to mount.[37]

Skinner frames his discussion so that readers might almost think that they are reading a guidebook, like the kind popular in Renaissance classrooms, which were illustrated with examples from ancient history and literature. Here's what you should do if you find yourself in such and such rhetorical dilemma, and – see – this is exactly what Lucrece has done. Skinner's second-person address to his reader ('*you* may be able to argue that...'), which comes as a slight surprise in a scholarly text, reinforces the impression that his scholarship has been partly, momentarily won over by the kind of how-to thinking that it analyses, by thinking that is designed for use.

What gets left out of this story is hard to talk about. There may be reasons for that.

Self, receding

Joel B. Altman identifies what he calls 'rhetorical selfhood' in the Renaissance. 'A rhetorical self', explains Altman, 'is one determined by its address to the world. It is defined by its attitude, literally its poise'.[38] What is said is contingent, dependent on the moment, on circumstance. Focusing on *Othello*, he argues that Shakespeare explores a deep self-estrangement at the heart of this sense of self, as well as a sense of 'nostalgia' for a more unified self. Altman finds a crucial origin of this conflict in Augustine, the rhetorician who abandoned his work as a teacher of oratory to devote himself to contemplation and eventually to become, of course, a Christian saint. Developing Paul's idea of there being two laws (a good one in God, a bad one in the body), Augustine depicted two wills in conflict with each other: one will that desires God's truth, and the other that turns away from God and desires the material things of this world. The first will is stable and unitary and true, the other is endlessly changing and multiple and false.[39] The former, the province of the inner self, is the place where 'my soul is bathed in light that is not bound by space' and where 'it listens to sound that never dies away'.[40] The latter, the province of rhetorical self-presentation, is designed to address shifting circumstances and variable audiences. What's problematic for Augustine about this rhetorical self is that it is based on interaction with (or, as he puts it, fornication with) the world – a world based on happenstance and contingency. This very multiplicity stands in the way of his coming to see his authentic self, the fragment of the divine that is his soul.

Altman is interested in how theatre brought to the attention of its practitioners what he calls 'the hidden phenomenology of the self that lurked within the rhetorical poetics out of which its [the theatre's] plays were constructed'.[41] Yet a version of this tension is evident in Shakespeare's *Lucrece*, too, where we also find two selves, one that can be externalized and the other that is interior and silent, aligning with alternative, non-rhetorical modes of literary discourse.

Consider the moment when Tarquin approaches Lucrece's door, encountering a series of objects that, in a previous literature, would have been signs warning him to stop. The door grates against the threshold as though 'to have him heard' (306); the wind blows the smoke from his torch into his face, as though 'to make him stay' (311); and, most interesting, he pricks his finger on a needle left in her dropped glove (319), wounding himself in a manner that has been traditionally associated with women's loss of virginity.[42] But to no effect: 'all these poor forbiddings could not stay him' (323). For him, these are mere things of chance, the kind of things that, as he goes on to explain, a merchant might face, such as 'huge rocks, high winds, strong pirates, shelves and sands' (335). Such things may impede his voyage, but eventually 'rich at home he lands' (336). Tarquin takes these all as mere 'accidental things of trial' (326).

The instrumentalizing assumption that the world exists independently of his psychic condition, and that the trials it throws Tarquin's way are merely 'accidental things', represents a major departure from, say, the world that Spenser's characters inhabit. *The Faerie Queene* seems to morph constantly in order to express the psychic states of the characters. If we want to understand the character of Redcrosse, for example, we cannot look for descriptions of his thought processes, as Angus Fletcher reminds us. Rather, we must examine the knight's various adventures in order 'to see, literally, what aspects of the hero have been displayed by the poet'.[43] That is, we should study how the external world manifests the hero's internal conditions.

In contrast, when Tarquin rapes Lucrece, he does not realize this interconnection with the world. He wants to satisfy his 'appetite', and he uses rhetoric to assess the gains and losses in trying to achieve what he desires. He deliberates extensively, but the purpose of this debate is not the satisfaction offered by contemplation; rather, the purpose is eventual action. He claims, 'thoughts are but dreams till their effects be tried' (353) and, more bluntly and efficiently, 'debating die!' (274). His rhetoric helps construct a world on which he can, eventually, act.

Only after the rape does Tarquin discover that the world was not composed just of 'accidental things of trial', as he had thought, but was made up of forces that turn out in retrospect to have constituted a kind of psychomachia. The poem had earlier built up the metaphor that, in raping Lucrece, he would be invading and conquering a city. The narrator compared Tarquin's hand on her breast to a 'rude ram' (464) that batters an ivory wall. Her pounding heart was a distressed citizen wounding itself to death as it rose and fell against this wall, producing a shaking that 'moves in him more rage and lesser pity, / To make the breach and enter this sweet city' (468–9).

But then, making an abrupt switch after the rape, Shakespeare radically disrupts the expectations that he has set up that she is a city to be overcome. We find that Tarquin has indeed made an invasion, but what he has invaded is none other than the edifice of his own soul:

> Besides his soul's fair temple is defaced,
> > To whose weak ruins muster troops of cares,
> > To ask the spotted princess how she fares.
>
> She says her subjects with foul insurrection
> Have battered down her consecrated wall,
> And by their mortal fault brought in subjection
> Her immortality, and made her thrall
> To living death and pain perpetual;
> > Which in her prescience she controlled still,
> > But her foresight could not forestall their will.

(719–28)

The 'spotted princess' is not Lucrece – '*she*' is, in fact, the soul of Tarquin. The metaphor of the body as the soul's temple has a long history, extending back to 1 Corinthians 3.16: 'Know ye not that ye are the Temple of God', as Burrow notes.[44] And a siege of a castle is one of the most common medieval forms for representing a psychomachia, according to Bernard Spivack. He cites Henry Medwall's fifteenth-century play *Nature*, where man 'abydeth wythin the garyson / of the frayll carcas and carynouse body', which the enemy tries constantly to 'bryng into captyuyte'.[45]

Shakespeare energizes the confusion of what edifice has been destroyed by referring to Tarquin's soul with a feminine pronoun, repeated nine times in the space of eight lines: 'how she fares'; 'she says'; 'her subjects'; 'her consecrated wall'; 'her immortality'; 'made her thrall'; 'her prescience'; 'she controlled'; 'her foresight'. Tarquin may have thought he was acting on the world, but he was also acting on a part of himself.[46] That Tarquin's soul-in-the-fortress is female might recall the female audience that is one of the traditional audiences for lyric, but here, taking up Fumaroli's and Altman's discussions, the female audience is aligned with the soul, or the contemplative part of the self. The (external) female audience imagined as an audience for lyric in Dante or Petrarch finds here an analogue in the (internal) female soul that contemplates itself.

It is suggestive that Tarquin's allegorical construction of self only emerges to the fore at the moment of its negation, at the moment when Tarquin has destroyed himself.[47] That is, his soul manifests only as it disappears. Indeed, immediately after this point, Tarquin vanishes from the narrative, skulking away like a dog into the night (736), and we learn no more about him. The focus of the remaining 1,105 lines of the narrative shifts to Lucrece. We seem to glimpse another, more private reality behind the rhetoric designed for public discourse. This is a reality that Shakespeare associates with the elusiveness of poetic imagery and with silence. In this reality, the self has not yet developed a subject–object orientation to the world but lives in a world that is always already (at least partly) an image of the self. The poem represents this allegorical reality as being left behind.[48]

In the case of Lucrece, the problem of rhetoric emerges perhaps most strongly in her repeated claim that she is unable to express her experience. What she has suffered exceeds, she says, the powers of her speech. 'For more it is than I can well express, / And that deep torture may be called a hell / When more is felt than one hath power to tell' (1286–8). Like Lucrece, Hecuba had suffered a grief that seemed to lie beyond words. Ovid writes, 'She was dumb with grief, her very grief had overwhelmed both her voice and her rising tears'.[49] As Lynn Enterline has explored, Shakespeare draws attention to this shared experience of silence. Lucrece blames the painter for 'giv[ing Hecuba] so much grief and not a tongue' (1463). An interesting conflation occurs here: Shakespeare associates Hecuba's silence with the inexpressibility of her great grief and, at the same time, with her existence as a representation, as a painting that, of course, cannot speak.

The pain of silence becomes inextricable from the condition of her being a poetic representation. The crime of rape is traditionally considered 'unspeakable'. What this silence says about perceptions of rape is important.[50] But so too is what this silence says about poetry. Philomela, after all, is one central creation myth for the origin of lyric. A story of rape provides an origin story for lyric that grounds it in silence and in inner dialogue.

Lucrece's silence is traditional in previous versions of her story; what Shakespeare has changed, as Enterline has emphasized, is that this experience of silence now occurs amid a lot of talking. 'Sometime her grief is dumb and hath no words, / Sometime 'tis mad and too much talk affords' (1105–6). That experience of silence amid speech is important because it is only through her talking, through her adept rhetorical performances, that Lucrece expresses her feeling of silence, the inexpressibility of her suffering. As a result, this experience does appear, but as a negation, as that which cannot appear. Enterline writes that 'the moving power of Lucrece's voice, like that of Philomela, the singing nightingale, derives from the idea of its impossibility'.[51] Thus, we are made to glimpse what cannot manifest *as* what cannot manifest.

In this essay, I have been considering the role of rhetoric in *The Rape of Lucrece*, especially rhetoric related to generating practical action in the world, and how the poem shows a different mentality looking out from behind its emphatic rhetorical surface, a mentality that is withdrawn. In trying to catch a glimpse of what lies behind the surface, I started the essay by noticing repeated images of audiences that recede from Lucrece: the raped stars, the men in the tower, the picture of Hecuba. Despite offering no possibility of practical help, these images seemed to offer Lucrece a sense of fellow-feeling. I suggested that, as she projected herself into these images, she became a kind of complex mirror for readers projecting themselves into the image of her. The interaction does not provide any possibility of practical help; the logic of this interaction (and the logic of this poetry) is non-instrumentalizing. Rather, the figures that she studies give her access to hidden parts of herself, specifically to contemplative parts of herself that cannot otherwise manifest in this world but that share in a collective human suffering. Although we associate a non-instrumental understanding of art with a post-Kantian world, we find this understanding emergent in Shakespeare's poem, appearing as a kind of shadow of rhetoric – as that which rhetoric cannot say. This poetry (and, along with it, the self that contemplates this poetry) is only glimpsed elusively peering out from behind the rhetoric, as though even now disappearing from view.[52]

Notes

1 Douglas Bush, *Mythology and the Renaissance Tradition in English Poetry* (New York: W.W. Norton & Company, 1963), 152. See also George Brandes, who comments on the poem's 'elaborate and far-fetched rhetoric' and says of Lucrece's lament that it is as 'copious and artificial as an oration of Cicero's'. George Brandes, *William Shakespeare: A Critical Study* (New York: The MacMillan Company, 1909), 59.

2 Especially important for its focus on rhetoric is feminist criticism of the poem's Petrarchan tropes; see especially Lynn Enterline, *The Rhetoric of the Body*, 152–97; and Nancy J. Vickers, '"The blazon of sweet beauty's best"', 95–115 and '"This Heraldry in Lucrece's Face"', *Poetics Today* 6.1/2 (1985): 171–84. Also crucial to the revival of interest in the poem's rhetoric: Joel Fineman, 'Shakespeare's Will: The Temporality of Rape', *Representations*, No. 20 (Autumn, 1987): 25–76; and Katharine Eisaman Maus, 'Taking Tropes Seriously'.

3 For recent scholarship exploring the role of forensic rhetoric in the poem, see for example Lorna Hutson, *Circumstantial Shakespeare* (Oxford: Oxford University Press, 2015) and Quentin Skinner, *Forensic Shakespeare* (Oxford: Oxford University Press, 2014).

4 See Lynn Enterline, *Shakespeare's Schoolroom* and William Weaver, *Untutored Lines*.

5 *Rhetoric* 1357a.

6 Hutson, *Circumstantial Shakespeare*, 70–101.

7 Weaver, *Untutored Lines*, 123–43.

8 Christopher Marlowe, *Doctor Faustus* in *The Complete Plays*, eds Frank Romany and Robert Lindsey (London: Penguin, 2003), 13.103–4.

9 *La Vita Nuova (Poems of Youth)*, trans. Barbara Reynolds (London: Penguin Books, 2004).

10 *Petrarch's Lyric Poems: The* Rime Sparse *and Other Lyrics*, ed. and trans. Robert Durling (Cambridge, MA: Harvard University Press, 1976).

11 On the importance of song to Shakespeare's marginal characters, see Heather Dubrow, *The Challenges of Orpheus: Lyric Poetry and Early Modern England* (Baltimore: Johns Hopkins University Press, 2008), 219.

12 Broken, worn, and silent, Hecuba appears almost like a fragment of ancient sculpture or other antiquarian artifact. See Chapter 5 of Rachel Eisendrath, *Poetry in a World of Things: Aesthetics and Empiricism in Renaissance Ekphrasis* (Chicago: University of Chicago Press, 2018).

13 *The Complete Sonnets and Poems*, ed. Colin Burrow (Oxford: Oxford University Press, 2002), 319.

14 6.2.26. All quotations of Quintilian from *Institutes of Oratory; or, Education of an Orator*, trans. Rev. John Selby Watson, 2 vols (London: Bell & Daldy, 1871–3).

15 6.2.34. Quintilian makes this same point at 6.2.27.

16 Enterline calls Lucrece a 'prototype' for Hamlet, *Rhetoric of the Body*, 166, and explores how in both texts Shakespeare's school training encouraged mediated forms of self-identification, or 'habits of alterity', *Shakespeare's Schoolroom*, 131–2.

17 Lucrece may also be the surrogate of the poem's author. See Enterline, *Rhetoric of the Body*, 152–97. Also, see Amy Greenstadt, who explores how the poem negotiates fantasies of authorial intention, '"Read it in me": The Author's Will in *Lucrece*', *Shakespeare Quarterly* 57.1 (Spring, 2006): 45–70.

18 *De optimo genere oratorum*, 1.4.

19 See, for example, Lorna Hutson, ed., *The Oxford Handbook of English Law and Literature, 1500–1700* (Oxford: Oxford University Press, 2017).

20 Marc Fumaroli, 'Les sanglots d'Ulysse', in *La diplomatie de l'esprit: De Montaigne à La Fontaine* (Paris: Gallimard, 1998), 2. Translations from the French mine.

21 Quintilian, 3.7.23.

22 Fumaroli, 'Les sanglots d'Ulysse', 3.

23 *Phaedrus* 275e.

24 Augustine, *Confessions*, 6.3.3.

25 'Narrative as Rhetoric in *The Faerie Queene*', reprinted in Harry Berger, Jr, *Situated Utterances: Texts, Bodies, and Cultural Representations* (New York: Fordham University Press, 2005), 177.

26 Ibid., 176.

27 *De oratore* 2.17.72; quoted in Skinner, *Forensic Shakespeare*, 20.

28 Aristotle, *Nicomachean Ethics*, trans. Martin Ostwald (Upper Saddle River, NJ: Prentice Hall, 1999), 1177b.

29 *Nicomachean Ethics*, 1178a. See Fumaroli, 'Les sanglots d'Ulysse', 6–7.
30 See Victoria Kahn, *Rhetoric, Prudence, and Skepticism in the Renaissance* (Ithaca: Cornell University Press, 1985), 37, 43.
31 Ibid., 20.
32 Fulke Greville, *Life of Sir Philip Sidney* (Oxford: Clarendon Press, 1907), 18.
33 The letter, which is written in Latin, is dated 1 March 1578. I am quoting the translation provided in *The Correspondence of Sir Philip Sidney*, vol. 2, ed. Roger Kuin (Oxford: Oxford University Press, 2012), 817.
34 Jeff Dolven, *Scenes of Instruction in Renaissance Romance* (Chicago: University of Chicago Press, 2007).
35 See especially *Forensic Shakespeare*, 154–60.
36 Ibid., 66.
37 Ibid., 129.
38 Joel B. Altman, *The Improbability of Othello: Rhetorical Anthropology and Shakespearean Selfhood* (Chicago: University of Chicago Press, 2010), 20.
39 Ultimately, even the rhetorical self represents for Altman 'a double sense of self', entailing, on the one hand, 'the assumption of a stable human identity that possesses the capacity for self-reflection and self-projection' and, on the other hand, 'the imitation of human multiplicity and that of the world – of the immanence of the human in the world and the world in the human – that challenges the idea of such stability' (19).
40 *Confessions*, trans. R.S. Pine-Coffin (London: Penguin, 1961), 10.6.
41 Altman, 15.
42 Cf. Britomart's wounds in the Castle Joyous (3.1.65) and in the House of Busirane (3.12.33), at the beginning and ending of Book III of *The Faerie Queene*.
43 Angus Fletcher, *Allegory: The Theory of a Symbolic Mode* (Princeton: Princeton University Press, 2012), 34–5.
44 *The Complete Sonnets and Poems*, 283.

45 Part 2, 10–11, 14. Quoted in Bernard Spivack, *Shakespeare and the Allegory of Evil* (New York: Columbia University Press, 1958), 73.

46 Ian Donaldson connects the self-destructiveness of Tarquin's crime, which renders him 'a captive victor that hath lost in gain' (730), with Ovid's address to Tarquin, '*Quid victor gaudes? Haec te victoria perdet*' (Why, victor, do you rejoice? This victory will ruin you). See his *The Rapes of Lucretia: A Myth and its Transformations* (Oxford: Clarendon Press, 1982), 52. For Tarquin's self-rape, see Sam Hynes, 'The Rape of Tarquin', *Shakespeare Quarterly* 10.3 (Summer, 1959): 451–3.

47 For Boccaccio, the aims of rhetoric and allegory were fundamentally different. Rhetoric was designed to persuade the crowd in the marketplace, but allegory was designed to conceal the precious kernel of truth for those worthy of receiving it. No pearls before swine. See Boccaccio, *Genealogia Deorum Gentilium XIV*, available in translation as *On Poetry*, trans. Charles G. Osgood (New York: The Liberal Arts Press, 1956). It should be noted, though, that Quintilian included allegory among the techniques available to the orator (8.6.44ff).

48 The allegorical construction of the world, which Tarquin rejects, may have started to sound by the 1590s 'old-fashioned'. See Brian Cummings on the ongoing use of allegory in a Protestant context, where the literal sense of words presumably dominated. 'Protestant Allegory' in *The Cambridge Companion to Allegory*, eds Rita Copeland and Peter T. Struck (Cambridge: Cambridge University Press, 2010), 177–90. That Shakespeare may have associated allegory in this poem with a bygone world might help substantiate the 'medieval' quality that several critics have noticed in this poem. See Bush, 154; C.S. Lewis, *English Literature in the Sixteenth Century, Excluding Drama* (Oxford: Clarendon Press, 1954), 500.

49 Ovid, *Metamorphoses*, 13.538–40. Quoted in Enterline, *Rhetoric of the Body*, 166.

50 See, for example, Mark Amsler, 'Rape and Silence: Ovid's Mythography and Medieval Readers', in *Representing Rape in Medieval and Early Modern Literature*, eds Elizabeth Robertson and Christine M. Rose (New York: Palgrave, 2001), 61–96.

51 Enterline, *Rhetoric of the Body*, 181.

52 For their insightful, generous and rigorous comments, I am grateful to Caryn O'Connell, Timea Széll and especially Heather James, who did some heavy lifting. Thanks also to Ardis Butterfield, Heather Dubrow and Susanne Wofford for their questions and comments in response to a shorter version of this paper at the 2018 Modern Language Association conference.

PART TWO

Debating *mimesis*

3

Epic Oenone, pastoral Paris

Undoing the Virgilian *rota* in Thomas Heywood's *Oenone and Paris*

Joseph M. Ortiz

In the second section of his *Apology for Actors* (1612), in the middle of a discussion of renowned classical actors, Thomas Heywood makes a brief and unexplained digression on the subject of English literary history: 'Here I might take fit opportunity to reckon up all our *English* writers, & compare them with the *Greeke, French, Italian, & Latine* Poets, not only in their *Pastorall, Historicall, Elegeicall, & Heroicall* Poems, but in their *Tragicall, & Comical* subjects, but it was my chance to happen on the like learnedly done by an approved good scholler, in a booke called *Wits Comon-wealth*, to which treatise I wholly referre you.'[1] This 'treatise', which Heywood never mentions again in the *Apology*, is Francis Meres' *Palladis Tamia* (1598), a work now known mostly for its seemingly prescient representation of Shakespeare as the English Ovid. While the passage on Meres has not received much serious critical attention (like much of the *Apology*, to be frank), it shows Heywood's keen awareness of the complex relationship between classical and Renaissance literature and the sense of competition that English writers often felt (in relation both to Continental writers and to each other) when attempting to imitate and translate classical material. Equally important, the passage shows Heywood's awareness of *genre* as a crucial reference point in the reception of classical literature. For Heywood, a formidable classicist himself, the successful imitation of Greek and Latin models (and, to a lesser extent, French and Italian) requires a careful understanding of their generic distinctions and objectives.

In this essay I use Heywood's poetic self-consciousness, and sensitivity to genre evident in his *Apology* and other works, as a context for reading his narrative poem *Oenone and Paris* (1594). The poem, when it has been discussed at all by modern critics, is nearly always read as a response to (and sometimes a slavish imitation of) Shakespeare's *Venus and Adonis*, which had appeared in print the previous year.[2] Not surprisingly, such readings tend to eclipse other aspects of Heywood's poem, most notably its nuanced and methodical handling of classical sources, particularly Virgil and Ovid. As I will show, Heywood's dramatization of a lovers' quarrel between Oenone and Paris reads very much like a debate over the comparative merits of different classical genres, particularly pastoral and epic. Moreover, the competing virtues that Heywood imputes to pastoral and epic through the poem's speaker and the speeches of its protagonists – leisure and fame, youth and maturity, reclusion and civic action – are made to point self-reflexively towards the poet himself. In this respect, Heywood's poem invariably evokes the idea of the Virgilian *rota*, the model of a poetic career that, in its simplest form, starts with pastoral and ends with epic.[3] Put another way, *Oenone and Paris* presents the image of a young, ambitious poet thinking about what he will do next.

As a poem typically classified as an epyllion or minor epic, *Oenone and Paris* may seem like a strange arena in which to weigh the claims of pastoral and epic. After all, the poems in this genre (however one chooses to characterize or define it) often appear to readers to reject epic's ideology from the start, or at least to dwell on those moments that epic, especially Virgilian epic, brands as 'deviant' or 'incoherent'.[4] For example, epyllia tend to focus on erotic desire, and they often eschew narrative closure. Yet, the question of what exactly constitutes a rejection of epic, or epic deviance, has special urgency for Heywood in *Oenone*, not only because he bases his poem on Ovidian material (the gateway drug of most epic dissidents), but because of something more recent: the 1590 publication of Spenser's *Faerie Queene*. The significance of this literary event helps to explain the manifold echoes of Spenserian language in *Oenone*, from its opening line to the end of the poem. William Keach argues that the 1590 *Faerie Queene* looms large over the Elizabethan epyllia in general, suggesting that the epyllion constitutes an ironic, problematizing response to Spenser's 'synthesizing poetry', his 'harmonious reconciliation' of epic heroism and erotic (Ovidian) experience.[5] Keach's argument is persuasive, though it can be qualified for Heywood, who sees Spenserian synthesis as a problem in itself, at least for someone who takes the Virgilian model of a literary career seriously. Many of Heywood's Spenserian allusions hone in on 'synthesizing' moments in *The Faerie Queene*, but they manage to frame this syncretism as a pastoral *regression* rather than harmonious union. At its most anxious, *Oenone and Paris* registers a sense of confusion about generic categories in the wake of the 1590 *Faerie Queene* – namely, that pastoral has contaminated epic for good, and that the Virgilian *rota* is no longer a practical model for English poets.

Oenone and Paris begins securely in the pastoral mode, in a setting that evokes landscapes familiar from both *The Shepheardes Calendar* and *The Faerie Queene*:

When Sun-bright Phebus in his fierie carre,
Ended his passage through the vernall signes,
And all the trees that on the mountaines are,
Aspyring Cedars, and the loftie pines,
And verdaunt flowers mantled all in greene
Newlye received their liveries from their Queene

(stanza 1)

Although this stanza has been glossed as an imitation of the opening of Shakespeare's *Venus and Adonis*, its first line contains a more specific echo of the beginning of Book One, Canto 2 of *The Faerie Queene*, in which '*Phoebus* fiery carre' is seen rising in the East (I.ii.1).[6] This imitation prepares the reader for another allusion to *The Faerie Queene* at the end of the stanza, in which the flowers that have 'newlye received their liveries from their Queene' recall the fairy knights in Spenser's poem who are commissioned by the Faerie Queene to perform heroic deeds. The stanza's anthropomorphic language ('aspyring Cedars', 'loftie pines'), at first seeming like mere poetic floridness, becomes subsequently legible as part of a recurring pattern of figures for worldly fame and nobility. In this way, the opening of *Oenone and Paris* enacts in miniature an impulse that recurs throughout the poem: the desire to replace pastoral tranquility with heroic action.

The second stanza of Heywood's poem, which formally introduces Paris, continues to move towards the heroic, and here again the scene is palpably Spenserian:

The Phrigian Paris earlie in a morning,
Rose from th'imbracements of his new-stolne bryde:
Him selfe in silkes, his steede with studdes adorning,
With speedie course fast to the groves he plyde,

Pursuing game as farre as Ida mountaine.
There hee alight's, and sitts him by a fountaine.

(stanza 2)

For all of the comparisons to Shakespeare this passage has engendered, Heywood's Paris is deceptively complex. He looks different from Shakespeare's Adonis, who is presumably wearing hunting gear, and even from Ovid's Paris, who, when first seen by Oenone in the *Heroides*, sports majestic purple (*fulsit mihi purpura*).[7] Rather, Heywood's Paris, dressed in 'silkes', looks much more like the knight of chivalric romance who has lapsed into sensuous passivity. His heroism is merely a pose. When he finally takes up the requisite 'bore-speare' a few stanzas later, he seems to carry it more as a fashionable accoutrement ('plated with golde') than for actual hunting (stanza 6). Even his horse, whose 'studdes adorning' recalls the 'studded bridle' of Adonis' horse in *Venus and Adonis* (stanza 2), wears his gear in dandyish fashion (37).

If Heywood's initial presentation of a heroic Paris is ironic, then it is significant that this undercutting is itself modelled on Renaissance epic. In particular, Heywood's Paris recalls a central figure in one of Spenser's primary models for *The Faerie Queene* – Ariosto's Ruggiero, who appears in a remarkably similar pose while dallying with the enchantress Alcina:

Che si godea il matin fresco e sereno,
Lungo un bel rio che discorrea d'un colle
Verso un laghetto limpido et ameno.
Il suo vestir delizioso e molle
Tutto era d' ozio e di lascivia pieno,
Che di sua man gli avea di seta e d' oro
Tessuto Alcina con sottil lavoro.

(7.53)[8]

[Who was enjoying the fresh and calm morning, beside a beautiful stream which ran down a hill opposite a limpid and peaceful lake. His sumptuous and soft clothing was all full of sloth and sensuality; Alcina had made the fabric with subtle work, by her own hands from silk and gold.]

Here, Ariosto makes clear the moral meaning of Ruggiero's amorous play with Alcina ('d' ozio e di lascivia', 'sloth and sensuality'). Heywood likewise suggests, though less explicitly, the libertine stature of Paris, who 'softly pace[s]' in a postcoital stupor and then lazily 'muze[s] on his beauteous rape' (stanzas 3–4). In addition, Heywood places Paris in a carefully arranged landscape that mirrors his languid contentedness: 'Flora bedecked it with eche smelling flower, / The Primrose, Cowslippe, and the Daffadillie, / The Pinke, the Daysie, Violet, and Lillie' (stanza 3). Paris has been in this landscape before, but so has Heywood's reader, if she has read *The Shepheardes Calendar*: 'Bring hether the Pincke . . . / Strowe me the ground with Daffadowndillies, / And Cowslips, and Kingcups, and loved Lillies'.[9] In a sense, epic imitation leads Heywood (and Paris) back to Spenserian pastoral, which in turn looks a lot like romance. The point is that, while Ariosto's Ruggiero can solidify his epic status by leaving Alcina (just as Virgil's Aeneas leaves Dido), at this point in Heywood's *Oenone*, epic is made to seem like a sham, a kind of pastoral role-playing.

That Heywood's poem inclines towards pastoral or romance is not in itself remarkable. As Clark Hulse and others observe, Renaissance minor epics regularly 'compare the erotic values of sonnet and pastoral with the heroic values of epic', often showing a greater affinity towards the former.[10] What is less typical is the extent to which Heywood inscribes the tension between pastoral and epic into the central drama of the poem. Equally important is the extent to which Heywood draws on Virgilian material to exacerbate the difference between the two genres. In fact, these two aspects of *Oenone* – the dramatization of generic conflict and the reliance on Virgil – are mutually reinforcing, given Heywood's choice of subject. For it is in Virgil's poetry that Paris above all is repeatedly presented as a generically liminal character – as someone who has a history in both pastoral and epic. Paris thus functions for Virgil as a uniquely convenient figure through which to signal generic mixing in his poetry, and through which to contemplate the ramifications of generic choices.[11] A brief consideration of Virgil's Paris will thus be instructive for reading Heywood's drama of generic conflict.

One of the ways in which Virgil emphasizes Paris' generic ambivalence is by teasing out the connotations of the various names and places typically associated with him. For example, in the *Eclogues*, at the height of Corydon's complaint against his desired Alexis, Virgil cites Paris as the single human example of a heroic figure who also lived comfortably in the woods:

quem fugis, a! demens? habitarunt di quoque silvas
Dardaniusque Paris. Pallas, quas condidit arces
ipsa colat.

(2.60–2)

[Ah, fool, whom do you flee? Even the gods have dwelt in the woods, and Dardan Paris. Let Pallas dwell by herself in the cities she has built.[12]]

As Stephen Guy-Bray astutely points out, Virgil constructs a carefully placed pun on 'Paris' and 'Pallas' to sharpen the contrast between the destructive violence of the Trojan city and the essentially benign violence of the woods.[13] Significantly, Virgil also emphasizes the 'urban', heroic side of Paris (thus helping to make Corydon's point) by referring to Paris as *Dardanius*. This modifier ties Paris securely to the line of Dardanus and Priam – a genealogy that was initially occluded when, because of a prophecy, Paris was sent out of Troy as a baby. The name also ties him, importantly, to Aeneas and the line of Trojans that would ultimately be translated to Italy.[14] In a similar fashion, but to different effect, Virgil uses a specific name for Paris in *Aeneid* 7, when the Latin queen Amata attempts to persuade her husband Latinus to oppose Aeneas' marriage with Lavinia:

at non sic Phrygius penetrat Lacedaemona pastor
Ledaeamque Helenam Troianas vexit ad urbes?

(7.363–4)

[Or, was it not thus that the Phrygian shepherd entered Lacedaemon and bore off Leda's Helen to Trojan towns?]

Amata's main argument centres on a notion of Latin superiority, but her brief dig at Aeneas via Paris is clear enough. He is a *pastor*, rustic and uncultivated, and, more damningly, he is *Phrygian*, a name that often functions in the *Aeneid* as an orientalizing term for someone associated with effeminacy, weakness, luxuriousness – in other words, someone entirely unsuited for dynastic marriage, or for epic. Indeed, this is an efficient pejorative that Virgil's Latins know how to use, as when the Latin Numanus taunts Ascanius and his companions:

bis capti Phryges ...
o vere Phrygiae, neque enim Phryges, ite per alta
Dindyma, ubi adsuetis biforem dat tibia cantum.
tympana vos buxusque vocat Berecyntia matris
Idaeae: sinite arma viris et cedite ferro.

(9.599–620)

[Twice-captured Phrygians ... O ye Phrygian women, indeed! – for Phrygian men are ye not – go ye over the heights of Dindymus, where to accustomed ears the pipe utters music from double mouths! The timbrels call you, and the Berecynthian boxwood of the mother of Ida: leave arms to men, and quit the sword.]

When Numanus briefly quotes the opening of the *Aeneid* (*arma viris*), his insult carries generic significance: Phrygian men (a term he treats as an oxymoron) have no place in epic.[15] And Numanus goes further, claiming that the Latins, when they are not waging war, work the earth and livestock 'with spear reversed' (*versaque . . . hasta*, 610–11). As far as Numanus is concerned, the Trojans are not even manly enough for georgic, the poetry of agriculture.[16]

Heywood is sensitive to the nuances of Trojan epithets, and he follows Virgil in strategically using these terms to suggest the generic ambivalence of his own Paris. In the same stanza in which he suggests Paris' luxuriousness, Heywood introduces him as 'the Phrigian Paris' (stanza 2), reinforcing the image's affinity with Ariostan romance. Heywood's Oenone herself seems to intuit the intimations of Paris' various names, addressing him in different ways depending on her mode of complaint. When she first sees him, she quickly brands him as 'ingratefull Trojan, cause of all my sorrowes', thus fixing him as a figure of infidelity and forever linking him to Helen (stanza 7). Three stanzas later, she softens her address, while still maintaining the fact of Paris' rapaciousness: 'Say gentle Trojan, wordes that may delight me, / And for thy former lust I will acquite thee' (stanza 10). Here, her use of 'gentle Trojan' is conspicuous not only because it skirts the bounds of an oxymoron, but also because it subtly reminds Paris of his newly regained nobility, his 'gentle' status. By this logic, a 'Trojan' Paris is still a faithless lover, but one whose status consciousness might goad him into more responsible behaviour.[17] However, Oenone soon changes her tack, instead reminding Paris of his essential softness, whether as lover or warrior:

> Whole worldes of warriours will besiege your citie,
> King Menelaus will not loose his Juell,
> Then fayre-fac'd Phrygian, if thou harborest pitie,
> Returne her backe, (the Greekes are fierce and cruel).
>
> (stanza 15)

Here, Oenone's alliterative epithet for Paris ('fayre-fac'd Phrygian') works in tandem with her rhetorical claim that he is capable of being moved sympathetically, but it also implies his physical difference from the 'fierce and cruel' Greeks who will respond to his rape with military force. (It also echoes, and re-appropriates, Paris' own representation of himself in Ovid's *Heroides*, where he repeatedly refers to himself as Phrygian while attempting to diffuse the associations of the name.)[18] Appealing both to his vanity and his fears, Oenone insinuates that 'Phrygian' Paris is a pretty boy unaccustomed to the 'worldes of warriors' that Menelaus will bring to Troy. In the next stanza, Oenone extends this idea of Phrygian softness and military inferiority to all of Troy, via a striking image that casts Trojan resistance to the Greeks as entirely feminine: 'Whereof the fayre Cassandra prophecied, / With her all Phrigia did thy rape withstand, / But mothers dreame right hast thou verified' (stanza 16). Oenone takes the fact of Paris' newfound nobility and uses it to compound his Phrygian-ness: all Trojans are Phrygians, but Paris is a Phrygian by both birth *and* upbringing – and thus profoundly unsuited for war.

Oenone's branding of Paris as Phrygian constitutes an attempt to fix him as a pastoral figure, in effect mitigating his generic ambivalence in Virgil. In this respect Heywood closely follows Ovid, whose Oenone also tells Paris that his affair with Helen will cause Troy's destruction, while at the same time subtly implying Paris' unsuitability for epic: 'Your case is one that calls for shame; just are the arms her lord takes up' (*causa pudenda tua est; iusta vir arma movet*, 5.98). Like Numanus' taunt in the *Aeneid*, Oenone's warning to Paris in the *Heroides* cleverly echoes the opening line of Virgil's epic (*arma virumque*) and suggests that Paris is dangerously venturing into the wrong poem. There is also the suggestion, signalled by a play on *pudenda*, that Paris belongs in erotic elegy. Heywood's Oenone takes the hint from her Ovidian model and amplifies the pastoral image of Paris. She replays the image of Paris 'in these verdaunt meddowes' (stanza 17) while recalling the fact that she last saw him 'on yonder banke of Croceate Jillyflowres ... with thy hooke in hand' (stanza 19).[19] Likewise, while evoking again the idea of Paris' physical softness, Oenone tries to redirect his pugnacious urges towards pastoral and elegiac modes:

That hand (faire hand) more soft and smooth then mine,
And yet my limber armes have azured wristes.
Once did Apollo more delight to have me,
Then did the Nimphes of Ida ever crave thee.

(stanza 23)

In programmatic, Ovidian fashion, Oenone recasts epic *arma* as her own 'limber armes', and the warlike, Python-killing Apollo as a Daphne-chasing Apollo, while reminding Paris of his exalted status in an Idaean (idyllic) landscape.

Paris' first response is surprisingly concessional. He initially confirms Oenone's characterization of himself, but he then elaborates on it in a way that suggests that her vision is limited. In the process, he reveals what is at stake for Heywood in the poem's figurations of genre. After corroborating Oenone's claim that she was 'Apolloes chiefest marke' and establishing her as a pastoral goddess ('grace to these hilles, and dales, & lovely brookes', stanza 29), Paris casts himself as a pastoral figure, in terms even more explicit than Oenone's: 'drowsilie leaning on my shepheardes crooke' (stanza 36). However, Paris' description of the pastoral Idaean landscape shows it to be more expansive and variegated than Oenone had portrayed it:

A place there is begirt with mighty oakes,
Where elders, elmes, and espine trees doe growe,
Whose ore-grown trunks withstand the hardest stroks,
    A nooke, where neither simple ewe doeth feede,
    Nor horned ramme plucks up the springing weede.

(stanza 34)

Paris' description of this glen, which harbours neither 'simple ewe' nor 'springing weede', places it outside the bounds of pastoral and georgic. Although he attempts to play the role of the singing shepherd ('that place I chused out to chaunt out a ryme', stanza 35), he finds that he has breached decorum: 'But rymes, nor odes, that place it was not for them' (stanza 35). Falling into a dreamlike stupor, Paris then receives a heavenly vision that reprises and amalgamates episodes from Books 4 and 6 of the *Aeneid*:

> When loe, the messenger of mightie Jove
> Did with his snakie wand appeare before me,
> . . .
> And now th'immortall oratour began
> To chere me up that had so sadlie drooped:
> Thou borne of Hecuba, take courage man.
>
> (stanzas 37–8)

As some critics note, Paris' account of the ensuing episode follows Ovid's version in *Heroides* 16, in which Paris tells Helen of his encounter with Mercury and the three goddesses. Yet, here again Heywood makes strategic changes. Ovid's Paris looks aspiringly at Troy's walls when the gods approach him; he is not striking a pastoral pose like Heywood's Paris.[20] Moreover, while Ovid's Paris is spooked enough to feel his hairs stand on end, Heywood's Paris experiences convulsions throughout his entire body: 'Head, heart, legges, limmes, my Jointures all did shiver' (stanza 36). In this respect, Heywood's Paris closely resembles Virgil's Aeneas meeting the Sibyl in *Aeneid* 6, and even more so Aeneas when he is himself visited by Mercury in *Aeneid* 4: 'Aeneas, aghast at the sight, was struck dumb; his hair stood up in terror and the voice clave in his throat' (*Aeneas aspectu obmutuit amens, / arrectaeque horror comae et vox faucibus haesit*; 4.279–80).[21] Heywood thus takes his Ovidian model and gives it a distinctly Virgilian spin. The generic implications of this move are profound. Despite the typical contrariety of pastoral and epic, Heywood shows that epic can encompass pastoral and make it comprehensible within a grander scheme. Even further, Heywood suggests that pastoral contains the potential for epic action – provided that it is influenced with the right inspiration.

By dramatizing and exaggerating a move from pastoral to epic, Heywood introduces a crucial element to the interplay of generic registers in his poem: the idea of progression. It is in this act of framing that Heywood most clearly invokes the principle of the Virgilian *rota*, the model of a literary career that increases in stature as it progresses from pastoral to epic. In fact, Paris emphasizes the evolutionary nature of this model by characterizing his pastoral past as a state of ignorance:

> I knew not this, when like a lowly swayne,
> I kept my goates within these neighbour bounds,
> Treading the measures in this grassy plaine,
> Viewing the Fayries hoppe their merrie round.
> I knew not this when first of all I knewe thee,
> Which had I knowne, I had disdain'd to view thee.
>
> (stanza 52)

Paris adopts Oenone's premise that, as a pastoral figure, he is better suited to her than to Helen. However, he goes on to say that such pastoral innocence is irrevocably shattered by the joint knowledge of his Trojan nobility and of his desire for Helen – two revelations that Paris elides in the course of his response. By this logic, there can be no retreat into pastoral in the light of epic knowledge, and epic's consequentiality ensures its superiority over pastoral:

> My former love was of sufficient force.
> But second to loves-selfe a sute commences.
> The second sute must beare away the pryse,
> Second excludes the first, and so it dyes.
>
> (stanza 31)

Paris' use of 'pryse' sustains the self-reflexive nature of the argument and recalls the conventional notion that among the various poetic genres, epic holds the best promise of literary fame. Broaching a pun on 'praise', this 'pryse' signals the *laudes* that Virgil imputes to warlike epic in the *Eclogues*.[22] Paris rests his case – his 'sute' – on Virgilian authority itself.

In its conventional deference to the Virgilian *rota*, Paris' response might seem effectively to end the debate over his generic identity. Except that it doesn't. He rejects pastoral well before the midpoint of the poem, which leaves ample room for complications. For one thing, Paris still *looks* like his pastoral self, despite sporting a few epic trappings. He may now be able to flaunt the 'noble offspring whence I am descended' (stanza 51), but he is just as otiose as before. He seems to confirm the truth of Venus' promise that, by choosing her, the 'shepheard' Paris would successfully avoid 'toyle, and travell' (stanza 44), a rhetorical formulation that suggests pastoral's imperviousness against georgic ('toyle') and epic ('travell'). Oenone picks up on these pastoral inclinations and, rather than conceding the argument, pursues the case for Paris' pastoral identity with even greater vigour. In particular, she pleads for Paris' return to pastoral (and to her) by deliberately *confusing* pastoral and epic. In this respect, William Weaver's astute claim that Paris and Oenone 'speak in different languages' – Paris with a schoolboy's rhetorical discipline and Oenone with overwhelming variety – is on the mark. But I would argue that Oenone's 'unmannerly speech' points to yet another Renaissance rhetorical mode: that of *contaminatio*, which she exercises in an attempt to destabilize the Virgilian *rota* propping up Paris' argument.[23] And it is illuminating that, in attempting to undermine the Virgilian *rota*, Oenone starts to sound like the one poem that had presented itself as the English realization of the *rota*: the 1590 *Faerie Queene*.

For an English poet in 1594, affirming the Virgilian rota was likely to evoke the example of Spenser. It is thus unsurprising that the conclusion of Paris' first speech, which nostalgically portrays his pastoral identity as an immature phase, triggers an echo of Spenser in the Virgilian mode. Paris refers to himself as a 'lowly swayne ... Treading the measures in this grassy plaine' (stanza 52), recalling the beginning of the *Faerie Queene*, particularly its opening imitation of the proem to the *Aeneid* and its well-known statement of the *rota*:

> Lo I the man, whose Muse whilome did maske,
> As time her taught in lowly Shepheards weeds,

Am now enforst a far unfitter taske,
For trumpets sterne to chaunge mine Oaten reeds.[24]

The Spenserian language seems to have an effect on Oenone, who immediately reacts as though she were a character in Spenser's poem. Mimicking Spenser's Una, who swoons at the thought that she has lost Redcrosse for good, Oenone falls prostrate 'on the playne, / That living, dyed: yet dead, reviv'th againe' (stanza 54).[25] She redoubles her efforts to cast Paris as a pastoral figure, reminding him of the 'verses' he once carved in 'rough rhyne' (stanza 57) and alternately calling him a 'flint-hearted Phrygian' (stanza 59) and the 'glorie of shepheards' (stanza 69), while simultaneously reanimating her earlier depiction of the pastoral landscape through a Spenserian lens:

The Satyres, and goat-footed Aegipines,
Will with their rurall musicke come and meete thee,
With boxen pypes, and countrey Tamburines,
Faunus and old Sylvanus, they will greete thee.

(stanza 66)

Presumably, Oenone's place in this Spenserian-Satyrian landscape would resemble that of Una amid the Satyrs. Indeed, Oenone casts herself as a second Una, repeatedly abandoned by her preferred champion and constantly under threat by a ravenous, Duessa-like figure: 'The lust of Læda summons thee to fight' (stanza 72).[26] A few lines later, Oenone performs a similar manoeuvre by ingeniously rewriting the opening of the *Faerie Queen* ('Fierce warres and faithful loves') as a restatement of Ovidian *militia amoris* – in the form of a chiasmus, no less: 'if thou needs wilt warre, then warre with me' (stanza 73). Her revision of Paris as a second Redcrosse reorients the meaning of Paris' desire while imitating the self-reflexive, pedagogical language of the *Faerie Queene*: 'Hath hurtfull Helen scooled thee so ill / That love for lust must thus be disinherited? / For ever, maie her whoorish trickes be scand' (stanza 87). With a kind of intertextual bravado, Oenone exposes Paris' epic ambition as *error*, and Paris as a Redcrosse simultaneously fooled by 'whorish' Duessa and 'schooled privily' by Archimago.[27]

Oenone's exuberant play with Spenserian language elucidates a subtle but important complexity in Renaissance epyllia. While epyllia (*Oenone* included) characteristically prefer Ovid over Virgil, and romantic or elegiac modes over epic ones, Heywood manages to show the constant proximity of Virgilian matter and the ease with which one *could* move between pastoral and epic. To put it another way, if, as Lynn Enterline suggests, 'writers of epyllia pointedly avoid Virgil's theme of *translatio imperii* and his plot of epic masculinity', then Heywood's poem is distinctive in its willingness to display openly the deliberations over such a choice.[28] It is able to do this because Spenser's poem explicitly announces itself (at least at the beginning) *as* an iteration of *translatio imperii*, while constantly lapsing into the pastoral or Ovidian mode. The *Faerie Queene*'s generic ambiguity is not unfamiliar to modern readers (nor would it have been revelatory to Renaissance readers who knew Ariosto's *Orlando Furioso* and the sixteenth-century debates over its generic status). Yet Heywood's aggressive harping on generic matters in *Oenone and Paris* perhaps gives a sense of the shockwave produced by the publication of the 1590 *Faerie Queene*. In this respect, it is worth considering how *that* version of Spenser's epic ends:

> But now my teme begins to faint and fayle,
> All woxen weary of their journall toyle:
> Therefore I will their sweatie yokes assoyle
> At this same furrowes end, till a new day:
> And ye faire Swayns, after your long turmoyle,
> Now cease your worke, and at your pleasure play;
> Now cease your worke; to morrow is an holy day.
>
> (III.xii.47a.3–9)

With this stunning anaphoric conclusion, Spenser manages to cast his poem as both georgic ('sweatie yokes', 'furrowes') and pastoral ('faire Swayns'), while still keeping in focus the larger 'worke' of epic. The cyclic, circular implications of the *rota* ('wheel') model for the Virgilian career are realized here, as epic turns back to georgic and pastoral – and, at the same time, becomes indistinguishable from them.[29] From this perspective, the Renaissance epyllion looks less like a rejection of epic than a wholehearted embrace of an expanded view of epic, *gratia* Spenser. From Oenone's perspective, the 1590 *Faerie Queene* inaugurates a brave new world of generic enrichment that authorizes her to appropriate epic language for pastoral ends: 'Woonder of Troy, Natures exactest cunning, / Glorie of shepheardes, Ideas chiefe Decorum' (stanza 69). Thus affirming Paris' generic hybridity and presenting Paris *as* a model for imitation, Oenone's language self-reflexively casts the epyllion as the sign of a change in the rules of poetic decorum rather than a breach of them.

And yet, Heywood does not allow Oenone's generic iconoclasm to stand triumphant. Paris' immediate response to her exuberant contamination is, appropriately, laughter: 'At this, the Trojan ganne to chase a laughter, / He would, and yet no longer could forbeare it' (stanza 79). Paris' reaction confirms Oenone's rhetorical indecorum and reifies the distance (personal and generic) between them. While Oenone's epic-pastoral flight is an expression of deep feeling, a language of 'teares' and 'mourning' (stanza 80), Paris hears it as only 'toyes', a loaded term used by Shakespeare and Marlowe to signal both the inconsequentiality of erotic elegy and its affront to poetic decorum.[30] Heywood, imitating Shakespeare, goes further in suggesting that the result of such a breach is not merely erotic disappointment but public humiliation: Shakespeare's Adonis merely 'smiles in disdain' (241) while Heywood's Paris laughs out loud. And although Paris later shows that he can still operate in the Ovidian mode if he wants to, producing a catalogue that rejuvenates Arachne's tapestry in *Metamorphoses* 6 (and Busyrane's tapestry in Book 3 of *The Faerie Queene*), he ultimately brands this digression as an instance of Cupid's 'foule abuses, / That rudely ruleth', an instance of order that is more regrettable than profitable (stanza 117).[31] This conservative impulse in Heywood's poem may point to an ambivalence, if not anxiety, about the possibilities for poetic fame in England after Spenser, particularly for those poets who cannot imagine a worthy English poetic tradition that does not have a coherent relationship with its classical models. Heywood, who in 1594 was keen to exercise his skills in classical imitation and yet keenly aware of the experiments of his fellow English poets, may have seen Spenser's project as anarchic rather than aspirational. In the preface to *Oenone and Paris*, Heywood tells his reader that he 'may in som other *Opere magis elaborato* apply my Veine to your humors', but the poem that follows raises doubts about what that greater work should look like.[32] After all, what does it mean if Oenone and Paris does sound an awful lot like *The Faerie Queene*? What is the point of writing an epic if it doesn't *go anywhere*, or if it puts you back where you started? What if in England the Virgilian *rota* really is a *rota* (a wheel)?

These last questions were Spenser's as well. In the six-book 1596 *Faerie Queene*, Spenser stages a dramatic, surprising return to pastoral in Book 6, most explicitly in the appearances of Pastorella and Colin Clout, and in Calidore's temporary abandonment of his quest in favour of pastoral reclusion. Spenser, who may very well have read Heywood's poem in the intervening years, self-reflexively comments on Calidore's turn to pastoral by evoking Oenone and Paris:

> Which *Calidore* perceiuing, thought it best
> To change the manner of his loftie looke;
> And doffing his bright armes, himself addrest
> In shepheards weed, and in his hand he tooke,
> In stead of steelehead speare, a shepheards hooke,
> That who had seene him then, would have bethought
> On *Phrygian Paris* by *Plexippus* brooke,
> When the loue of fayre Oenone sought,
> What time the golden apple was vnto him brought.

(6.9.36)

There has been much debate over whether Spenser's return to pastoral at the end of the 1596 *Faerie Queene* signifies a rejection of the Virgilian *rota* or a complex re-envisioning of it.[33] For this essay, it will suffice to conclude that the story of Oenone and Paris was legible in the 1590s as a figure for the stratification of poetic genres implied by the *rota*, and that it offered self-conscious, humanist poets like Heywood and Spenser a medium in which to think through the relationship between classical imitation and poetic fame. By the time Heywood explicitly commented on the current state of English poetry in his *Apology* in 1612, he had produced several Ovidian works and performed countless feats of generic experimentation. Yet he was also aware that, for all his Ovidian credentials, Meres had named someone else as the English Ovid. Thus, if Oenone and Paris had expressed an anxiety about the prospects of literary fame for a classicizing poet, then this anxiety might have seemed retrospectively to have been well-founded – insofar as Heywood felt that he had ended up, like Oenone in the last line of his poem, 'unregarded'.

Notes

1 Thomas Heywood, *An Apology for Actors* (London: Nicholas Okes, 1612; reprint New York: Garland, 1973), Sigs. E3–E3v.

2 Douglas Bush, one of the earliest modern critics of the poem, calls it a 'plagiarized' version of Shakespeare's *Venus and Adonis*. See *Mythology and the Renaissance Tradition in English Poetry* (Minneapolis: University of Minnesota Press, 1932), 309. Likewise, the poem's first modern edition flatly states that 'verbal plagiarism of Shakespeare's poem is everywhere conspicuous' and deems it interesting mainly as an artefact of early Shakespeariana. Thomas Heywood, *Oenone and Paris*, ed. Joseph Quincy Adams (Washington, DC: Folger Shakespeare Library, 1943), xi. (While it is clear that Heywood read and alluded to *Venus and Adonis*, some of the imitations adduced by Bush and Adams seem strained or specious, at least to my ears.) Some recent criticism has been more generous to Heywood and, while still privileging

Shakespeare as a main reference point, has fruitfully expanded the scope of intertextual readings of *Oenone*. William Weaver reveals the complexity, previously unremarked, of the way Heywood handles Ovid's *Heroides*, arguing that the poem charts a progression of rhetorical styles that suggests a specifically English humanist curriculum (*Untutored Lines*, 94–119). Lynn Enterline, on the other hand, offers an original and perceptive reading of *Oenone* as a response to Thomas Lodge's *Scillaes Metamorphosis* (1589) ('Drama, Pedagogy, and the Female Complaint: or, What's Troy Got To Do With It?', 185–210).

3 Weaver notes the applicability of the Virgilian *rota* to Heywood's poem, but focuses instead on Heywood's dramatization of the *progymnasmata*, the humanist educational programme by which students advanced through the different types of rhetoric (*Untutored Lines*, 109–12).

4 These are David Quint's terms. See his *Epic and Empire: Politics and Generic Form from Virgil to Milton* (Princeton, NJ: Princeton University Press, 1993), esp. 31–41. The influence of the epic-romance dichotomy on the Elizabethan epyllion has often been discussed, especially where the question of genre is concerned. See for example Clark Hulse, *Metamorphic Verse*.

5 William Keach, *Elizabethan Erotic Narratives*, 219–20.

6 Edmund Spenser, *The Faerie Queene*, ed. Thomas P. Roche, Jr (New York: Penguin, 1978).

7 Ovid, *Heroides*, trans. Grant Showerman (Cambridge, MA: Harvard University Press, 1977), 5.65. All quotations are from this edition.

8 Ludovico Ariosto, *Orlando Furioso*, ed. Pietro Papini (Florence: Sansoni, 1957), my translation. To the extent that Heywood's Paris imitates Ariosto's Ruggiero, he also resembles Adonis – though Ariosto's, not Shakespeare's. A few stanzas after revealing the languid Ruggiero, Ariosto compares him to a concupiscent Adonis: *Acciò che dopo tanta disciplina / Tu sii l'Adone* (7.57, 'was all this schooling to no better purpose than to make you play Adonis?').

9 Edmund Spenser, *The Shorter Poems*, ed. Richard A. McCabe (New York: Penguin, 1999), 'April', 136–41.

10 *Metamorphic Verse*, 6.

11 Critical attention to moments of generic mixing, or generic imitation, in Virgil's poems has become almost a subfield of Virgil studies in the last few decades. See Gian Biagio Conte, *The Rhetoric of Imitation: Genre and Poetic Memory in Virgil and Other Latin Poets*, trans. Charles Segal (Ithaca, NY: Cornell University Press, 1986), esp. 100–29.

12 Virgil, *Eclogues. Georgics. Aeneid*, ed. H. Rushton Fairclough, 2 vols (Cambridge, MA: Harvard University Press, 1916; rev. ed. 1935). All quotations are from this edition.

13 Stephen Guy-Bray, *Homoerotic Space: The Poetics of Loss in Renaissance Literature* (Toronto: University of Toronto Press, 2002), 47.

14 On the significance of Dardanus as a link between Troy and Italy, particularly in the context of Virgilian epic, see K.F.B. Fletcher, *Finding Italy: Travel, Nation, and Colonization in Vergil's* Aeneid (Ann Arbor: University of Michigan Press, 2014), 110–11.

15 Turnus uses the term in a similar way, referring to the Trojans as *semiviri Phrygis* ('Phrygian half-men', *Aeneid* 12.99).

16 Quint shows how the distinction between Roman manliness and a feminized, orientalized luxuriousness becomes a generically defining structure in the *Aeneid* and in all subsequent epics, though he does not emphasize the term Phrygian (*Epic and Empire*, esp. 24–41). For an excellent discussion of the connotations of 'Phrygian' and Phrygia in classical Roman poetry, see Philip Hardie, 'Phrygians in Rome / Romans in Phrygia', in *Tra Oriente e Occidente: Indigeni, Greci e Romani in Asia Minore*, ed. Gianpaolo Urso (Milan: Edizioni ETS, 2007), 93–104. Hardie shows that 'Phrygian' functions in Roman poetry, especially Virgil and Catullus, as a 'term for the barbarian Other', but Phrygia is also a crucial *starting* point for journeys necessary for the establishment of Roman civilization – and thus, from a generic standpoint, a starting point for epic.

17 See Enterline, who reads the legalistic language in this section as evocative of rhetorical practices associated with the Inns of Court and thus, by extension, of the rhetorical exercises that were fundamental to Tudor education ('Drama, Pedagogy, and the Female Complaint', 193).

18 See Ovid, *Heroides*, 16.198–203.

19 Weaver notes that Paris' 'hooke' can also refer to a weeding hook, which would suggest a 'georgic' version of Paris (*Untutored Lines*, 106). I suspect that Heywood is being deliberately ambiguous here and that the combined pastoral-georgic image of Paris works to intensify his incompatibility with epic.

20 As Weaver notes, the image of the drowsy Paris derives from Benoît de Sainte-Maure's *Le Roman de Troie*, which Heywood may have known directly or through its inspiration of later visual and verbal depictions of Paris (*Untutored Lines*, 104). In these cases, however, Paris is usually taking a break from hunting, not resting on his 'shepherd's crook' as Heywood has him.

21 The passage echoes Ovid's description of Oenone in *Heroides* 5.37–8, which is not surprising since Ovid is appropriating Virgilian material for elegiac purposes. Impressively, Heywood seems to recognize the Virgilian imitations in Ovid's poem and amplifies them while adding other Virgilian imitations of his own. For example, his addition of Paris' supplicating response to Mercury ('I gave my selfe precisely to devotion', stanza 36) imitates Aeneas' response to the Sibyl after experiencing a bodily shiver (*funditque preces rex pectore ab imo*, *Aeneid* 6.55). Likewise, Mercury's 'take courage man' in *Oenone* is closer to the Sibyl's injunction to Aeneas (*nunc pectore firmo*, 6.261) than to its Ovidian model.

22 *Eclogues* 6.6. For a discussion of this passage, along with a larger discussion of the *rota Virgiliana* in Virgil's own works, see Michael C.J. Putnam, 'Some Virgilian Unities', in *Classical Literary Careers and their Reception*, eds Philip Hardie and Helen Moore (Cambridge: Cambridge University Press, 2010), 17–38.

23 Weaver, *Untutored Lines*, 112–13. On the nature of *contaminatio* in the Renaissance, see Thomas M. Greene, *The Light in Troy: Imitation and Discovery in Renaissance Poetry* (New Haven, CT: Yale University Press, 1982), 156–62.

24 *The Faerie Queene*, 1, Proem, 1.1–4. According to the fourth-century commentator Servius, the *Aeneid* originally began with these autobiographical lines: *Ille ego, qui quondam gracili*

modulatus avena / carmen, et egressus silvis vicina coegi / ut quamvuis avido parerent arva colono, / gratum opus agricolis; at nunc horrentia Martis ('I am he who once tuned my song on a slender reed, then, leaving the woodland, constrained the neighbouring fields to serve the husbandmen, however grasping – a work welcome to farmers: but now of Mars' bristling'). Renaissance editions of the *Aeneid* typically included these lines at the beginning of the poem.

25 Cf. *The Faerie Queene*, I.vii.24.1–4: 'Then downe againe she fell unto the ground; / But he her quickly reared up againe: / Thrise did she sink adowne in deadly swownd, And thrise he her revived with busie paine.'

26 In a brief, provocative reading of the poem, Jim Ellis suggests that the branding of Helen as 'whorish' (in contrast to her potential status as the victim of rape) marks a movement from epic to pastoral. He further argues that, in a sense, Paris tries to have it both ways, by simultaneously enjoying the fruits of his epic action and invoking an Ovidian ideology to absolve himself of moral responsibility (*Sexuality and Citizenship*, 200–4).

27 Spenser, *Faerie Queene*, I.viii.29.2 and I.i.46.5. For a brilliant discussion of Spenser's intervention in Renaissance discourses of education, see Jeff Dolven, *Scenes of Instruction in Renaissance Romance* (Chicago: University of Chicago Press, 2007), 135–72.

28 Enterline, 'Drama, Pedagogy, and the Female Complaint', 196. See also Enterline's longer discussion of the relationship between Virgilian imitation and the epyllion in *Shakespeare's Schoolroom*, 74–88.

29 Richard McCabe notes how this generic mixing is already prepared for by Spenser's etymologizing of George as 'georgic' in Book One, and he further connects this act of 'sympathetic parody' to a potential generic ambivalence in the October episode of the *Shepheards Calendar*. See 'Parody, Sympathy and Self: A Response to Donald Cheney', *Connotations* 13.1 (2003): 10–12.

30 See *Venus and Adonis*, 34, 106. On Marlowe's use of 'toy' to designate erotic elegy's transgressiveness, see Heather James, 'The Poet's Toys: Christopher Marlowe and the Liberties of Erotic Elegy', *Modern Language Quarterly* 67.1 (2006): 103–27.

31 This passage also suggests Heywood's familiarity with George Peele's *The Araygnement of Paris: A Pastorall* (1584), which features a similar Ovidian catalogue, though spoken by Oenone. In *The Dramatic Works of George Peele*, ed. R. Mark Benbow (New Haven, CT: Yale University Press, 1970), 73–4.

32 Heywood, *Oenone and Paris*, ed. Adams, 3.

33 Patrick Cheney sees Calidore's actions as part of a larger program in which Spenser 'reinvents' the Virgilian *rota*, expanding it in order to Christianize it. See *Spenser's Famous Flight: A Renaissance Idea of a Literary Career* (Toronto: University of Toronto Press, 1993), 7, 205–11. Similarly, A. Leigh DeNeef argues that Spenser 'ultimately reaffirms the Virgilian model' in Book 6, but only after complicating the meaning of pastoral and chivalric action in terms of a Christian ethos. See 'Ploughing Virgilian Furrows: The Genres of Faerie Queene VI', *John Donne Journal* 1 (1982): 151–68. M.L. Donnelly also sees Spenser as modifying the *rota*, but for professional rather than spiritual reasons ('The Life of Vergil and the Aspirations of the "New Poet"', *Spenser Studies* 7 [2003], 1–35).

4

'Arte with her contending, doth aspire T'excell the naturall'

Contending for representation in the Elizabethan epyllion

Andrew Fleck

In an otherwise unremarkable poem printed as part of a 1566 broadside, Bernard Garter praises the 'comelie corps' and 'christall face' of England's virgin queen.[1] Her perfection appears in a statue created centuries earlier in a contest between two legendary artists and to which Dame Nature 'gaue... lyfe' in England's time of need. Garter's poem begins with the painter Apelles and the sculptor Pygmalion 'striu[ing]' to make the perfect woman. Apelles 'strayed euerie where, / To marke and viewe ech courtlie Dame', sketching the 'cumliest parte' of Greece's most beautiful women and eventually a 'thousand wights knit vp in one', producing an ideal 'paterne such, as earst was none'.² His rival, 'Pigmalion eke, to shew his arte' carefully transforms ivory into a statue so alluring that he 'did run mad'. On its surface, Garter's poem treats a contest between the most talented sculptor and most talented painter from the ancient past; they had become exemplars of artistic excellence, as the roughly contemporary dedication of William Fulwood attests: 'Think not Appelles paynted peece, / ne yet Pigmalions skill, / In present volume here to view, / fine fansies to fulfill.'³ Apelles, assembling the best parts of many imperfect women, produces a painting more beautiful than any particular woman; Pygmalion carves an uncanny sculpture so like a woman that he falls in love with it. Although the sculptor loses his mind, he defeats the painter in the contest. Confronted with Pygmalion's creation, 'Appelles shut his booke', conceding that his rival's sculpture 'did passe ech other wight'.

As he stages the contest between a painter and a sculptor, Garter also acknowledges the limitations of visual artists: the statue remains inanimate and cannot reciprocate its maker's love; Apelles' painting remains a figure on a flat plane that 'lyfe did lacke'. Only later, when people have begun to admire Apelles' painting of lascivious Venus, does Dame Nature return Pygmalion's chaste sculpture to earth.⁴ She breathes 'lyfe' into it to give England its perfect young queen. Fickle Dame Nature intends to humiliate the arrogant artist and 'g[i]ue the workemannes worke a fall', but the circumstances of sixteenth-century England force her to 'g[i]ue it life to bear'. Pygmalion may not be able to animate his art, but he can make art that requires little from nature to take on life. Of course, Nature remains superior because animation happens only with her intervention. Garter does not dismiss the power of artists to create beauty, but he concedes that painters and sculptors do have their limits.

Even as ancient painters and sculptors strove to surpass their rivals in trials of art, Elizabethan poets imagined themselves contending with them for superiority. Christopher Marlowe's epyllion, *Hero and Leander*, describes several scenes of visual artistry, subordinating these to the power of his verse.[5] In the poem's opening, the narrator focuses on Hero's garments, including sleeves embroidered with the scene of Venus seducing Adonis and a kirtle stained with the blood of 'wretched Lovers' (I.5, 16).[6] Hero wears a veil, an ambiguous garment that modestly covers beauty even as it calls attention to it.[7] It consists of 'artificiall flowers and leaves, / Whose workmanship both man and beast deceaves' (I.19–20). These representations of natural material deceive sensible animals and rational humans alike, pointing to the risks of pitting art against nature. Indeed, her veil's pastoral embroidery deceives even the bees, creatures that should have a keen ability to tell the difference. Marlowe describes Hero's sweet aroma, attributed to the alluring smell of these botanical images. Bees come to the plants on Hero's veil 'for honie', but they search 'in vaine' to satisfy their desire (23). Not easily undeceived, these frustrated honey bees 'lighted there againe', assuming that their heightened senses must be faulty (24). In incorporating this praise of the power of art to rival nature and deceive viewers, Marlowe – a humanist bee – transforms a commonplace about imitating the artists of antiquity.[8] In fact, Francis Meres, who collected commonplaces, arranged several of them under the heading 'Painters'. Apelles supposedly painted 'a Mare and a Dogge so liuelie, that Horses and Dogges passing by would neigh and barke at them'.[9] Meres includes two anecdotes about Zeuxis, who was 'so excellent in painting'. One scandalous tale – the one Garter assigned to Apelles – mentions that in order to paint an image of the world's most beautiful woman, Zeuxis had 'fiue Agrigentine Virgins naked by him' as models (287). The other story, one that Marlowe might have had in mind, was that 'hee painted Grapes so liuelie, that Birdes did flie to eate them' (287). In adopting the commonplace about masterful painters who depict nature so effectively that it deceives other creatures, Marlowe implies that his own poem surpasses the work of those ancient painters.

In place of epic violence, writers of epyllia frequently turn to other forms of competition. The plots, of course, typically involve verbal combat. But epyllia themselves raise the expectation that their art will rival, and perhaps outperform, nature. Their victory over the natural occurs, as in Marlowe's description of Hero's veil, in the power to deceive nature, whether sensitive beasts or rational human beings. Many of these poets make claims that, or create episodes in which, the poet's art surpasses the work of a painter or sculptor. All of these forms of struggle and contest – between figures in the poem, between art and nature, between poets and painters, and between the poets themselves – shape the Elizabethan epyllion. Indulging in brief narratives that focus on erotic seduction rather than martial destruction, minor epic poets – trained in rhetorical rivalry in humanist schoolrooms, the Inns of Court, and the print culture of late-Elizabethan England – layer contests atop one another in poems that otherwise lack the traditional victories of epic valour.

Not entirely dead things: the power and limits of poetry

The rationale for poets' contest with painters emerged, in part, from their understanding of Horace, who begins his *Ars Poetica* by directing poets to consider how painters succeed or fail. The grotesque image with which Horace opens his treatment of the poet's calling, imagining a painter who has 'adioyne[d] / vnto a womans heade / A longe maires necke, and ouerspred / the corps in euerye steade / With sondry feathers of straunge huie', pits the two forms of representation – pigments and words – against one another as they strive to capture the natural in their art.[10] Early modern poets often justified their calling by pointing to Horace's explanation that 'Poets seeke to proffit the, / or please thy fansie well, / Or at one time things of proffit / and pleasunce both to tell' (B3r). In pointing to Horace's defence of the poet's ability to inculcate moral values and 'good counsaile' in readers who consume their 'delectable' words, they found themselves in competition with the painters Horace praised for their mimetic ability. 'A Poesie is picture lyke', Horace tells his readers; as a result, some poets found themselves striving with painters to hold the mirror up to nature (B4r).[11] Poets of all stripes had Horace in mind. John Walsall prefaced his translation of *Batrachomyomachia* with a 'commendation of Poetry', in which he evokes Horace's *dictum* to defend the necessity of poetry's figures, lest it '[d]oth not mens hearts with such affection hold'.[12]

In *Venus and Adonis*, Shakespeare directly confronts the power of painters. Adonis' aroused horse pursues the breeding jennet, a figure that Venus will use to instruct Adonis in the necessity of procreation.[13] The poet stops the narrative action of pursuit with a lyric blazon, showing the ways this horse did 'excel a common one / In shape, in courage, colour, pace and bone' (293–4). This horse is

> Round-hoofed, short-jointed, fetlocks shag and long,
> Broad breast, full eye, small head and nostril wide,
> High crest, short ears, straight legs and passing strong,
> Thin mane, thick tail, broad buttock, tender hide:
> Look what a horse should have he did not lack . . .
>
> (295–9)

The imperative 'Look' twice emphasizes this perfection, an imperative that evokes the conflict between artists and the natural world. Readers cannot literally 'look' at the horse, except in the mind's eye where the poet and his audience collaborate to create a visual image. He asks readers to compare the horse's exemplarity to any other 'common' horse of their experience: 'Look when a painter would surpass the life / In limning out a well-proportioned steed, / His art with nature's workmanship at strife, / As if the dead the living should exceed' (289–92). But as the reader considers the unnerving possibility that the artist might surpass nature, the poet subtly denigrates the painter as he elevates himself: 'As if the dead the living should exceed . . . So did this horse excel a common one' (293). 'This horse' is not a painting, not a Rubens or a Caravaggio. This horse is the poet's invention, a simile that creates an image for the mind's eye. Adonis' horse is akin to the 'prowd horse' in Marlowe's epyllion (II.141) and perhaps gets the poet's attention because Sidney, and before him Horace, devote so much attention to horses at the outset of a meditation on poetry.

Competing with painters and sculptors meant that poets confronted two potential shortcomings. Horace acknowledges the first difficulty when discussing dramatic poetry. Prevented from staging the most striking aspects of certain tales, such as 'Progne turn[ing] into a bird', theatrical poets learn that 'things reported to the eares / moue not the mynd so sone / As lyuely set before thyne eyes / in acte for to behold' (A6r–A6v). Visual spectacle seems to grant painters an advantage over a poet's words; Horace encourages writers to employ 'ready eloquence' to overcome this disadvantage. Elizabethan poets – perhaps inspired by Ovid whose love of grotesque transformation defies Horace's decorous strictures – intimate that their words create powerful images in the mind that more effectively move audiences than stone or pigment.[14] Poetry, in its use of 'figure', affects its readers through *enargia* and *energia*.[15] *Enargia*, George Puttenham explains, 'delight[s] th'eare' through its beautiful sounds, and gives pleasurable verse 'a glorious lustre and light', while *energia* has the forceful power to 'stirre the mynde', teaching and moving its audience with a 'strong and vertuous operation' (142–3). Visual art can affect an audience, but the effect can be unpredictable and temporary. The poet, however, chooses precise words to move the reader to virtuous responses. Defending poetry in the preface to *Ouids Banquet of Sence*, George Chapman praises the ability to create *enargia*, 'or cleernes of representation, requird in absolute Poems'.[16] While most artists can create an image others will recognize, a great poet endows it with 'motion, spirit and life', even though 'ignorants will esteeme [it] spic'd, and too curious' (A2r).

A second obstacle for poets, one that they shared with their rivals, arises from their subordination to nature. Horace and

Aristotle treated the ability to imitate nature's perfection mimetically as a sign of artistic achievement. Art would seem to be unable to exceed nature. Although this trope takes on pointed urgency in epyllia, that rivalry recurs throughout Elizabethan texts. It pervades Spenser's *Faerie Queene*, for instance, where the seductive power of Acrasia's art transforms nature into her treacherous bower. Acrasia pits these two creative forces against each other, 'striuing each th'other to vndermine', but art and nature's contest to improve on each other ultimately 'did the others worke more beautify'.[17] Later, the poet yokes the creative power of nature and art together at the Temple of Venus, where 'all that nature by her mother wit / Could frame in earth' appears 'and all that nature did omit, / Art playing second natures part, supplyed it' (IV.x.21). As the speaker of the proem to Book Three concedes, no 'living art may ... expresse' the real meaning of chastity. Neither Zeuxis nor Praxiteles can portray the nature of this virtue in art, and even 'Poets witt, that passeth Painter farre', must worry that he may 'through want of words her excellence ... marre' (III.Pr.2).

Praising art, even verbal art, risks erecting an idolatrous rival to God's creation. When he argued that poets had access to the divine and were prophets or neoplatonic 'makers', Sir Philip Sidney acknowledges the danger that by 'balanc[ing] the highest point of man's wit with the efficacy of nature' he might seem to be challenging the power of the heavens.[18] Stephen Gosson, who dedicated his *School of Abuse* to Sidney, was not alone in worrying about the morality of deceptive verbal art. As Linda Gregerson shows, 'the verbal image was often thought to be as dangerous in its potential as was the visual' and that words, 'like pictures or statuary, were suspect for the very reason that they were powerful, capable of shaping and thus of waylaying the human imagination'.[19] Elizabethan preachers often treated representation as a distraction from morality. William Burton pointed to the inferiority of artists' works compared to God's, recalling the story that Apelles painted a portrait with a fly on the subject's face in 'such artificiall and liuely manner, that diuers coming to looke vpon the picture of the man, tooke the sayd painted flye for a liuing flye indeede'.[20] When someone tried to brush the fly from the portrait 'they did greatly wonder at the excellent cunning of the painter'. That might seem like a neat trick, but Burton rails against the deception: 'what is Apelles to the Almightie?' He expresses amazement that anyone would take notice of this 'painted flye, which is no flye' rather than 'prais[ing] the Lord' for his workmanship in something as insignificant as this insect (9).[21] John Walshall praises the 'verie true and effectuall hearers' who listen to 'this prophete Christe and his holy gospell', finding satisfaction in the Gospel's *enargia* 'liuely discribed by the holy Ghost', in contrast to 'the birdes, and the vain hearers' who marvel at the 'cluster of grapes' that 'Zeusis so artifically painted'.[22] And yet, even sceptical moralists resorted to the power of representation to make a point. In delineating the 'vanitie of earthly delights', one preacher imagines that he has painted the portrait of personified Vanity, thinking it 'good to drawe aside the Curtaine, and to shewe you the picture of Vanitie it selfe, as though none but Appelles had painted it'.[23] The appeal of subordinating the painter to the rhetorician in arguing about the primacy of God's natural world may have been too great for this preacher to resist.

If nature is the target for the artist's mimetic talent, it would seem that nature must always excel art, as Burton implies. But as Sidney would argue, the artist's – and especially the poet's – wit could surpass nature's bounded creative ability. Other callings remain dependent on nature, but Sidney argues that '[o]nly the poet, disdaining to be tied to any such subjection, lifted up with the vigour of his own invention, doth grow in effect *another* nature' (78, my emphasis). The realization in this world of the great poets' 'ideas or fore-conceits' may falter as a result of 'our infected will', but the 'heavenly Maker' created human beings to use their 'erected wit' to rule over 'all the works of that second nature', the limitless imagination (79). For Sidney, true poets use their art to access a better nature than the one around them.

Modulating between neoplatonic idealism and the mimetic aspirations of Horace and Aristotle, Sidney's arguments for the possibility that a poet's art could surpass nature inspired William Scott to argue forcefully for poetry's superiority to painting. For Sidney, poetry employs the 'art of imitation, for so Aristotle termeth it in the word "mimesis" – that is to say, a representing, counterfeiting, or figuring forth – to speak metaphorically, a speaking picture – with this end, to teach and delight' (79–80). In his manuscript *Model of Poesy*, Scott amplifies Sidney's articulation of poetry's significance, intensifying its superiority to the visual arts.[24] Taking up Sidney's references to the 'speaking or wordish picture' of Simonides and Horace's dictum *ut pictura poesis*, 'poesy and painting are almost one and the same thing', Scott shows how 'much more worthy is the poet than the painter'.[25]

For Scott, painters create appealing images but they cannot reach the mind and move the audience as effectively as poets can. Painters produce 'those dead and tongueless shapes set out in colours only' and 'cannot presume to be understood in that he hath artificially expressed, much less in all he would have thereupon inferred' (6). The poet, on the other hand, uses 'words (the proper servants of reason)', and these are the 'most immediate and faithful unfolders both of the scope of him that imitates and of the thing portrayed in the imitation' (6). As Scott's argument unfolds, he refers to the famous painters of antiquity, often praised for exceeding nature, only to show that they fall short by comparison to poetry. He recounts two commonplaces about Zeuxis. In the first, the painter depicted a realistic boy beneath a realistic grapevine. Zeuxis chastised himself paradoxically because 'the artificial grapes had allured the birds, cozened by their counterfeited show' (17). If he had succeeded, the birds would have been frightened by the boy and stayed away from the grapes. Second, Scott recalls Aristotle's judgement against Zeuxis that a painter could not 'so well express those features and graces of sensible life and passion, those sweet forms of countenance and presence' (17–18). In Scott's estimation, poets can succeed where painters fail: the range of verbal figures available are the 'greatest grace and glory of the poet, the light and last shadows which are the life of our speaking picture, that add complete grace and perfection to all the rest' (46). The most important of these figures contribute to *enargia*, to 'the forcibleness and efficacy, when the conceit is so uttered and expressed as the readers are moved and passionately affected with the lively quickness of style' (64–5). A painter may be able to depict 'the length and breadth of the bodies he represents in a plane', and if skilful enough he may 'represent to your eye the third dimension' through perspective and the play of light and shadow. Poets, however, can 'express the images of our conceits so properly and lively in style that the words and phrase bear the true character and stampe of the moving passions, and seem to deliver over to the sense of the reader the affection expressed' (65). Poets defeat painters, in Scott's view, because they better control an audience's emotional reaction.

Art with her contending: the moving, speaking poetic picture

Some theorists of the late Elizabethan period, then, made an aggressive case for the superiority of their art. Not only could poets access a second, 'golden' nature better than the 'brazen' one in which humans lived, but paradoxically, their words created more powerful images in the mind's eye than those merely pleasing to the visual sense. The writers of epyllia similarly assert this claim for poetry's superiority. Marlowe's poetically transformed bees offer one instance. An even earlier example occurs in Spenser's *Muiopotmos*, which William Scott praises as the best Elizabethan example of brief, heroic verse that 'handle[s] small-seeming matters in high and stately manner' (20). Spenser's brief epic of the butterfly's death synthesizes airy Ovidian material and motifs with the seriousness of epic. Its appealing Ovidian digressions resemble other epyllia, while the mock-epic catalogue of flowers in Clarion's garden pits nature and art against each other in ways familiar from Spenser's romance.[26] Clarion, surveying his father's domain, enters these 'gay gardins' among flowers that evoke the tokens of Spenser's invention of an origin for butterflies' beautiful wings.[27] Suspended in the midst of the narrative, this lyric *florilegium* allows the reader to luxuriate in 'the pleasures of that Paradise', including 'wholesome Saulge', 'refreshing Rosmarine', and twenty-four other flowers and herbs (186–200).[28] Growing in a kind of paradise, the plants appear together as part of a 'riotous excesse' that 'doth there abound', but since they are actually 'there set in order', they also testify to husbandry and artifice (168, 172). In fact, the narrator praises the garden's fecundity, since 'lauish Nature in her best attire, / Powres forth sweete odors, and alluring sights', but he also notes that 'Arte with her contending, doth aspire / T'excell the naturall, with made delights' (165–6).

In *Venus and Adonis*, Shakespeare directly engages in an Ovidian exploration of the boundary between nature and art. His poem confronts the difficulty of giving life to another contest: Venus' attempt to overcome young Adonis' stony reluctance. In a miniature epic that replaces most of the martial hallmarks of epic – even Spenser's *Muiopotmos* gestures to the *Iliad* when Clarion dons an excellent breastplate 'No lesse than that, which Vulcane made to sheild / Achilles life from fate of Troyan field' (63–4) while Shakespeare's Venus boasts of emasculating the 'direful god of war' (98) by 'Leading him prisoner in a red-rose chain' (110) – Shakespeare's poem concentrates on the drama of Adonis' rejection. The 'lovesick queen' debases herself, desperately pleading for Adonis to reciprocate her desire (175).[29] Selfishly turning away from the pleasure or purpose of physical beauty, Adonis, like 'Narcissus' (161) or the young man of the sonnets, enters the category of 'Things growing to themselves' which 'are growth's abuse' (166). As Adonis rebuffs Venus, her denunciations become increasingly heated, while he remains cold as a Petrarchan beloved.[30]

His stony refusals enrage Venus: she accuses him of being unnatural, calling him 'flinty, hard as steel' as if he were not made of flesh (199). As she warms to this subject, Venus accuses Shakespeare's protagonist of being the creation of a different artist, Pygmalion. The impervious boy strikes Venus as a purely artificial, 'lifeless picture, cold and senseless stone, / Well-painted idol, image dull and dead, / Statue contenting but the eye alone, / Thing like a man, but of no woman bred' (211–14). Venus here evokes the famous instance of a desirable 'senseless stone' statue 'contenting but the eye'; ironically, he resembles the statue Venus once endowed with life and movement.[31] Shakespeare's Venus does not directly acknowledge her own part in the mythology of Adonis' ancestry, but she might also have another of Ovid's tales in mind, one in which an impervious youth rebuffs a female's charms as a statue. In the fourth book of the *Metamorphoses*, Hermaphroditus resists the advances of Salmacis. In *Salmacis and Hermaphroditus*, Francis Beaumont, drawing on Ovid while frequently alluding to Shakespeare's epyllion, heightens the young man's efforts to struggle against a strong woman. In Salmacis' melancholy pool, Hermaphroditus, whom Salmacis had earlier 'lockt . . . fast' in her arms, 'Struggled apace to overswimme the mayd', only to be fused with her in response to her prayer to the gods (873, 896). For Ovid, and to a lesser extent Beaumont, Hermaphroditus might give Venus hope that 'a man an Iuorie Image' might come to life.[32] When Shakespeare's Adonis finally does accept some of Venus' kisses, the relieved narrator compares his wearing down to the first stirrings of life in Pygmalion's statue. With Adonis' once-stony flesh now stirring, the narrator asks 'What wax so frozen but dissolves with temp'ring / And yields at last to every light impression?' (565–6). The poem had run the risk of turning nature into art, of flesh into stone, in its determination to keep its Adonis impervious to desire.

The tension between Adonis' attempts to move and Venus' attempts to hold him still suggest the tension between painted images and the fluid movement of verse. The verbs the poet most often uses to describe Adonis' actions relate to 'struggle' and 'resist' while the verbs that cluster around Venus involve 'force' or restraint. When Adonis first dismisses her advances,

Venus will not accept a negative answer: 'Backward she pushed him, as she would be thrust, / And governed him in strength, though not in lust' (41–2). The poet compares the boy to a bird 'tangled in a net, / So fastened in her arms Adonis lies' (67–8). Their struggles, his to move and hers to subdue, are on display in a stanza describing their opposed interests:

> Sometime she shakes her head, and then his hand,
> Now gazeth she on him, now on the ground.
> Sometime her arms enfold him like a band:
> She would, he will not in her arms be bound.
>   And when from thence he struggles to be gone,
>   She locks her lily fingers one in one.
>
> 'Fondling', she saith, 'since I have hemmed thee here
> Within the circuit of this ivory pale,
> I'll be a park, and thou shalt be my deer.'
>
> (223–31)

The conceit that follows, with its bawdy innuendo involving the favourite puns of Elizabethan love poetry, display the skills of the erotic poet.

This tension between movement and stasis provides further matter for invention, both for the voluble goddess and the poet. As Marlowe's narrator explained, 'love resisted once, growes passionate' (II.139). Venus reaches the end of her poetic ability once she has described her body as a wonderland and been spurned again by her stony lover. Panicked, the poet asks, 'Now which way shall she turn? What shall she say? / Her words are done, her woes the more increasing' (253–4).[33] Finding her momentarily silenced, Adonis 'springs' away to his horse, only to find that it has abandoned him (258). The boy sits down to pout and the horse's escape provides Venus with new subject matter. Her dissertation on the horse's passions as they relate to Adonis', just like her command to 'Lie quietly ... Nay, do not struggle' while expounding the analogies to be drawn from hunting hares and boars, provides Venus with new excuses to imprison her prey and wear him down with lessons (709–10, 713).[34] She praises him as 'fairest mover on this mortal round' (368), ironically giving him the name he wants – 'mover' – though he does not currently deserve it, sitting in the field. The poet's playful tension around stillness and movement continues until Adonis finally escapes 'break[ing] from the sweet embrace' (811) and 'shoot[ing]' across the night like a 'bright star' (815) not unlike the bright planet Venus. Unlike the static paintings and sculptures that may have inspired Shakespeare to transform Ovid's tale of Venus and Adonis' mutual desire into a one-sided pursuit, this poem has movement and vitality.[35] Ultimately, the broken tension of movement and stasis points to the liveliness of Shakespeare's figural language and to his poem's superiority to even the best painter's 'lifeless picture'.

Lively expressions of nature's lineaments: ekphrasis and epyllia

The competition between writers of epyllia and their rivals in painting and sculpture occurs most pointedly in one of the hallmarks of the Elizabethan miniature epic: the turn to ekphrasis. Usually considered to be the poetic description of a work of visual art, ekphrasis may gesture to famous episodes of poetic mastery in classical epic. Homer's description of the images on the shield of Achilles and Virgil's description of the pathetic figures of the Trojan War carved on the Temple of Juno offered models for Elizabethan poets.[36] Writing in praise of travel as an opportunity to witness personally what others report, the French author Jerome Turler digresses into a discussion of poets and painters, recalling the significance of the ekphrasis in the *Aeneid*: Virgil, he writes, created verbal images 'very lyuely expressinge the lineamentes of nature... seeming to contain in them verye motions of mind, affections, and true teares indeede' so that 'those painted and counterfeited bodies were mooued with compassion one of them towards another'.[37] Shakespeare's *Lucrece*, in which the 'conceited painter' so effectively creates a vivid scene of Troy's destruction that 'In scorn of nature, art gave lifeless life', might stand as the epitome of the contention embodied in ekphrasis: a poet creates a painter whose art surpasses nature (1371, 1374).[38]

Marlowe's description of lively carvings on the Temple of Venus in *Hero and Leander* set a high bar for subsequent writers of epyllia. Deceptively carved in coloured stone, the walls of this temple show 'the gods in sundrie shapes, / Committing headdie ryots, incest, rapes' (I.143–4). Marlowe describes the artist's depiction of Ovidian tales that unveil the Olympians' intemperance. Jove 'slylie steal[s] from his sister's bed' while 'Blood-quaffing Mars, heav[es] the yron net / Which limping Vulcan and his Cyclops set' (I.147, 151–2). Once again, the poet surpasses his rival artists, however, in using words to capture the sculptures and paintings of the temple. After all, a sculptor or painter cannot create activity or movement in his or her work: stone or pigment may capture only one version of the supposedly mutable Proteus (I.137). But a poet can evoke the shape-shifting deity, even as he describes 'Proteus carved' in the jasper stone of the temple. The many 'wanton unseene stealths of amorous Jove' that the narrator describes 'paynted all above' the throne of Astrea in Beaumont's *Salmacis and Hermaphroditus* show the persistence of this motif among epyllia (213–14). Spenser's epyllion makes even more powerful use of ekphrasis. Embellishing Ovid's etiology of the spinning spider in Minerva's punishment of Arachne, Spenser develops an origin for spiders' animosity toward butterflies. Arachne, the 'most fine fingered workman' in the world (260), had earned a reputation that reached the top of Olympus. Minerva, as patron of the arts, descended to earth to bestow 'due reward / For her prais-worthie workmanship' upon the most skillful mortal at her loom (267–8). The 'presumptious' weaver 'rashly dar'd' to 'chalenge' the goddess to 'compare with her in curious skill' (269–71). The mortal and the goddess weave images in tapestry, aspiring to outperform each other and to surpass nature. In two ekphrases, Spenser describes these images in verse, putting himself in control over the contestant's visual art. The poet calls their strife a 'paragon' (274), technically a term for competition among artists for superiority.

Arachne's contest with Minerva, transformed on Spenser's poetic loom, participates in a long tradition of artists competing with each other. The most famous of these paragones derives from Pliny's *Natural History* and appears in many early modern texts. In expanding his idiosyncratic *Dictionary* into the elaborate *Bibliotheca*, for instance, Sir Thomas Elyot added a second, expanded entry for 'Parrhasius'. Originally he called him simply 'an excellent payntour'.[39] Having encountered Pliny's story about Parrhasius' triumph over Zeuxis, Elyot adds a second entry, out of alphabetical order, beneath his new entry for Paris: Parrhasius, 'contendinge with Zeusis, which of them had most kunnyng', defeated his rival in a contest for the most lifelike painting.[40] Famously, Zeuxis appeared to have the upper hand when the surface on which 'he had so craftely paynted grapes' enticed nearby birds who 'flew to them and pecked on them'. Zeuxis then turned to his opponent and 'required Parrhasius, that he should take away the sheete' covering his contribution to their contest and 'shew forth his wark'. The sheet, 'so fynelye wrought that all men iuged it to be a verye shete', was, in fact, Parrhasius' painting. The arrogant Parrhasius 'laughed and iested on Zeuxis meryly', while his rival 'granted to Parrhasius the victory'. His concession, 'yesterday I deceyued birdes, but to day thou haste deceyued me being a craftes man', acknowledges his rival's superior skill, making Zeuxis seem as foolish as the birds who mistook pigment on a flat plane for nature's grapes.

Zeuxis' painted grapes became a commonplace for the artist's skill. Turler, for instance, praises the sculptures on Juno's Temple in Virgil's ekphrastic scene only to recall that 'Zeusis & Parrasius the Painters, fell in contention for the excellencie' (28). Zeuxis 'painted Grapes so liuely that hee deciued Birdes with them', but Parrhasius painted a veil 'so workemanly that he deceaued him that had deceaued the birds' (28). The contest shows an artist with the power to create something to deceive the heightened senses and rational capacity of another artist; it eventually became short-hand for art's deceptive power. Henry 'Silver-Tongued' Smith, for instance, would inveigh against the appeal of worldly goods and honour, dismissing riches as 'like painted grapes, which looke as though they would satisffy a man, but do not slake his hunger or thirst'.[41] Zeuxis' defeat at Parrhasius' hands often does not feature in references to painted grapes. But in the case of William Scott, the victory of one artist over another, in the context of his own argument for the superiority of poets to painters, has a greater impact. Parrhasius, Scott notes, 'beguiled Zeuxis as Zeuxis did the birds,' and as a result 'he carried the garland from all painters of his time by their own confession' (45–6). Pliny holds Parrhasius up as a model because his painterly skill allowed him to 'give the beholder occasion to conceive beyond that is expressed' (46).[42] The true poet, as Scott goes on to argue, can have an even greater effect on his readers. And the activity of artistic competition itself allows for the most affecting representations to emerge.

The contest between Arachne and Minerva in *Muiopotmos* depends on their ability to rival nature. Arachne initiates the competition, weaving an image of the rape of Europa. Her tapestry, framed by images of flowers and ivy, depicts Europa weeping as Jove the Bull carries her to the sea. Her creation is a masterwork: the narrator attests that she makes the central figures 'so lively' that 'ye would weene' that she had made 'true Sea, and true Bull' (279–80). The pathetic Europa 'in everie member shooke' as Arachne imparts to inanimate threads the trembling of a frightened virgin (285). This mortal artist's 'goodly worke', rivalling nature's vitality, astonishes Minerva and sparks her envy. Spurred on by her opponent's talent, and perhaps hoping for inspiration from depicting a previous trial in which she had emerged victorious, Minerva creates a 'meta-paragone' of sorts, an image of her competition with Neptune for the patronage of Athens. Having depicted a miraculous creation of olive trees, the first source of Athenian prosperity, Spenser's Minerva stitches a wreath of peaceful olive leaves as a frame, rivalling the ivy adorning Arachne's tapestry. 'Fluttering among the Olives wantonly', Minerva weaves a butterfly 'that seem'd to live' (331–2). Like the image of Europa trembling on the back of the bull, this uncanny butterfly could be mistaken for its natural counterpart. Minerva's butterfly receives a blazon of its perfect features: the narrator describes the 'velvet nap which on its wings doth lie, / The silken downe with which his back is dight, / His broad outstretched hornes, his hayrie thies', as well as its 'glorious colours' and 'glittering eyes' (333–6). Just as Apelles acknowledged the superiority of Pygmalion's creation in Garter's broadside poem, Arachne concedes defeat in the face of the 'workmanship so rare' and silently the 'victorie did yeeld' to her opponent (338, 342). As in the case of Garter's Apelles, who threw 'his bookes in to the fire: / He feared les the Gods did grutch, / That wurkemen should so high aspire', Arachne learns a painful lesson, transformed into an arachnid with 'crooked crawling shankes', a 'fowle and loathsome' face with a 'bag of venim' (350–2). Ekphrasis allows Spenser to depict the paragon of two visual artists; but at the same time, he subordinates them to his own poetic prowess. After all, in describing Clarion's 'shinie wings as siluer bright, / Painted with thousand colours' (89–90) and inventing the Ovidian story of Venus' capricious transformation of Astery into a butterfly adorned with wings bearing the colours of the flowers she had gathered 'for memorie / Of her pretended crime' (142–3), the poet professes the ability to create something 'passing farre / All Painters skill' (91).

A poet's claim to defeat a rival painter need not involve extended ekphrastic description: it could also simply evoke ancient stories about artistic competition. Shakespeare invokes such an agon at the centre of *Venus and Adonis*. When Venus hears that rather than spend the day with her, Adonis will go on a boar hunt, she nearly faints a second time, 'sink[ing] down, still hanging by his neck, / He on her belly falls, she on her back' (593–4). Though she finally has him where she wants him, 'Her champion mounted for the hot encounter', she sees that 'He will not manage her, although he mount her' (596, 598). She concedes that having plied Adonis with every feminine wile at her disposal, the desire she hoped to find 'is imaginary', reflecting only her own passion (597). As this recognition sinks in, she acknowledges that she has been narcissistically deluding herself. Alluding to Zeuxis, the poet adds:

> Even so poor birds, deceived with painted grapes,
> Do surfeit by the eye and pine the maw;
> Even so she languisheth in her mishaps,
> As those poor birds that helpless berries saw.
> The warm effects which she in him finds missing
> She seeks to kindle with continual kissing.
>
> (601–6)

No longer the proud but 'empty eagle, sharp by fast' (55) that gorges herself on Adonis, 'a bird ... tangled in a net' (67–8), Venus realizes that, like the birds Zeuxis attracted to his grapes or the bees that sought honey among the plants on Hero's veil, she has deceived herself with the image of mutual desire, thereby evading the thing itself. She, and perhaps the poem's aroused and frustrated readers, remains incomplete and unsatisfied.[43] Shakespeare's reflections on early modern debates about the power of poetry capture desire's many facets more potently than any painter could depict them.

Poets of epyllia strive to outdo their rivals among visual artists in outdoing nature. In Marlowe's celebration of poetic art over gullible nature, Shakespeare's poetic triumph over painters, or Spenser's ability to make a goddess depict a creature that seems to flap its wings on a tapestry, we read scenes that underscore the poet's medium – words – while declaring that he has created a speaking picture that outshines a mute image. By invoking the material of visual artists, these poets attempt to surpass rivals, whether painters, sculptors, or other writers. The ability to give movement to pictures, through narrative, gives the art at the heart of minor epics a claim to superiority. Sceptics remained. Some considered it obvious that the visual immediacy of paintings were more effective than the poet's wordy, speaking pictures. Prefacing his memorial of Nicholas Bacon, George Whetstone modestly concedes that Apelles depicted Alexander much better than Plutarch could, and that Zeuxis 'perfectly painted Hellen, but Ouid erred in penning her wantonesse'.[44] Whetstone reprovingly evokes the poetry of Ovid, whose own tales of eros and artistic contest inform these popular narrative poems. Perhaps these Elizabethan writers hoped that their epyllia might help change some minds.

Notes

1 Ber[ned] Gar[ter], 'A Strife betwene Appelles and Pigmalion', in J. Canand, *The fantasies of a troubled mannes head* (London, 1566).

2 This story is usually associated with a different painter, Zeuxis. Elizabeth Mansfield argues that the myth of the painter selecting models 'records and perpetuates a persistent cultural anxiety about the use of mimesis in visual representation' in *Too Beautiful to Picture: Zeuxis, Myth, and Mimesis* (Minneapolis: University of Minnesota Press, 2007), xv. She argues that the artist 'cannot work without a model. In other words, he requires a stable referent to perceived reality. But he realizes that a real model cannot serve as a bridge to an ideal' (28–9).

3 *The Enimie of Idleness: Teaching the maner and stile how to endite, compose and write all sorts of Epistles and Letters* (London, 1568), Aiir. Wilfrid Holme's poem denouncing rebellion yokes Apelles, 'the Pictor principall', and 'Pigmalion, the Mason in crafte artificiall', as painter and sculptor par excellence. *The fall and euill successe of rebellion* (London, 1572), B1v.

4 Stephen Hamrick argues that Garter broke with his otherwise puritanical scepticism about images in order to praise the young queen. *The Catholic Imaginary and the Cults of Elizabeth, 1558–1582* (Farnham: Ashgate, 2009), 104.

5 Judith Haber notes the tension in the poem between the reader's desire for narrative progress and the poet's desire to showcase his virtuosity (*Desire and Dramatic Form*, 42).

6   Many scholars remark that Hero's sleeves provided inspiration for Shakespeare's own epyllia. See for instance Keach, *Elizabethan Erotic Narratives*, 93.

7   Enterline explores the fetishistic power of veils, particularly in her analysis of Petrarch (*The Rhetoric of the Body*, 111); Weaver notes that veils reveal or conceal, depending on the speaker's purpose (*Untutored Lines*, 56); and Brown argues that the poem's celebration of the veil is also a celebration of the poet's art (*Redefining Elizabethan Literature*, 163).

8   Three excellent recent studies demonstrate what humanist educational training – including the keeping of commonplace books with material young men would transform just as bees take flowers to make honey – contributed to the development of epyllia. See Heather James, 'Flower Power', *Spenser Review* 44.2 (2014). Weaver notes the risks of Erasmus' adaptation of Quintilian in the development of *copia* in the commonplace book (*Untutored Lines*, 29). Enterline argues that Elizabethan schoolrooms taught young men that rhetorical *copia* was insufficient for the more complex *imitatio* required of them, which led to some of the theatrical developments of the early modern period (*Shakespeare's Schoolroom*, 132).

9   *Palladis Tamia: Wits treasury being the second part of Wits common wealth* (London, 1598), 287r.

10 *Horace His arte of Poetrie, pistles, and Satyrs Englished*, trans. Thomas Drant (London, 1567), A1r.

11 On the 'creative misprison' in the way early modern poets treat Horace, see Christopher Braider, 'The Paradoxical Sisterhood: "ut pictura poesis"', in *Cambridge History of Literary Criticism*, ed. Glyn P. Norton, vol. 3 (Cambridge: Cambridge University Press, 1999), 170.

12 *The Strange, Wonderfull, and Bloudy Battell betweene Frogs and Mise* (London, 1603), B3r. In the margins, Walsall adds '*Vt Pictura Poesis erit*'.

13 Enterline notes the valences of the humanist schoolroom in this scene (*Shakespeare's Schoolroom*, 89–90). Katherine Duncan-Jones shows that early readers of the poem might have found the situation of an aged, pedagogical Venus besotted with a young man comedic but not impossible. 'Much Ado with Red and

White: The Earliest Readers of Shakespeare's *Venus and Adonis*', *RES* 44 (1993): 501.

14 I thank Lynn Enterline for suggesting that Ovid defies Horace in this way. Stephen Guy-Bray argues, contrary to my argument below, that despite Shakespeare's efforts to represent depth in his epyllia, the poet glories in beautiful surfaces. 'Nondramatic Style', in *Shakespeare in Our Time: A Shakespeare Association of America Collection*, eds Dympna Callaghan and Suzanne Gossett (London: Bloomsbury, 2016), 304.

15 *The Arte of English Poesie*, eds Gladys Doidge Willcock and Alice Walker (Cambridge: Cambridge University Press, 1970), 143. Francois Rigolot treats the complex ambivalence involved in pursuing the 'enthrallment or astonishment' of *enargia* which could overwhelm 'the reader's belief' in 'The Rhetoric of Presence: Art, Literature, and Illusion', in *Cambridge History of Literary Criticism*, ed. Glyn P. Norton, vol. 3 (Cambridge: Cambridge University Press, 1999), 165.

16 *Ouides Banquet of Sence* (London, 1595), A2r.

17 *The Faerie Queene*, ed. A.C. Hamilton (Harlow: Longman, 2001), book II, canto xii, stanza 59.

18 *Miscellaneous Prose of Sir Philip Sidney*, eds Katherine Duncan-Jones and Jan Van Dorsten (Oxford: Clarendon, 1973), 79.

19 *The Reformation of the Subject: Spenser, Milton, and the English Protestant Epic* (Cambridge: Cambridge University Press, 1995), 3.

20 *The Rowsing of the Sluggard in 7 Sermons* (London, 1595), 8.

21 John Marston playfully toys with this danger when his narrator compares Pygmalion's passion for his statue to 'peevish Papists [who] crouch, and kneele / To some dum Idoll with their offering / As if a senceles carved stone could feele' (*The Metamorphosis of Pygmalion's Image*, stanza 14).

22 *A Sermon Preached at Paules Crosse* (London, 1578), D1v.

23 S.I., *Bromelion, A Discourse of the Most Substantial Points of Diuinitie* (London, 1595), 30. The irony of S.I. praising his own rhetorical skill by linking it to the ancient world's greatest painter seems to have been lost on him.

24 Sarah Howe, '"Our Speaking Picture": William Scott's *Model of Poesy* and the Visual Imagination', *Sidney Journal* 33.1 (2015): 37.

25 William Scott, *The Model of Poesy*, ed. Gavin Alexander (Cambridge: Cambridge University Press, 2013), 6.

26 For a discussion of this complex catalogue, see James, 'Flower Power', para 8.

27 Edmund Spenser, '*Muiopotmos*: or The Fate of the Butterfly', in *The Shorter Poems*, ed. Richard McCabe (New York: Penguin, 1999), 161–2. Further references are to this edition. The garden's flowers and herbs appear only a few stanzas after Venus punishes Astery, slandered by her peers in their contest to 'gather flowers, [Venus'] forehead to array' (117).

28 Clark Hulse sees a mixture of Virgilian and Ovidian impulses in this episode (*Metamorphic Verse*, 259).

29 As Richard Rambuss argues, Venus' pursuit may be in vain since 'this boy as a boy might desire something else' than a woman. 'What it Feels Like for a Boy: Shakespeare's *Venus and Adonis*', in *A Companion to Shakespeare's Works,* eds Richard Dutton and Jean Howard, vol. 4 (Malden, MA: Blackwell, 2003), 244.

30 For Heather Dubrow, Venus' deployment of traditional Petrarchan tropes allows Shakespeare and his audience to take satisfaction in the reversal of the usual situation. See *Captive Victors: Shakespeare's Narrative Poems and Sonnets* (Ithaca: Cornell University Press, 1987), 34. Enterline notes that importing Petrarch into this Ovidian tale sets Venus up for a failure that the readers, if not the goddess, can predict (*Shakespeare's Schoolroom*, 66). Richard Halpern cautions that despite its appeal to an elite male audience, the poem found a popular and female one in '"Pining Their Maws": Female Readers and the Erotic Ontology of the Text in Shakespeare's *Venus and Adonis*', in *Venus and Adonis: Critical Essays*, ed. Philip Kolin (New York: Garland, 1997), 379.

31 Halpern recalls Adonis' descent from Pygmalion, and the irony surrounding Venus in this moment ('Pining Their Maws', 380).

32 *The .xv. bookes of P. Ouidius Naso*, fol. 43v.

33 Danielle Clark notices that Venus continues to make situations for herself so she can keep talking. See 'Love, Beauty, and Sexuality', in *The Cambridge Companion to Shakespeare's Poetry*, ed. Patrick Cheney (Cambridge: Cambridge University Press, 2007), 187.

34 Heather Dubrow sees the captive Adonis' struggle to escape Venus as pointing to an interiority to which the goddess has no access (*Captive Victors*, 46–7).

35 Hulse argues that Shakespeare might have known Titian's treatment of Venus and Adonis, which can only imply narrative movement, even as it depicts the moment of Adonis' departure (*Metamorphic Verse*, 163). John Doebler suggests that Titian's focus on conflict rather than satisfaction may have inspired Shakespeare. 'The Reluctant Adonis: Titian and Shakespeare', *Shakespeare Quarterly* 33.4 (1982): 488.

36 Rigolot surveys the influence of these episodes in early modern poetry ('Rhetoric of Presence', 164). English poets may have seen ekphrasis as a chance to create that second nature described by Sidney, according to Claire Preston in 'Ekphrasis: Painting in Words', in *Renaissance Figures of Speech*, eds Sylvia Adamson, Gavin Alexander and Katrin Ettenhuber (Cambridge: Cambridge University Press, 2007), 120.

37 *The traueiler of Ierome Turler deuided into two bookes* (London, 1575), 28.

38 On the superiority of the ekphrastic poet to the tactile work of art, see Preston, 'Ekphrasis', 124.

39 Sir Thomas Elyot, *The Dictionary of syr Thomas Eliot knyght* (London, 1538), Q4v.

40 Sir Thomas Elyot, *Bibliotheca Eliotae. Eliotis Librarie* (London, 1542), Aa8r.

41 *The Preachers Proclamacion, Discoursing the Vanity of all Earthly Things* (London, 1591), B3v.

42 Howe sees this discussion as part of Scott's effort to translate Italian terms of painting, particularly *chiaroscuro*, for an English audience ('Our Speaking Picture', 60–1).

43 Halpern argues that Shakespeare's allusion to Zeuxis points to the ambition of poets, one that ultimately leaves their readers unsatisfied ('Pining Their Maws', 384).

44 *A remembraunce, of the woorthie and well imployed life, of the right honorable Sir Nicholas Bacon Knight* (London, 1579), A2v.

5

Learning to read with *Lucrece*

Catherine Nicholson

At the pseudo-suspenseful climax of Shakespeare's *The Rape of Lucrece* (1594), as the Roman prince Tarquin looms over the chaste Roman matron in her bed, Lucrece turns to the rhetoric of the schoolroom as a last, futile defense. 'If but for fear of this, thy will remove', she urges: 'For princes are the glass, the school, the book, / Where subjects' eyes do learn, do read, do look' (614–16). The couplet's crossing of objects and verbs underscores their entanglement in the sixteenth-century imagination: like the looking glass or the classroom, where Elizabethan schoolboys learned to speak and write by imitating the schoolmaster's Latin, the book was an engine of mimetic transfer, a site for the reduplication of words and ideas, verbal techniques and moral and cultural values. One of the most popular collections of English poetry in Shakespeare's lifetime, *The Mirror for Magistrates* (first ed. 1559), used the same conjunction of images as a frame for British history, offering first-person verse reflections by exemplary figures from the Roman conquest to the Tudor dynasty. Most of their stories were cautionary tales: 'For here', writes William Baldwin in the prefatory epistle to his 1574 continuation of the series, *The Last Parte of the Mirour for Magistrates*, 'as in a mirror or looking glasse, you shal see if any vice be fou[n]d, how the like hath bene punished in other heretofore, whereby admonished, I trust it will be a good occasion to moue men to the soner amendment'.[1] A more direct source for Shakespeare's poem, William Painter's 1566 *The Pallace of Pleasure*, which contains the first English translations from Livy's Roman histories, offers a similar defence of its salacious contents:

> [A]lthough by the first face and view, some of these may seme to intreat of vnlawfull Loue, and the foule practises of the same, yet being throughly read and well considered, both olde and yong may learne howe to auoyde the ruine, ouerthrow, inconuenience, and displeasure, that lasciuious desire, and wanton will, doth bring to the suters and pursuers of the same.[2]

To see one's worst self reflected in one's reading is, by this logic, an incentive to act otherwise.

But this confidence that the narration of evil necessarily dissuades readers from it is one Shakespeare's Lucrece does not share. 'And wilt thou be the school where lust shall learn?'. She continues:

> Must he in thee read lectures of such shame?
> Wilt thou be glass wherein it shall discern
> Authority for sin, warrant for blame,
> To privilege dishonour in thy name?
>
> (617–21)

Lucrece here worries over what Jeff Dolven has identified as the shaping anxiety of sixteenth-century pedagogy, fuelled by 'the stubborn undertow of mere repetition', which 'is arguably the essence of education and arguably its opposite'. The difficulty isn't simply knowing whether learning has occurred, but also knowing what has been learned: who is to say if the lessons a student derives from an example are those the teacher meant to convey? The imminent threat of sexual violence gives Lucrece's articulation of this anxiety a visceral edge: if 'education itself', as Dolven writes, 'is a project of reproduction', what offspring will be born of Tarquin's lawless instruction?[3]

For those of us who read, study and teach *The Rape of Lucrece* in the present, such anxieties persist. Like Lucrece, we may worry over what warrant is ascribed to sexual violence when associated with an unmatched cultural authority – not the authority of a Roman prince, but of William Shakespeare. *Lucrece* is not, to be sure, a poem in defence of rape, but it is a poem that derives significant aesthetic appeal and rhetorical power from the elaborate staging of a rape and its aftermath. And Shakespeare, more than any other author, is a figure we regard as Elizabethan schoolboys were taught to regard Cicero or Virgil: as a literary exemplar and as an ethical or even existential pattern. What follows is not a consideration of whether or how to teach *Lucrece* in a manner that respects the sensitivities of student readers. But I foreground the problem at the outset, partly because it seems to me an inescapable and worthwhile one, and partly because it is related to the question I do take up. That is: what perspective does *Lucrece* itself offer on the ethics and efficacy of readerly mimesis?

Within the poem the ability to read well – particularly as sixteenth-century pedagogical theorists defined reading well – appears as both an essential skill and a crushing vulnerability. Perhaps because our own identities are so bound up in the valorization of readerly skill, scholarly interpreters have tended to pay more attention to the former assessment than the latter. In contrast to earlier readings of *Lucrece* that found both the poem and its heroine wanting, more recent accounts have tended to focus on Lucrece's achievements, particularly her passage from linguistic incapacity to interpretive and expressive sophistication.[4] Once criticized as rhetorical excess or misogynist self-loathing, Lucrece's lengthy soliloquies after her rape have been reclaimed as bold articulations of Ovidian subjectivity, republican stoicism, self-deciphering female sexuality, writerly will, the authority of the commonplace, the desire to transcend representation, or simply of literacy itself.[5] Such readings usefully complicate any impulse to reject *Lucrece* on simplistic ethical grounds: Shakespeare refuses to treat his heroine as a mere victim, endowing her with an impressive capacity for self-reflection and self-assertion. But even as *Lucrece* invites us to read its titular act of violence as an education of a sort, it remains deeply sceptical of that education – not only for the obvious reason that rape is an appalling abuse, but because the interpretive and expressive capacities with which Lucrece is endowed in her suffering are as disabling as they are empowering. Learning to read with *Lucrece*, I argue, is simultaneously a lesson in the advantages of declining to read as one has been taught.

'Read it in me': empathy, imitation and the tragedy of understanding

As scholars of early modern reading have emphasized, humanist pedagogy placed a premium on three interrelated modes of readerly response: attention, empathy and imitation. At the highest levels of literate culture, among what Lisa Jardine and William Sherman term 'professional reader[s]' – scholars, secretaries, and bureaucratic officials – reading was prologue to performance: 'studied for action', as Jardine and Anthony Grafton put it in their influential account of Gabriel Harvey's lifelong re-reading of the Roman historian Livy. Such reading was active 'in a strong sense': 'conducted under conditions of strenuous attentiveness' and 'intended to *give rise to something else*'.[6] Such readers were exceptional (and the obsessively diligent Harvey an exception among them), but even at an elementary stage, reading both entailed and anticipated action, channelled into what John Colet, founder of St Paul's School, termed 'besy imitacyon with tonge and penne'.[7] As Lynn Enterline argues, the inculcation of literacy was embodied and emotive: 'the platform of *imitatio* – the demand that boys imitate the schoolmaster's facial movements, vocal modulation, and bodily gestures, as much as his Latin words and texts – was designed to train young orators in physical as well as verbal techniques that would touch the "hearts" of those who heard and saw them'.[8] Learning to read meant learning to feel like and with others, especially the protagonists of classical literature. By expressing those feelings in his own words and gestures, the student might incorporate both the stylistic graces and the virtuous disciplines of the past.

Such active, attentive, immersive reading was not without risk. To begin with, it cultivated and privileged precisely those passionate influxes education otherwise subordinated to the control of reason. And, as Enterline shows, the theatrical character of grammar-school pedagogy blurred distinctions of gender, class, religion and moral character that were elsewhere strenuously enforced.[9] There was, moreover, always the danger that the wrong lessons might be learned and the wrong habits imparted. As the period's most influential pedagogical and rhetorical theorist, the Dutch humanist Erasmus, notes in his 1511 treatise *De ratione studii*, it will take 'mental agility on the teacher's part ... if some passage is encountered which may corrupt the young'. For instance, a schoolmaster planning to teach Virgil's second *Eclogue*, with its account of Corydon's desire for Alexis, should therefore 'prepare or rather protect the minds of his audience with a suitable preface', recasting the poem's homoerotic plot as a cautionary tale of friendship between unequals.[10] Although he insists that even in this case 'the minds of his audience will suffer no ill effects, unless someone comes to the work who has already been corrupted' (687), Erasmus is plainly alert to the possibility that reading might deform the mind and tongue: 'Nothing to be sure is acquired more easily than what is right and true', he declares. 'But once bad habits get a grip on a character, it is remarkable how they cannot be eradicated' (666).

When her defence against Tarquin fails, Lucrece imagines herself as just such a vitiated reader, and her experience a vicious text, '[t]he story of sweet chastity's decay' (808). She recoils from the lessons that will follow: 'Yea, the illiterate that know not how / To cipher what is writ in learned books, / Will quote my loathsome trespass in my looks' (810–12). Even as she agonizes over the easy legibility of her injury, however, she also worries over the hidden insult to her husband: 'O unseen shame, invisible disgrace! / O unfelt sore, crest-wounding private scar!' (827–8). Indeed, the realization that her violation might be kept secret, known only to its perpetrator, horrifies her as much as the thought of its becoming common knowledge: 'Reproach is stamped in COLLATINUS' face, / And TARQUIN's eye may read the mot afar, / How he in peace is wounded, not in war' (829–31). It is to forestall both these possibilities – the defamatory circulation of her 'good name' (820) and the secret devaluation of her husband's honour – that Lucrece determines to kill herself. In place of the narrative scripted by Tarquin, 'the story of sweet chastity's decay', which readers might claim as 'excuse' (1715) for their own lustful crimes, she offers her self-murdered body as exemplary text: 'How TARQUIN must be used, read it in me' (1195).

It is possible to hear that declaration as an assertion of rhetorical mastery – or even 'a new ideal of literary authorship'.[11] Certainly, by the poem's conclusion, Lucrece seems to have turned the imitative structure of reading to her own ends. This marks a significant change in character, for virtually the first thing we learn about Shakespeare's Lucrece is that she is a woefully inexpert interpreter of her adversary. As Tarquin greets her in the poem's opening stanzas, there is, as the poem's narrator observes, a caution in the 'sometime too much wonder of his eye, / Which, having all, all could not satisfy' (95–6). Lucrece, however, fails to comprehend it:

But she that never coped with stranger eyes
Could pick no meaning from their parling looks,
Nor read the subtle-shining secrecies
Writ in the glassy margins of such books.

(99–102)

Here Lucrece appears as a borderline illiterate, incapable of picking any but the very plainest sense from the text before her; lacking a learned interpreter, she takes Tarquin's intention as she finds it. In the following stanza that lack of linguistic facility manifests as literal dumbness, as Lucrece responds to Tarquin's stories of her husband's battlefield success with a pantomime of pleasure: 'Her joy with heaved-up hand she doth express, / And wordless so greets heaven for his success' (111–12). It isn't until she awakens to Tarquin's presence in her bedroom that Lucrece's tongue is loosed, issuing a flood of pleas, rebukes, laments and curses that continues right up to the moment of her death. Unlike Ovid's Philomela, who loses her tongue, and her access to language, with her virginity and to whom Lucrece addresses herself, promising to 'imitate thee well' (1137), Shakespeare's heroine receives eloquence and insight in apparent recompense for her sexual violation.

Or perhaps this *is* to imitate Philomela well. '[T]he primary formal models of Lucrece's speeches are to be found in the rhetorical exercises and textbooks of Elizabethan grammar schools', William P. Weaver observes.[12] Despite her eventual outburst against the 'idle words' of 'skill-contending schools' (1016–18), Lynn Enterline concurs, 'after her rape Lucrece behaves much as any early modern schoolboy would, searching for classical exemplars to imitate and so find words to express her "woe"', and her effusions continue 'along institutionally predictable lines', from *prosopopoeia* to *disputatio* and back again.[13] Philomela's song has a suggestive kinship to such schoolroom exercises: 'for the generation of schoolboys that included Shakespeare', as Sean Keilen has argued, 'the nightingale's virtuosity becomes a theory and an *exemplum* of eloquence', precisely because her metamorphosis conjoins violence and sweetness, the ravishing of the body and the ravishment of the ear.[14] The implications of that association, which figures rape as a rite of passage into poetic language – an extreme version of the kind of bodily violation regularly dispensed in the schoolroom as beatings – ought to give us pause, and the long interim between Lucrece's rape and her death suggests that they gave Shakespeare pause as well. For even as he depicts Lucrece as heir to Philomela's broken music, Shakespeare also suggests that her new capacities of expressivity and insight are perilously self-cancelling, a version of eloquence that threatens to become merely an echo.

Before she makes her decisive speech to Collatine and the other Roman lords, Lucrece addresses herself to three other interlocutors, two human and the third a work of art. This last interaction, in which she generates a dazzling ekphrastic reading of a tapestry showing the fall of Troy, has received abundant notice from critics, but the first two have tended to pass unremarked.[15] Reading them as a linked sequence transforms the significance of Lucrece's deft and emotional reading of the painting, however, for the two earlier scenes cast doubt on the virtues of readerly sympathy and skill. Instead, the subtlety and sensitivity of the well-trained reader appear in each as vulnerabilities, amplifying suffering without arriving at any means of relieving it.

Lucrece's first interaction is with her maid, whom the narrator describes as a perfect student of her mistress's woe. Responding with 'swift obedience' to her summons, she 'sorts a sad look to her lady's sorrow', and when Lucrece begins to weep, the maid weeps in turn, 'enforced by sympathy' (1215, 1221, 1229). The narrator is tickled by this display of imitative emotion – 'A pretty while these pretty creatures stand' (1233) – while remaining aloof from it, a difference he ascribes to gender: 'For men have marble, women waxen minds' (1240). But it wasn't only women whose minds were supposed to be waxen; pedagogical theorists had long used wax as a figure for the malleability of the ideal pupil. In *The Scholemaster* (1570), Roger Ascham commends 'the pure cleane witte of a sweete yong babe', which 'is like the newest wax, most hable to receiue the best and fayrest printing'.[16] But Shakespeare's description of Lucrece's maid exposes the dangers of such susceptibility: 'th'impression of strange kinds / Is formed in them by force, by fraud or skill' (1242–3). As the metaphor itself is pressed into new form, maid and mistress become harder to distinguish, dissolving into a common grief and a common guilt, akin to original sin: 'Then call them not the authors of their ill, / No more than wax shall be accounted evil / Wherein is stamped the semblance of a devil' (1244–6). But the extended figure concludes in an image that transforms women into texts inscribed with a guilt that is definitively their own: 'Poor women's faces are their own faults' books' (1253). Now the maid's attentiveness and sensitivity look more like predispositions to moral laxity. The effect of this contagion is both to increase suffering and to devalue it: transfigured in Lucrece's image, 'the poor counterfeit of her complaining' (1269) is at once pitiable and impoverished, an unconvincing simulacrum of grief. Lucrece claims of that grief that 'repetition cannot make it less' (1285), but the poem hints that repetition does lessen suffering – not by easing, but by cheapening it.

As if sensing the dilemma, Lucrece changes tack, telling the maid to fetch '[o]ne of my husband's men' and bid him 'be ready by and by to bear / A letter to my lord' (1291–3). Suddenly speed is of the essence: 'The cause craves haste, and it will soon be writ' (1295). But when the 'sour-faced groom' appears to receive this 'short schedule' of her woe, the momentum of the narrative stalls in another eddy of imitative emotion (1334, 1312). Taking the note from Lucrece, the groom 'blush[es] on her with a steadfast eye' – an action the narrator ascribes to 'bashful innocence' but Lucrece interprets as consciousness of her despoliation: 'But they whose guilt within their bosoms lie / Imagine every eye beholds their blame; / For LUCRECE thought he blushed to see her shame' (1339, 1342–6). So thinking, she blushes more deeply, and the pair are briefly suspended in a cycle of mutual embarrassment:

> His kindled duty kindled her mistrust,
> That two red fires in both their faces blazed;
> She thought he blushed as knowing TARQUIN's lust,
> And blushing with him, wistly on him gazed.
> Her earnest eye did make him more amazed:
> > The more she saw the blood his cheeks replenish,
> > The more she thought he spied in her some blemish.
>
> (1352–8)

As with the spectacle of the weeping women, the narrator's perspective on the scene is bemused and gently condescending, and the reader is invited to share that perspective, standing at an ironic remove. There is cruelty in that detachment, but also a kind of pragmatic wisdom: those who feel with Lucrece only intensify her distress.

Such imitative circuits of emotion also structure the scene that follows, in which Lucrece performs her bravura reading of the painted tapestry of Troy. In contrast to her initial encounter with Tarquin, when she proved incapable of picking any secret or subtle meaning from his looks, Lucrece now shows herself a skilled and supremely sensitive interpreter of the master narrative of Western tradition. Her text is complex, the narrator reveals, 'For much imaginary work was there: / Conceit deceitful, so compact, so kind', and much 'left unseen, save to the eye of mind' (1422–3, 1426). Lucrece deftly fills in those gaps, as the immersive experience of reading becomes an engine of expressivity: 'So LUCRECE, set a-work, sad tales doth tell / To pencilled pensiveness and coloured sorrow; / She lends them words, and she their looks doth borrow' (1496–8). But the episode ends in disillusionment, as Lucrece spies a figure whose 'face, though full of cares, yet showed content. / . . . So mild, that patience seemed to scorn his woes' (1503–5). Thinking, perhaps, that she has found a pattern for her own grief, she peers closer and realizes that this is the treacherous agent of Troy's destruction:

> The well-skilled workman this mild image drew
> For perjured SINON, whose enchanting story
> The credulous old PRIAM after slew;
> Whose words like wildfire burnt the shining glory
> Of rich-built ILION.
>
> (1520–4)

Narrative is exposed as murderous deception, attentiveness and sympathy as credulity; language spreads like wildfire.

Lucrece initially recoils from this revelation, '[s]aying, some shape in SINON's was abused' (1529):

> 'It cannot be', quoth she, 'that so much guile' –
> She would have said 'can lurk in such a look'.
> But TARQUIN's shape came in her mind the while,
> And from her tongue 'can lurk' from 'cannot' took:
> 'It cannot be' she in that sense forsook,
>   And turned it thus: 'It cannot be, I find,
>   But such a face should bear a wicked mind.'
>
> (1534–40)

The 'turn' that yields the stanza's conclusion might be taken as proof of Lucrece's newfound rhetorical sophistication, her mastery of the transformative power of tropes. But it is less of a transformation than it seems: having learned the folly of readerly sympathy, Lucrece replaces it with an inverse law of readerly suspicion, undergirded by the same mimetic logic. We are still within the regime of *imitatio*:

> For even as subtle SINON here is painted,
> So sober-sad, so weary and so mild,
> As if with grief or travail he had fainted,
> To me came TARQUIN armed to beguild
> With outward honesty, but yet defiled
>   With inward vice. As PRIAM him did cherish,
>   So did I TARQUIN, so my Troy did perish.
>
> (1541–7)

Even as Lucrece embraces a radical scepticism about representation, she clings to a deeper faith in analogy: as Sinon, so Tarquin; as Troy, so myself. Likeness remains the foundation of understanding: to read one sad story is to read them all.

Likeness is also the foundation of Lucrece's revenge plot, her 'meritorious fair design': 'How TARQUIN must be used, read it in me', she bids. 'Myself, thy friend, will kill myself, thy foe, / And for my sake serve thou false TARQUIN so' (1195–7). But in the aftermath of her suicide, the circuit of imitative feeling produces not action but paralysis: Collatine simply collapses, 'and bathes the pale fear in his face, / And counterfeits to die with her a space' (1775–6). His mournful cries, and those of Lucrece's father, beget further imitations, as 'the dispersed air ... answer[s]' with echoes of 'My daughter' and 'My wife' (1805–6). Once again, imitation yields dissipation: here, as in Ovid, echo is a figure of helpless mimicry, of reflexive and self-consuming yearning. Crucially, the task of executing Lucrece's will falls to an onlooker who stands outside this circuit of imitative emotion; to Brutus, who frankly rejects the mimetic logic of sympathy: 'Why, COLLATINE, is woe the cure for woe? / Do wounds help wounds, or grief help grievous deeds' (1821–2)? And in the stanzas that follow, despite Lucrece's urging that Tarquin's fate be patterned on her own, he is *not* 'serve[d] ... so': the poem ends not with his death but with his banishment, and with the establishment of a new civic order, Brutus' fair and meritorious design.

None of this is Shakespeare's invention: Lucrece's suicide prompts the expulsion of the Tarquins and the institution of the republic in all of the poet's classical and vernacular sources. But for all its familiarity, Shakespeare makes this outcome in some sense unexpected, departing as it does from what he elsewhere represents as the inevitable imitative structure of readerly response. For although Lucrece's initial lack of readerly skill dooms her, Brutus makes imperviousness to instruction his primary credential for leadership: 'Let my unsounded self, supposed a fool, / Now set thy long experienced wit to school' (1819–20). Brutus' wisdom is indistinguishable from his resistance to the regime of *imitatio*, his efficacy within *Lucrece* at direct and paradoxical odds with the pedagogical culture from which the poem emerges. Indeed, we might say that Brutus enters the poem to end it; the *FINIS* that appears beneath its final stanza is his contribution.

'I have enough': ineptitude, anticlimax and the comedy of disengagement

'Time's glory is ... / To feed oblivion with decay of things', Lucrece reflects after her rape, 'To blot old books, and alter their contents' (939–48). What is a bitter revelation to her, however, might be taken as more cheerful counsel to Shakespeare's readers: painful stories end, and they also, occasionally, change. Late in his career, Shakespeare returned to the story of Lucrece and imagined it with a new and happier ending, enabled by the very limits of imitative reading. The plot begins as before, in a bedchamber, with a villainous intruder: creeping from his hiding place in Act Two, scene two, of *Cymbeline*, Iachimo conducts a duplicitous inventory of Imogen's possessions, gathering the intimate observations he later will wield as proof that the sleeping princess welcomed him as her lover. 'I will write all down', he announces: the pictures hanging on her walls, the placement of a window, the contents of a tapestry, the book at her bedside, the bracelet on her arm – which he stealthily removes – and, most telling of all, the form of a mole on her left breast, 'cinque-spotted, like the crimson drops / I' th' bottom of a cowslip'.[17] Back in Italy, Iachimo unpacks his arsenal, detonating each suggestive image before Imogen's exiled husband, Posthumus. He leaves the description of the mole for last, proof of his illicit 'knowledge' of Posthumus's bride: 'You do remember / This stain upon her?' he asks. Posthumus indeed remembers, and responds as if what Lucrece calls 'the story of sweet chastity's decay' is one he has always already known: 'Ay, and it doth confirm / Another stain as big as hell can hold, / Were there no more but it'. 'Will you hear more?' Iachimo teases, but Posthumus has heard plenty: 'Spare your arithmetic; never count the turns. / Once, and a million' (2.4.138–44).

The 'arithmetic' that enrages Posthumus is an arithmetic Shakespeare's Lucrece knows well. It is both the unforgiving calculus of female chastity, whereby a single lapse contaminates all past and future conjunctions, and the perilously generative arithmetic of allusion, whereby a glancing reference – to an image, story, or bodily trace – conjures a train of damning associations. Allusion plays a crucial role in Iachimo's plot: Posthumus may claim that knowledge of the mole alone is sufficient proof of Imogen's lapse, but he is primed to make that leap by Iachimo's elaborate description of her bedchamber: the tapestry depicting 'Proud Cleopatra when she met her Roman', the chimney piece showing 'Chaste Dian bathing', and the silver andirons, 'two winking cupids' (2.4.70, 82, 89). Even Posthumus is not so gullible as to regard such intelligence as tantamount to carnal knowledge, but the scene Iachimo sets is scripted in advance with references to adulterous passion, violated chastity, and winking hypocrisy, preparing him to accept cuckoldry as a foregone conclusion. Once again, to read one sad story is to read them all: once, and a million.

The producers of the First Folio classed *Cymbeline* among Shakespeare's 'Tragedies', although most modern editions describe it as a tragicomedy or romance: an experimental hybrid whose resolution privileges reconciliation over revenge, grace over grief. This is because the dark likelihoods forecast by Iachimo's allusions are not borne out: Imogen is not faithless; Posthumus's attempt to kill her is luckily thwarted; the pair are reunited; and Iachimo himself is restored to society, to 'Live, / And deal with others better' (5.5.419–20). There is a lingering bad taste in all this sweetness, to be sure; the cloud of tragic possibilities Iachimo conjured hovers over the celebratory final scene. 'In *Cymbeline*', as J.K. Barret observes, '[a]llusions conjure past narratives, and those narratives stick to the present as unforgotten prospects'.[18] Barret argues that the task of forestalling these disastrous futures falls partly to *Cymbeline*'s readers, who must resist Posthumus's temptation to know its outcome in advance. But within the play such not knowing is often the product of less strenuous mental and moral effort. Allusion may be a devastating form of rhetorical ammunition, but Iachimo's lackadaisical execution of his scheme suggests that some are damp squibs.

The inconsequentiality of his ominous hints – the inchoateness of the play's tragic plot – is not simply apparent in retrospect; on the contrary, the momentum of Iachimo's allusions is foreshortened from the start. There is, to begin with, the undignified manner of his arrival in Imogen's bedchamber in Act Two, Scene Two. Having failed at seduction, he resorts to smuggling himself inside a trunk, to which he returns at scene's end. The lofty rhetoric with which he emerges from the trunk is at comic odds with the action itself, and Shakespeare heightens the contrast by having Iachimo liken himself to a prestigious literary forebear:

> The crickets sing, and man's o'er-laboured sense
> Repairs itself by rest. Our Tarquin thus
> Did softly press the rushes ere he wakened
> The chastity he wounded.
>
> (2.2.11–14)

'Our Tarquin' is Livy's Tarquin, Ovid's Tarquin, Plutarch's Tarquin, and, in English, Chaucer's Tarquin, but also, of course, Shakespeare's Tarquin: the violent and volubly tormented antagonist of *Lucrece*. Early audiences could have been counted on to catch the self-promoting reference: by 1611, when Simon Forman saw *Cymbeline* on the London stage, *Lucrece* had already appeared in five print editions, and extracts from it circulated widely in anthologies like John Bodenham's *Belvedére* and Robert Allot's *England's Parnassus* (both 1600).[19] Although it couldn't match the popularity of the 1593 *Venus and Adonis*, *Lucrece* was a solid publishing success and – given its pedigree – an index of Shakespeare's literary aspirations.[20] Iachimo's reference reminds audiences that the playwright had already made a name for himself as a skilful anatomizer of male sexual aggression and imperilled female virtue.

But the reminder is a red herring. In the lines that follow, Iachimo emulates Tarquin's volubility but displays no hint of his violence: after singing the praises of Imogen's complexion, lips, breath, and eyelids, he arrives at last at his 'design': 'To note the chamber. I will write all down' (2.2.23–4). For readers or audience members primed by the allusion to *Lucrece*, this comes as a stunning anticlimax – and a relief. Iachimo's 'design' is not rape at all, but writing: 'Such and such pictures, there the window, such / Th' adornment of her bed, the arras, figures, / Why, such and such, and the contents o' th' story' (2.2.25–7). Having braced us for a return to the scene of Lucrece's violation, Shakespeare instead gives us the scene of the poem's composition: the banal readerly and writerly routines that precede the fabrication of narrative urgency and tragic irreversibility. Unlike Lucrece's reading of the tapestry, moreover, this reading is cursory and vague. And unlike that reading, or the retrospective account Iachimo later produces for Posthumus, it is detached in both senses of the word: unemotive, and disjunct from any necessary or apparent connection to the future. Far from granting predictive power to the literary past, Shakespeare here suggests that to know 'the contents o' th' story' – of any one story – is to know just that, and no more.

To drive the point home, Iachimo concludes his inventory by noting Imogen's bedtime reading, from Ovid's *Metamorphoses*: 'She hath been reading late / The tale of Tereus: here the leaf's turned down / Where Philomel gave up' (2.2.44–6). It is perhaps pedantic to wonder whether Imogen stopped reading before or after Philomel gives up – whether the turned down leaf marks the last page she read or the next to be read – but given her precarious situation, her unconscious suspension on the brink of tragedy, the question seems relevant. And the possibility that she hasn't arrived at the story's tragic turn is strengthened by Iachimo's response, for he leaves off as well: 'Here the leaf's turned down / Where Philomel gave up. I have enough; / To th' trunk again, and shut the spring of it' (2.3.45–7). That determination, that it is 'enough' to malign chastity, without assaulting it, makes possible the play's turn toward romance. All the elaborate actions by which its happy ending is eventually achieved stem from this moment of allusive restraint, from Iachimo's (and Shakespeare's) willingness to let a sleeping figure lie.

Act Two, scene two, of *Cymbeline* offers a compressed comic rewriting of *Lucrece*, a version of her story in which sexual aggression is held in check by the fortunate failure of readerly determination. Like Imogen's partial reading of Philomela's story, Iachimo's abortive reference to 'our Tarquin' is a truncated parody of the imitative disciplines of the Elizabethan schoolroom. Were she a more diligent student of Ovid, or he of *Lucrece*, *Cymbeline* would have a different, and darker, conclusion. But we might also see Iachimo's turn from action to annotation – 'I will write all down' – as a realistic rendering of what humanist *imitatio* practically entailed: not, for the most part, the literal re-enactment or reanimation of literary antiquity, but the diligent amassing of notes.[21] 'Whatever you read, have ready a notebook', the fifteenth-century Italian humanist Guarino of Verona instructs his student, Leonello d'Este. 'For the notebook will be at hand like a diligent and attentive servant to provide what you need.'[22] Erasmus likewise devotes a long chapter near the end of his *De copia* (published together with *De ratione studii* in the authorized edition of 1512) to the arrangement of such a book, the material storehouse for the 'ample supply' of examples, illustrations, comparisons, metaphors, epithets and allegories on which the abundant style depends. 'Having made up your mind to cover the whole field of literature in your reading (and anyone who wishes to be thought educated must do this at least once in his life)', he writes, 'first provide yourself with a full list of subjects'.[23]

This is among the most influential sentences in the history of humanism, but it is also a funny one. The quasi-comical lapse from the sweeping ambition of Erasmus' introductory clause to his mundane conclusion serves as an apt reminder that the anticlimactic structure of Iachimo's soliloquy in Imogen's bedchamber – from 'Our Tarquin...' to 'I will write all down' (2.2.12, 24) – is also the anticlimactic structure of humanist education. Both on the continent and in England, humanism's grandest visions of intellectual and moral refinement, cultural transformation and national or imperial prowess were linked to ordinary, even tedious, rituals of readerly self-discipline: the keeping of a notebook, marking of commonplaces, extraction of quotations and memorization of useful phrases. Humanists were sensitive to this gap between rhetoric and practice. Having impressed the absolute necessity of careful note-taking on his aristocratic pupil, Guarino adds, 'Now you may find it too boring or too much of an interruption to copy everything down in such a notebook. If so, some suitable and well-educated boy – many such can be found – should be assigned this task'.[24] Even Erasmus, great advocate and exemplar of the art of commonplacing, prefaces his instructions in *De copia* with a note of self-deprecation, professing his unwillingness to expend 'a great deal of labour on topics which, in spite of their considerable contribution to serious subjects, themselves seem unimportant'.[25]

But Iachimo's example invites us to see the trivial and temporary status of annotation differently: not as a dull precursor to more meaningful and lasting endeavours, but as a practice detachable from any further outcome, an autotelic exercise whose application to future occasions, rhetorical or pragmatic, might remain purely notional.[26] The prospect of such inconsequential activity was in one sense the bane of humanist culture, particularly when it came to the study of literature, just as waste – wasted time, wasted effort, wasted words – was the inevitable shadow image of *copia*. '[T]o the first' objection against reading and writing poetry, 'that a man might better spend his time', Philip Sidney acknowledges in his *Defence of Poesie* that this 'is a reason indeed', were it not for the fact that such learning 'teacheth and moveth to virtue'.[27] Nonetheless, the stigma of waste adhered with particular force to the minor genre of the epyllion, as Barbara Correll shows elsewhere in this volume. But if Iachimo's example is deflating, both of humanist ambitions and of our own closely-held beliefs in the moral value and political efficacy of reading, it may also come as something of a reassurance: allusion is not action; reading is not rape. Here humanist anxieties about the impressibility of schoolboy readers might intersect with our own concerns about imposing a poem about sexual violence

on readers in our own classrooms. It is possible to enlist
Lucrece against itself in this respect, for learning how to limit
or refuse the influence of a text on one's thoughts, feelings and
actions is one of the poem's central lessons. Empathy and
imitation are values we still ascribe to the reading of poetry,
and above all to the reading of Shakespeare, but they are not
the only readerly responses worth cultivating. Imperviousness,
inattention and aimlessness have their virtues, too.

Notes

1 William Baldwin, 'To All the Nobilitie', in *The Last part of the Mirour for Magistrates* (London: Thomas Marsh, 1574), *3r.
2 William Painter, 'To the Right Honorable', in *The Palace of Pleasure* (London: Richard Totell and William Jones, 1566), *3v.
3 Dolven, *Scenes of Instruction*, 25, 26.
4 Early critics tended to dismiss *Lucrece* as an aesthetic folly: see F.T. Prince, 'Introduction' to *William Shakespeare: The Poems* (London: Longmans, 1963), 12–17; Douglas Bush, *Mythology and the Renaissance Tradition in English Poetry* (New York: W.W. Norton, 1963), 152–4; and Richard Wilbur, 'The Narrative Poems: An Introduction', in *William Shakespeare: The Complete Works*, ed. Alfred Harbage (London: Penguin, 1969), 8–22. Two relatively early and still influential critiques of the poem on feminist grounds are Coppélia Kahn, 'The Rape in Shakespeare's *Lucrece*', *Shakespeare Studies* 9 (1976): 45–72, and Nancy Vickers, '"The blazon of sweet beauty's best"'. See also Katherine Eisaman Maus, '"Taking Tropes Seriously"; Joel Fineman's dense rhetorical analysis of the poem' in *The Subjectivity Effect in Western Literary Tradition* (Cambridge, MA: MIT Press, 1991), 165–221; and Jane O. Newman, '"And Let Mild Women To Him Lose Their Mildness": Philomela, Violence, and Shakespeare's *The Rape of Lucrece*', *Shakespeare Quarterly* 45 (1994): 304–26.
5 In 'Women, Language, and History in *The Rape of Lucrece*', *Shakespeare Survey* 44 (1992): 33–9, Philippa Berry discovers in Lucrece's 'private use of language', a 'secret and powerful

feminine eloquence' that is also 'the clearest indication of republican ideals in the poem' (34), while in *The Rhetoric of the Body*, 152–97, Lynn Enterline hears a self-wounding Ovidian eloquence in her duet with Philomela. On Lucrece as a figure of self-deciphering female sexuality, see Miriam Jacobson, 'The Elizabethan Cipher in Shakespeare's *Lucrece*', *Studies in Philology* 107.3 (2010): 336–59; on authorial self-possession, see Amy Greenstadt, '"Read It In Me": The Author's Will in *Lucrece*', *Shakespeare Quarterly* 57.1 (2006): 45–70; on the rival authority of the commonplace, see Jeffrey Hehmeyer, 'Heralding the Commonplace: Authorship, Voice, and the Commonplace in Shakespeare's *Lucrece*', *Shakespeare Quarterly* 64.2 (2013): 139–64; on the transcendence of representation see Margaret Rice Vasileiou, 'Violence, Visual Metaphor, and the "True" Lucrece', *SEL* 51.1 (2011): 47–63; on Lucrece's literacy, see Eve Sanders, *Gender and Literacy on Stage in Early Modern England* (Cambridge: Cambridge University Press, 1998), 138–40.

6   Lisa Jardine and William Sherman, 'Pragmatic Readers: Knowledge Transactions and Scholarly Services in Late Elizabethan England', in *Religion, Culture, and Society in Early Modern Britain*, eds Anthony Fetcher and Peter Roberts (Cambridge: Cambridge University Press, 2006), 102; Lisa Jardine and Anthony Grafton, '"Studied For Action": How Gabriel Harvey Read His Livy', *Past and Present* 129 (1990): 30–1; emphasis in original.

7   Quoted in T.W. Baldwin, *William Shakespere's Small Latine & Lesse Greeke*, 2 vols (Urbana: University of Illinois Press, 1944), 1:95.

8   Enterline, *Shakespeare's Schoolroom*, 4. On the schoolmaster as facilitator and object of imitation, see also Walter Ong, 'Latin Language Study as a Renaissance Puberty Rite', *Studies in Philology* 56 (1959): 103–24; Richard Halpern, *The Poetics of Primitive Accumulation: English Renaissance Culture and the Genealogy of Capital* (Ithaca: Cornell University Press, 1991), 29–32; and Anthony Grafton, 'The Humanist as Reader', in *A History of Reading in the West*, ed. Guglielmo Cavallo and Roger Chartier, trans. Lydia G. Cochrane (Amherst: University of Massachusetts Press, 2003), 199.

9   On these dangers, see Enterline, *Shakespeare's Schoolroom*.
10 In *The Collected Works of Erasmus* [*CWE*], vol. 23, ed. Craig R. Thompson (Toronto: University of Toronto Press, 1978), 683.
11 Greenstadt, 46.
12 Weaver, '"O Teach Me How to Make Mine Own Excuse"', 422.
13 *Shakespeare's Schoolroom*, 124. See also Enterline, *The Rhetoric of the Body*, 155–6.
14 Sean Keilen, *Vulgar Eloquence: On the Renaissance Invention of English Literature* (New Haven: Yale University Press, 2006), 114.
15 On the significance of the tapestry scene, see Vasileiou; Christopher Johnson, 'Appropriating Troy: Ekphrasis in Shakespeare's *The Rape of Lucrece*', in *Fantasies of Troy: Classical Tales and the Social Imaginary in Medieval and Early Modern Europe*, eds Stephen D. Powell and Alan Shepard (Toronto: Centre for Reformation and Renaissance Studies, 2004), 193–212; Richard Meek, 'Ekphrasis in *The Rape of Lucrece* and *The Winter's Tale*', *SEL* 46.2 (2006): 389–414; Preston, 'Ekphrasis', 115–29; Catherine Belsey, 'Invocation of the Visual Image: Ekphrasis in *Lucrece* and Beyond', *Shakespeare Quarterly* 63.2 (2012): 175–98; and Alison A. Chapman, 'Lucrece's Time', *Shakespeare Quarterly* 64.2 (2013): 180.
16 Roger Ascham, *The Scholemaster* (London: John Day, 1570), fol. 10v.
17 *Cymbeline*, ed. Valerie Wayne (London: The Arden Shakespeare Series, 2017), 2.2.24, 38. All subsequent citations are from this edition.
18 J.K. Barret, 'The Crowd in Imogen's Bedroom: Allusion and Ethics in Cymbeline', *Shakespeare Quarterly* 66.4 (2015): 442.
19 Extracts from *Lucrece* dominate the selections from Shakespeare in *England's Parnassus*; on the remaking of the poem by anthologies in the seventeenth century and after, see Kate Rumbold, 'Shakespeare Anthologised', in *The Edinburgh Companion to Shakespeare and the Arts*, eds Mark Thornton Burnett, Adrian Streete and Ramona Wray (Edinburgh: Edinburgh University Press, 2011), 88–107.

20 On the importance of *Venus and Adonis* and *Lucrece* in establishing both Shakespeare's reputation as a poet and his marketability in print, see Roger Chartier and Peter Stallybrass, 'Reading and Authorship: The Circulation of Shakespeare 1590–1619', in *A Concise Companion to Shakespeare and the Text*, ed. Andrew Murphey (London: Blackwell Publishing, 2007). Blackwell Reference Online. Accessed 19 May 2017. www.blackwellreference.com/subscriber/tocnode.html?id=g9781405135283_chunk_g97814051352833.

21 On note-taking as an essential medial step in the transmission of European culture, see Ann Blair, 'Note Taking as an Art of Transmission', *Critical Inquiry* 31.1 (2004).

22 Quoted in Grafton, 198–9.

23 *CWE* 23.635.

24 Quoted in Grafton, 199. Others, like Francis Bacon and Jeremias Drexel, author of a popular seventeenth-century guide to annotating and excerpting, warned against such arrangements, but as Ann Blair suggests, the very existence of such cautions indicates that the labour of annotation was frequently delegated (103–4).

25 *CWE* 23.297.

26 In fact, Blair writes, 'young student readers were encouraged to take notes with no specific purpose', 100.

27 Philip Sidney, *The Defence of Poesie* (London: William Ponsonby, 1595), [F4]v.

PART THREE

Epyllia, masculinity and sexuality

6

From discontent to disdain

Thomas Lodge's *Scillaes Metamorphosis* and the Inns of Court

Jessica Winston

In his verse miscellany *Scillaes Metamorphosis* (1589), Thomas Lodge twice describes himself as a gentleman of Lincoln's Inn and he dedicates the work to fellow innsmen, Master Raph Crane and other 'Gentlemen of the Innes of Court and Chauncerie'.[1] In this way, Lodge signals that his audience is members of the early English law schools and legal societies. Yet it is not clear how the collection might connect with this group, since the verse seems to have little to do with the law or the social world of the Inns. The title poem, *Glaucus and Scilla*, is set in Oxford, far from the bustling metropolis of London. While that poem introduces Themis, goddess of law and social order, she appears only briefly as a chaperone for lovesick nymphs.[2] And, although the language often seems legal – 'proof', 'attaint', 'case', 'report' – the terms have other, non-legal meanings and are used in these other ways.³ Elsewhere in the volume, verses like 'In Praise of the Countrey Life' (D3v–D4v) and 'In Commendation of a Solitarie Life' (E1r–E2r) express the speaker's desire to separate himself from a competitive, cosmopolitan world, such as the one at the Inns.⁴ How then might this volume speak to innsmen?

The aims and appeal of Lodge's collection emerge when it is considered in the context of the transformative social and professional culture of the Inns of Court in the late 1580s and early 1590s. For families in the aristocracy and gentry (and some well to do merchants and yeomen), the Inns were known as societies that offered their sons the possibility of personal, social and professional transformation – places where sons could acquire urban and sophisticated wit and attain the expertise needed to become a lawyer, magistrate, or to serve the state in some other useful capacity. Parents hoped this transition would allow their sons to move from dependency to financial security, and from lower to higher on the social scale, as they developed the social connections and legal skills to serve in the government or return to the provinces to assist with a family estate or the governance of the local polity. Too often, however, this transition took a less exemplary form, with sons falling from promise into ruin. Lodge's earlier prose fiction, *Alarum against Usurers* (1584), vividly portrays this possibility, offering a cautionary tale about a naïve and gullible new member of the Inns who, trapped into debt by a wily usurer, succumbs to a life of dissipation and crime. *Scillaes Metamorphosis* similarly responds to this context.⁵ Unlike *Alarum*, however, which depicts what fellow innsmen should avoid, *Scillaes Metamorphosis* aims to inculcate in readers a disposition or attitude towards the world – one that could help members of the Inns to resist the potentially harmful allurements and enticements around them.

This essay analyses the volume's featured poem, *Glaucus and Scilla*, in relation to the Inns in the 1580s and 1590s to demonstrate that Lodge's epyllion is less a work about change than how to resist it. Such an assertion may seem counterintuitive, since the poem's source is Ovid's *Metamorphoses* and transformation is a crucial topic. In the opening stanzas, Glaucus asserts that change is the only constant: 'Take moist from sea, take colour from his kinde, / Before the world devoid of change thou finde' (A2r). Yet as we shall see, constant change does not indicate a main theme, but establishes the problem Lodge seeks to address: a world where enticements towards transformation are everywhere and inevitable. Lodge uses the poem – and especially its narrator – to model how his gentlemen readers might move through, engage with, but also resist the potentially harmful transformative world around them: by developing a disdainful attitude towards this world and its temptations.

Critics usually regard *Glaucus and Scilla* as the first English epyllion. By reading Lodge's poem in relation to the volume in which it appeared, his other work, and the social environment in which it circulated, it becomes possible to reconsider the relationship between Lodge's epyllion and the genre he appears to have inspired, which continued to be written with the Inns in mind.[6] Critics have long recognized that Lodge influenced the form, tone and subject matter of later epyllia; but when epyllia are discussed as a genre, critics tend to view them in terms of their similarities rather than their differences. Yet later minor epics, such as John Marston's *Metamorphosis of Pigmalions Image* (1598) or Christopher Marlowe's *Hero and Leander* (1594), also seem different from Lodge's *Glaucus and Scilla*. For one, those works are more explicitly erotic than Lodge's. While *Glaucus and Scilla* contains a titillating reference to 'trembl[ing]' water when it touches nymphs' 'teates' (A2v) and some suggestion of homoeroticism, none of this is explicit or sustained. By contrast, Marston openly proclaims in the dedication of *Pigmalion*, 'My wanton muse lasciviously doth sing / Of sportive love, of lovely dallying' (1).[7] In this sense Lodge may have inspired a type of verse that reflected attitudes that were different from his own. Specifically, Lodge's *Glaucus and Scilla* raises a question about how individual innsmen might relate to the world around them – a world implicitly defined as the Inns of Court and more broadly London. As we shall see, later authors, including Shakespeare in *Venus and Adonis*, responded to this topic, and their poems present views that reinforce, diverge from, or even challenge those in Lodge.

Thomas Lodge – reveller and Innsman

Beyond this point about Lodge's influence on literary history, I want to offer a revised sense of the complex relationship between the literary and social cultures of the Inns. Traditionally, critics argue that this literary culture grew out of social divisions at the Inns, but this may not always have been the case. The Inns were complex institutions, functioning as legal societies and law schools for young men seeking careers in the common law, but they were also finishing schools for young men of the aristocracy and gentry who sought to acquire an urban polish and to develop a network of connections that would help them at court and in other elite social circles.[8] Early modernists have argued that the literary culture of the legal societies emerged out of and responded to this distinctive intellectual and social environment. Wilfrid Prest explains: 'Simply by concentrating large numbers of students in an exceptionally lively metropolitan environment, virtually free of academic or any other supervision, the Inns could have hardly failed to play an important part in the English Renaissance.'[9] Those who came to the Inns for social networking, who did not intend a career in law – those whom Francis Beaumont dubbed 'revellers' – used literature to distinguish themselves from the serious lawyers and law students, whom Beaumont termed 'the plodders'.[10] In this view, literary activity was pursued mostly by young men who, having little intention of studying the common law, came to the schools because of their location in London and proximity to the court. As Prest observes, 'The status of common lawyers in Tudor and early Stuart England was not high' and literary activity was one of numerous styles and behaviours adopted by young gentlemen 'which would clearly distinguish them from the common lawyers with whom they were nominally associated'.[11]

Seen in this light, Lodge's volume might be understood as an effort to distinguish himself as a 'reveller', not a 'plodder'. *Scillaes*' dedication to members of the Inns seems to speak directly to revellers – appealing to those whose interests during term time lay less in legal study than in the pamphlets and poems in the bookstalls of Paul's.[12]

This view makes some sense in light of Lodge's biography. After taking his BA at Trinity College, Oxford, Lodge was admitted to Lincoln's Inn in 1578, and immediately expressed his affinity for poetry, asserting in 1579 that 'I affirme that poetry is a heavenly gift, a perfit gift than which I know not greater plesure'.[13] He also associated himself and his writings with the Inns' social and literary world: prior to *Scillaes Metamorphosis*, he addressed his *Alarum Against Usurers* (1584) to 'my right courteous friends, the Gentlemen of the Innes of Court', and signed off, 'Thomas Lodge, of Lincoln's Inn' (A2r; A3v). The title pages of two later works, *The Life and Death of William Long Beard* (1593) and *A Fig for Momus* (1595), also call attention to the author's institutional affiliation.

Lodge's interest in poetry also distanced him from the legal workings of the Inns. Lodge's mother's will, drawn up in 1579, stated that Lodge's inheritance was conditional: 'if he does not continue a good student at Lincoln's Inn', then 'his portion is to be divided among his brothers'.[14] Lodge seems not to have met this condition. He went into debt, and in 1583, he granted his expected inheritance to his brother, William, in return for payment of debts he owed. In 1585, he was excluded from his father's will, a move that has been read as the father's disapproval of his son's life.[15] Lodge's lack of interest in law was hardly unusual. According to one well-accepted estimate, about 85 per cent of those admitted to the Inns were never called to bar.[16]

Yet Lodge himself does not appeal to such social divisions. In *Scillaes Metamorphosis*, Lodge inclusively salutes 'the gentlemen of the Inns of Court and Chancery', gesturing to the whole of the Inns of Court and their affiliated institutions. For Lodge, such inclusiveness is not unusual. He used similar rhetoric in the epistle to *Alarum*, where he addressed all members of the Inns as 'your loving friend' (A3v). There, he also appreciates studiousness, wishing his dedicatee Sir Philip Sidney 'the benefits of happie studie' (A1r), and hoping that innsmen have 'prosperous successe in their studies, and happie event in their travails' (A2r). While Lodge's writings must have distinguished him from other members who did not avidly write or publish, he does not present his publications as a sign of difference. Instead, he uses them to forge connections with men of the Inns as an undifferentiated group.

If *Scillaes Metamorphosis* speaks to this entire group, it offers a model for meeting and reacting to the transformative world of London. Viewed this way, the work suggests a revised framework for thinking about literature at the later sixteenth-century Inns. To be sure, much of this writing treats innsmen satirically and critically. Such derision, however, is less the effect of social divisions (although these certainly existed) than an attempt to reform and shape the culture of the Inns and the attitudes and behaviours of everyone associated with the societies.

Lodge's effort to shape the culture of Inns comes in the form of the narrator of *Glaucus and Scilla*, an initially discontented character who, by the end of the poem, turns his discontent into disdain, developing a critical, derisive distance from the world around him. In this respect, his model innsman is, surprisingly, not a man *of* the Inns. Rather, it is of a man who keeps his distance from that community and from London as a whole. This figure thus raises a question: Can such a distant, isolated figure be a model for how all men at the Inns should relate to the community and city around them?

London's a harlot

Early modernists have long understood the Inns were a transformative space; however, it is less commonly acknowledged that explicit representations of the Inns as places of potentially negative transformation are associated with a specific era, the later sixteenth and early seventeenth centuries. In the 1560s, writers at the Inns engaged with that environment, seeking to shape the ideas, values and behaviours of fellow members.[17] Yet these works rarely take the Inns or innsmen explicitly as their subject, and when they do, such representations are serious or playful, but not critical or alarmist. Serious critique emerges in the 1580s and early 1590s. For instance, John Davies' *Epigrammes* (written c. 1592–5) present satirical caricatures of the 'clamorous frie of the Inns of Court' known for taking the best seats at the theatre, or Publius, student of common law, who abandons his law books for revelling and is 'ravisht' with the 'delectation' of bear baiting.[18]

Multiple dynamics fostered this new awareness and censure. Perhaps the most important involves the demographic growth of the Inns, an increase spurred by the rapid rise in litigation in England, beginning in the 1550s.[19] As the need for lawyers grew, the Inns expanded in population, with the first major period of accelerated growth from 1579 to 1584 and another sustained period from 1594 onwards.[20] Because of the possibility of employment and prestige, the Inns grew in size and altered in terms of demographics. The Inns were already historically associated with aristocracy and the gentry, but they also began to attract more sons of yeomen and merchants. Writing in 1586, John Ferne complained that only 'gentlemen of bloud' should be admitted to the Inns.[21] In 1615, Sir George Buck also griped about the sons of 'graziers, farmers, marchants, tradesmen, and artificers' coming to the societies.[22]

The Inns expanded in population and changed in demographics, resulting in new and expanded buildings, but little else altered.[23] The societies still had no clear admissions qualifications, no required learning and no real disciplinary oversight. As this legal and social world grew more populous and more diverse, the formal and informal oversight of individuals by senior members or by the community necessarily diminished. The chances of getting lost in this environment increased, an outcome made more likely by the allurements of a quickly expanding London – prostitutes, commodities, fashion and the growing entertainment industry of the public theatre. To provide some additional oversight and guidance, many parents hired private tutors to assist their sons. Others relied on makeshift arrangements with relatives, friends and contacts.[24] Yet such arrangements did not prevent young men from being taken in, even ruined, by the diversions of town. In the figure of Publius, student at common law, Davies represents this decline in terms of Publius' increasing filth: 'His satten doublet and his velvet hose' are 'bespread' with 'spittle', and 'rightly too', since he for 'filthie sports his books forsakes'.[25]

In the 1580s and 1590s, writers like Davies repeatedly used literature to respond to the Inns as places of transformative potential, providing models of behaviour and decorum to follow or, more frequently, to avoid. One extended example of such prescriptive literature is Lodge's own *Alarum against Usurers*. Here, an usurer wins the confidence of a naïve and gullible junior member of the Inns, a 'young novice' (B2r), who 'count[s] all golde that glysters, and him a faithfull frend that hath a flattering tongue' (B2v). The usurer gives the man a loan and introduces him to a 'friend', a 'minxe' and 'harlot', who encourages him to spend yet more money. In short time, the man is riotous in his apparel, lavish in his banqueting, loose in his living, and again, out of money (B3r). Thus, through a series of schemes, the usurer drags the young man into debt and, ultimately, into a role as an accomplice in the similar seduction and demise of other young men.

In *Alarum*, the principal agent of the young man's downfall is the usurer. Yet it is notable that a contributing figure is the 'harlot', a seductive force in her own right. As Peter Lake observes, this sort of character frequently stands as a metonym for the enticing pleasures of London, a symbol of the city's 'corrupt alter ego, brazenly selling its often corrupting commodities and loans, things which ... seemed eminently desirable, but which ... were riven with consuming corruption and disease'.[26] In this way, Lodge's *Alarum* taps into a longstanding, cross-cultural tradition of associating cities with the evidently distracting temptations of women.[27] Innsmen themselves register this connection. In his play *Supposes* (c. 1566), George Gascoigne (member of Gray's Inn) presented a city as gendered temptation when Erostrato goes to Ferrara to study and ends up immediately in a love affair. Likewise, *Gismond of Salerne*, performed by members of the Inner Temple in the mid-1560s, links the town to the temptations of love in an offhand reference to the Trojan War:

> Whil'st Paris kept his heard on Ida downe
> Cupid nere sought him out, for he is blinde.
> But when he left the field to live in towne,
> He fel into his snare [...].[28]

Here, the temptations of city lead to personal destruction, but they also undo a civilization.

While those passages refer to cities in general, in later sixteenth- and early seventeenth-century literature, London itself is gendered, and she is not just any woman, but as Lodge implies in *Alarum*, she is a harlot. In 1592, Thomas Nashe asks, 'is there any place so lewde as this Ladie London?'[29] In 1606, Thomas Dekker writes that London 'hast all things in thee to make thee fairest, and all things in thee to make thee foulest: for thou art attir'de like a bride ... but there is much harlot in thine eyes'.[30] This seductive space is especially dangerous to those involved in the law, an idea present in *Alarum* and reinforced elsewhere. In Dekker's dialogue *Dead Term* (1607), a personified city of Westminster complains that in between legal terms, London entices law students and lawyers away from their duties, encouraging drunkenness, quarrelling, gaming and other vices. Westminster says to London, '[T]he wantonesse of thine eye, and the musicke of thy voyce allurest people from all the corners of the land, to throng in heapes, at thy fayres and thy theators'.[31]

If we keep such a perception of London in mind, we realize that the narrative of Lodge's poem is the opposite of *Alarum*. Where the treatise details the downfall of an innsman in

London's seductive pleasures, *Glaucus and Scilla* presents a young, male protagonist dealing with the allurements of a woman, but it focuses the story not on temptations *per se*, but on how one might deal with them. In this reading, the narrator emerges as the ideal model. Yet his role takes shape in relation and as an alternative to the story of Glaucus, the figure who, in terms of number of lines and point of view, dominates the poem.

Glaucus complaining

Lodge adapts his poem from books 13 and 14 of Ovid's *Metamorphosis*. There we learn that Glaucus was a fisherman, who landing on an unknown coast, ate a magical root that turned him into a merman sea-god. One day, he spies the lovely Scilla and immediately desires her. She spurns his advances. Glaucus, discouraged but not dismayed, visits Circe, asking her to use her powers to make Scilla love him. But Circe, herself desiring Glaucus, poisons Scilla, turning her into a half-woman, half-dog monster. The horrified Glaucus flees from Circe. Scilla remains rooted in place, eventually metamorphosing into the legendary rocky coastal hazard. Ovid emphasizes multiple, sudden transformations and reversals: Glaucus from fisherman to sea god, and from sea god to lover; Circe from goddess to vengeful, spurned lover; and Scilla from carefree girl to monster.

In Lodge, the story retains the kernel of the god's desire for Scilla, but is otherwise entirely different. The story takes place in Oxford, on the edge of the river Isis. There, an unnamed narrator walks 'alone (all onely full of griefe)' (A2r). Suddenly, Glaucus appears, lamenting his unrequited desire for Scilla. A group of nymphs emerge from the river to present their own tales of love, although they are far less affected than Glaucus appears to be. The god's mother, Thetis, also appears. Seeing her distraught son, she calls upon Venus and Cupid to cure him. Cupid shoots a bow into Glaucus, apparently in the same place where he had before wounded him. Glaucus is cured. Yet Thetis, angered by Scilla's rejection of her son, has Cupid wound Scilla too. Now Scilla desires Glaucus, who rejects her, and Scilla, surrounded by Fury, Rage, Wan-Hope, Despair and Woe, remains dejected. What happens next is ambiguous: Scilla either becomes, or is confined to, a rocky 'haunt', which serves as a place for 'this mournful Nimph to weepe in' (C4r). Glaucus charges the still melancholy narrator to write his story as a warning to women.

Some of Lodge's most striking alterations involve the female figures, a signal that he is creating a story less about the tribulations of desire than the struggle to overcome it. For instance, Lodge eliminates Circe, a figure who in her ability to transform men into beasts would seem to emblematize the threat of London, as she does in other early modern texts.[32] Yet by eliminating Circe, and introducing a parental figure, Lodge shifts the focus from threats to the male self to methods and models of response to them. To enhance this focus, Lodge reworks Scilla, eliminating the part where Glaucus first sees her. He begins the narrative only after Glaucus is already in the throes of desire. He also structures the poem so that Scilla seeks Glaucus' affections, testing his ability to resist her.

In Lodge's telling, Glaucus' story concerns his inability to control his passions. In one critical reading, Glaucus has been understood as a kind of schoolmaster who chastises the narrator for failing to learn the lessons of his schoolbooks, that 'times change by course of fate' (A2v).[33] Glaucus does insistently guide the narrator throughout the poem. Yet Glaucus' schoolmasterly position is more posture than permanent role. Indeed, for much of the poem he is more dependant than master. To control his own passions, he requires the assistance of his mother, a parental chaperone reminiscent of the network of social relations and family often asked to watch over sons at the Inns. It is notable that Thetis does not ask Venus from the outset to help Scilla return Glaucus' affections; Scilla is a distraction. Rather, Thetis asks the goddess to remove her son's desire, a reversal that returns him to an earlier state of being.

Then Thetis initiates Scilla's transformation, apparently out of a 'now you'll know how it feels' revenge and, the text suggests, perhaps envy for Scilla's beauty (C2r). The change also tests the integrity of Glaucus' reversal – he truly no longer desires Scilla. When Scilla 'claspe[s]' (C2r) her arms about him, he sits 'starke as stone' and 'list not prove her' (C2v). To the extent that Glaucus' story concerns metamorphosis, it is only as reversal of a previous transformation. It is telling in this regard that Lodge suppresses another Ovidian detail: Glaucus was once mortal. In Lodge, Glaucus is a once and future sea god. By omitting his original metamorphosis, Lodge creates for Glaucus a turnaround in which he returns to his original, pre-desiring state.

With respect to this return to a seeming state of control, Jim Ellis argues that Glaucus provides a model of male citizenship, one that equates mastery of heterosexual desire with the autonomous political self.[34] Yet this autonomous self-mastery is in fact only tenuous and impermanent. To control his desire, Glaucus requires parental assistance, suggesting that his seeming independence relies upon maternal (here perhaps suggesting familial) dependency. Moreover, it is not clear how long this tenuous state of monitored self-control lasts. In the volume of *Scillaes Metamorphosis*, just following *Glaucus and Scilla*, Lodge presents another poem, the 'Glaucus Complaint', in which the sea god pines again for Scilla's love. In terms of the chronology of Glaucus' narrative, the complaint belongs to an earlier part of his story, where the sea god describes his enthrallment to love.[35] But in terms of the organization of the volume, the complaint appears at the end of the epyllion. The effect is to suggest that Glaucus' independence does not last. If the poem presents a model of the male mastery of desire, it is one where the master's mastery is elusive, since it depends on a state of perpetual parental guidance, which cannot last. The tale of Glaucus is a fantasy about resisting transformation, even as it also suggests that, without parental supervision, it is impossible to resist those things that unravel the self and lead to an enervating state of desire.

The discontented narrator

Glaucus and Scilla, however, presents another narrative of metamorphosis that stands as a sterner model for dealing with temptation: the narrator's transformation from unhappy lover to disdainful critic. At first, the narrator's story seems to parallel that of Glaucus, since he too begins discontented and then returns to his original state. Yet over the course of the poem the narrator does change: he turns from a passive, melancholic figure, subject to the opinions and emotions of those around him, into an author who maintains a calculated distance from this world.

When we first meet the narrator, he is, like Glaucus, discontented, although the poem does not give a reason for the narrator's weary sadness. The location near Oxford signals one possible source, since it implies that the narrator is a scholar, and thus perhaps suffers from the melancholia often associated with scholars.[36] Another might be that the narrator also suffers from frustrated desire. He sees himself reflected in Glaucus' story, saying upon hearing Glaucus' tale, 'when he wailed, I straight forgot my woe' (A2r). Later, after learning just part of the sea god's tale, the narrator says that 'Comparing his mishaps and moane with mine', he (the narrator) 'Gan smile for joy' (A2v). In the narrator's relationship with Glaucus, there is latent homoeroticism, further reinforcing the sense of the narrator's unrequited longing. The narrator feels both better and weaker when Glaucus 'reposd his head upon my faintfull knee' (A2r). He tells us that he has been through this before, saying 'Alas woes me, how oft have I bewept / So faire, so young, so lovely, and so kinde' (B4r), but the latter phrase seems to refer as much to Glaucus as to these previous loves. Despite these various possibilities, the narrator does not explicitly state a cause for his discontent. Rather, he just suffers, and his suffering is beyond him. Like Glaucus, he has no agency or control. The randomness of the setting only reinforces the narrator's lack of agency. As the poem opens, we find the narrator walking on the banks of the river Isis. What is he doing there? Why is he there? We conclude that he is a scholar, but we do not know that for certain; other than the detail that he has 'bewept' before, he has no backstory and no forward-looking aims.

For much of the poem, the narrator remains subject to the world around him, continuing as the auditor and observer of Glaucus, whose point of view, as R.W. Maslen observes, shapes much of the narrative. When Glaucus enters, he commands the narrator to 'mourne no more, but moane my haples state', thus insisting on the supremacy of his own perspective.[37] Later, after Cupid shoots Scilla with his bow, the narrator's feelings become bound up with Scilla's. He responds to her state of restless desire, stating that her miserable situation 'did hartely aggreeve me' (C2v). Yet Glaucus, seeing the narrator 'pencive', quickly distracts him, taking him for a ride on a dolphin, thus pulling the narrator's focus back to him and his point of view. Indeed, this reassertion of Glaucus' point of view on the narrator's seems connected to the sexual consummation implied in the dolphin ride. Glaucus 'horst' the narrator on the back of a phallic dolphin, where they ride 'hand in hand' (C3r). Later, they ride a dolphin again, while Glaucus sings a 'sonnets song' to him (C4v). The narrator is now Glaucus' lover, and thus again emotionally aligned with Glaucus, rather than with Scilla or anyone else. If the poet is Glaucus' lover, he is also the god's spokesman: he adopts Glaucus' idea that women should always accede to men's desires: 'Ah Nimphes thought I, if every coy one felt / The like misshappes their flintie hearts would melt' (C4r).

Lodge reinforces the idea that the narrator has adopted Glaucus' point-of-view near the close of the poem. When Glaucus leaves, the narrator reverts to his original, unhappy state. While Glaucus is 'full of glee' (C4r), the narrator returns to a state of discontent, again 'alonely' and 'with many a sigh and heart full sad and sorie' (C4v). At this point, the narrator's sadness seems to stem from Glaucus' departure. In this sense, the narrator continues to be – however willingly – dependent on Glaucus, and thus generally to the vicissitudes of the world around him. He is not fully in control of his own story. As with

Glaucus and Scilla, Lodge's narrator has no control over his own peace of mind. For both Glaucus and the narrator, when external forces change, they revert to their original state of melancholy, disconsolate longing.

Or at least, in the narrator's case, that is what seems to occur. Yet the poem does not endorse the narrator's dependence on Glaucus. If the poem positions Glaucus as a guide to the narrator, it also makes Glaucus' mastery dependent on his mother, thus ironizing and undercutting him as an authoritative guide. Furthermore, in the final stanza, the narrator changes, developing his own perspective on the figures and events dominating his life. In the closing stanzas, Glaucus charges the narrator to write about 'Scillas pride', a command that provides a direction for the narrator's discontent, channelling it towards bitter, misogynist railing. Thus he concludes the poem with a moralizing envoy:

> That Nimphs must yield, when faithfull louers straie not,
> Least through contempt, almightie love compel you
> With Scilla in the rockes to make your biding
> A cursed plague, for womens proud back-sliding.
>
> (C4v)

At this point, the narrator remains guided by Glaucus, since his moral reflects the god's view; he writes as Glaucus 'wild me tell you' (C4v). Even so, the role of author and railer is one that the narrator then takes on for himself. He follows Glaucus' advice and writes the epyllion itself, thus demonstrating a mastery over his own desire, as well as that of Glaucus and Scilla.

More than that, he uses his newfound bitterness to produce other verse. It is notable that in the volume, the first poem following *Glaucus and Scilla* is the 'Glaucus Complaint'. As mentioned above, this complaint returns Glaucus to the mode of disconsolate lover, but the author of the complaint is none other than the narrator, as it is written 'by the said Gent'. In the context of the volume, this 'gent' is the narrator of the previous poem, although this attribution aligns the narrator with Lodge, described as a 'gentleman' on the title page of *Scillaes Metamorphosis*. At this point, the narrator-cum-Lodge controls the narration, and he continues to control it for the remainder of the volume, turning his melancholy and disdain outward. For instance, in 'The Discontented Satyre Written by Thomas Lodge, Gent,' the narrator meets a satyr in the woods and 'vow[s] to honor discontent' (D3v). In 'In Praise of Solitarie Life', a narrator commends a life free from the ambitions, desires and misfortunes of the world of the court (D3v–D4v). In other words, over the course of *Glaucus and Scilla*, the narrator changes his attitude towards and his level of independence from the world. He adopts a keen, knowing persona that rather than succumbing to the temptations of the world remains distant from it, able to judge it without (seemingly) being affected by it. Furthermore, while the narrator briefly identifies with Scilla in the poem, there are no other poems in the volume where he represents or identifies with a woman's point-of-view, a fact that reinforces his critical distance from everyone around him – both men and women.

This understanding of the narrator as model, however, raises a question about the treatment of Scilla in Lodge's epyllion. In her initial indifference towards Glaucus, she would seem herself to model the very distance from, and disdain towards, desire that the narrator ultimately adopts. Why is she punished? One reasonable explanation is that Scilla's fate stems from the gender politics of the poem. Lodge focuses on male selfhood, one marker of which is the ability to control one's attitude towards the world, and indeed to control others. Thus, *Glaucus and Scilla* states that women must give in to the desires of men, 'Nimphs must yield, when faithfull louers straie not' (C4v). Women must be subject to men, must change in response to men, not the other way around. At the same time, Scilla's fate is to be a persistent danger and, hence, warning to men. Her rocky 'bowre' is 'shun[ned]' by the 'sea-man . . . with fear dispairing' (C4r). In this sense, the despairing seaman is a version of the narrator, who shuns Scilla – and all the allurements of women – to navigate the dangers of the world.

Conclusion: 'vindicating self-will'?

Reading *Glaucus and Scilla* as a response to the transformative world of the Inns of Court and London provides a way to unite analyses of the poem's generic innovation with a sense of social contexts and to reconsider Lodge's relationship to later epyllia. Scholars have argued that he blended the established genre of medieval and early Tudor complaint with Ovid's wry eroticism, and in so doing, instigated a new style of Elizabethan poetry that satirized the popular Petrarchan conceits of the day and appealed to a new generation of readers. Clark Hulse exemplifies this line of argument: 'In 1589 Thomas Lodge was, under the influence of the lyric, able to transform the moral and satiric complaint into a vehicle of erotic delight appropriate to the new literary coterie shaped by Sidney and Spenser.'[38] Other criticism addresses the poem's relationship to contemporary social and political contexts. Maslen asserts that Lodge transforms Ovidian tradition to express discontent with (but not outright criticism of) monarchic power. Ellis contends that Lodge sets the stage for other epyllia by presenting a model of political selfhood imagined in relation to the way that the male self maintains autonomy by avoiding the entanglements of heterosexual desire (51–64). Lynn Enterline argues that the epyllion functioned quite differently. Authors of the epyllia first learned Ovid in grammar school, in a curriculum that was supposed to train them into the type of masculine, civic selfhood Ellis describes. Yet, in embracing Ovid's eroticism and ventriloquizing his female voices, authors of epyllia used their humanist learning to question its values, uses and consequences.[39]

The present argument links genre and context, suggesting that Lodge's literary innovation was central to the poem's social project and immediate context, the Inns of Court. It also identifies a difference between Lodge's epyllion and the later narrative poetry he influenced. For Lodge promotes a certain image of controlled masculinity, one developed through the narrator's connection with the quasi-mentor Glaucus, but which by the end of the poem exists independently of him.

At the same time, this male self can only be sustained through disengagement from, rather than engagement with, romantic allurements and civic obligations. But later authors of epyllia did not necessarily endorse the model of the male self (or the poet) that Lodge presents.

In his epyllion, Lodge satirized the frustrated, ever desiring lover of Petrachan poetry, a model perhaps for men subject both to women and to all the feminized allurements of London. To create this satire, Lodge turned to and adapted Ovidian verse – stories about sudden change and forced transformation – to fashion a poem that could offer its initial readers a model for how innsmen might deal with the transformative dangers of London. In so doing, Lodge also provided a literary model that other writers – including Shakespeare – could follow. But did they? Ellis and William Weaver have argued that all of the authors of epyllia transformed Ovidian narratives in order to offer moralizing commentary on appropriate behaviour and ways of being in the world.[40] Yet I would suggest that we see the relationship of Lodge's epyllion to the later epyllia in a different way – not solely in terms of imitation, but in terms of response and even critique.

It is worth recognizing that Lodge's model of male selfhood seems to have been viable for at least one person – him. As one biographer remarks, Lodge's is 'the life of an incurably assertive individualist vindicating self-will and private opinion against all the forces of environment'.[41] In *Glaucus and Scilla*, Lodge represents a version of his own persona, showing, in Hulse's words, how 'a melancholy gentleman . . . blots out the degraded world around him' (48). Yet the poem – and the rest of the volume – are not *just* a reflection of Lodge's own self-fashioning. Instead, Lodge's narrator models an attitude that could be adopted by other innsmen, if they too wish to avoid the metamorphosing temptations of London. They should not look to their parents (or even friends and associates) for guidance. Rather, they should rely on their own 'will' and 'opinion' to disdain the financially and morally threatening forces of their environment.

Ultimately, however, Lodge's model is puzzling: he attempts to admonish and reform the members of his community by promoting a model figure who is not a part of this very community. The narrator of *Glaucus and Scilla* becomes an accomplished poet, but this poet constantly demands further separation from the world, appearing in the rest of the collection of poetry that is *Scillaes Metamorphosis* to want a solitary and country life. This narrator does not seek to be a part of London, let alone the Inns of Court. It is thus worth asking: what would happen if all men at the Inns adopted the attitude of Lodge's 'gentleman narrator' in *Glaucus and Scilla*, and more extensively in *Scillaes Metamorphosis*? What would such an attitude really get them? And here we can see Lodge's relationship to the later epyllion in a new light. For later authors do not simply imitate Lodge. They return to and explore the possibilities and failings of the very model that Lodge presents.

For one example, Shakespeare wrote *Venus and Adonis* with junior members of the Inns in mind, and perhaps one particular member, Henry Wriothesley.[42] His epyllion might be understood as both response to and critique of Lodge's vision: Shakespeare presents a character who, like Glaucus, must struggle with both sexual temptations and maternal admonition – both embodied in Venus. In the face of such figures, Adonis asserts his difference, his independence and freedom, a state of being that the poem figures as hunting. Because the poem represents Venus as a gigantic, aggressively sexualized woman and Adonis by contrast as a small, petulant youth, it seems clear that Adonis and Venus are mismatched and that Adonis is, therefore, right to reject Venus. Yet in rejecting Venus, what does he reject?

One might see Venus, like Scilla, as representing the allurements of London. After all, she tempts Adonis to neglect what he sees as his duty, and she is consistently associated with a language of the city – trading, buying, selling and debt. She tells Adonis, 'one sweet kiss shall pay this countless debt' (84); she holds out her lips 'ready for his pay' (89). This language appears throughout the poem: 'int'rest' (210), 'sell' (513), 'buy' and 'buys' (514, 517), 'good dealing' (514), 'honey fee' (538), and 'price' (551). Furthermore, when she 'pluck[s]' Adonis from his horse (30) and seeks to 'sell myself' (513), her language recalls period descriptions of London's prostitutes. To give just one example, which also involves aggressive selling and 'plucking': William Camden complains of those London 'harlots' who 'after the manner of ravening she-wolves catch hold of silly wretched men and plucke them into their hooles' (434). Like the narrator of Lodge's poems, Adonis rejects Venus and the sexual enticements and economic entanglements she represents: ''Tis much to borrow, and I will not owe it' (411).

Instead, Adonis pursues hunting, an activity that might be understood as a countrified, solitary attraction, in contrast to the citified temptations Venus offers. Critics usually interpret the boar in *Venus* as a symbol of Adonis' homosocial and homosexual desires: hunting is a masculine pursuit; the boar with his red and white foaming mouth is a parody of the Petrarchan beloved; and Adonis' manner of death – penetrated in the thigh by the tusk of the boar – is both phallic and sexual. Alongside these readings, the boar may also stand as figure for country (instead of the city), and Adonis' hunting as less homosocial than isolated and lonely, the very sort of activity that Lodge's narrator craves when he desires a 'solitary' and 'countrey' life. Thus Adonis asks Venus to 'leave me here alone' (382) and to 'sleep alone' (786). In this respect, Adonis may be a version of Lodge's narrator: disdainful, independent and socially isolated. In this sense, Shakespeare's epyllion may be a response to *Glaucus and Scilla*, and specifically to the model the narrator represents. Unable to deal with the erotic temptations of the city and, seeking the isolation of a country life, Adonis' fate demonstrates that such a model has no future. At the same time, in the outsized depiction of the economic and sexual Venus, Shakespeare perhaps also parodies the association of women with the city and its exaggerated temptations.

How might other authors have responded to Lodge's model of male selfhood in relation to the community of the Inns and

London in general? That question is beyond the scope of this essay, but it is one that readers might keep in mind as they explore the rest of the essays in this volume. For now, as the example of *Venus and Adonis* suggests, it is worth acknowledging that while authors of the epyllion may have presented models of male development and civic selfhood, as Ellis and Weaver argued, they did more than that. Indeed, they also analysed and challenged the model put forward by Lodge in the first English epyllion. Lodge may have written for members of the Inns, with the whole of the Inns in mind, and with a desire to connect himself more strongly to that community. Yet, in the end, in *Glaucus and Scilla* he did not present a viable model for how to relate to London or the social community that is the Inns of Court. In *Venus and Adonis* Shakespeare returns to Lodge's vision, exploring its underlying assumptions and limitations. It would seem that for Shakespeare, Lodge's narrative vindication of self-will fails to offer a workable sense of how men might actually relate – to other men, or women, or to the city where they lived.

Notes

1 Because I discusses *Scillaes Metamorphosis* as a whole, all references to the collection and to individual poems within it are to the first edition, *Scillaes Metamorphosis: Enterlaced with the Unfortunate Love of Glaucus* (London: Richard Jones, 1589), STC 554, title page, *1r, A1r. While the present volume uses Donno's *Elizabethan Minor Epics* as the standard reference work, for consistency of reference to the epyllion and other poems in *Scillaes*, I instead refer throughout to the copy of the above edition in EEBO. Scholars frequently use the same name to refer to the full collection and its feature poem (e.g. Donno 21). To avoid confusion, I refer to the collection as *Scillaes Metamorphosis* and the epyllion as *Glaucus and Scilla*, a shortened, regularized form of the poem's initial title, *The Most Pithie and Pleasant Historie of Glaucus and Silla*.

2 The appearance of Themis is so incongruous that one editor suggests that Lodge may have confused the name Themis with

Tethys, the wife of Oceanus and mother of rivers, a reference that would make sense given that the poem features the sea god Glaucus pining on the banks of a river. See Nigel Alexander, *Elizabethan Narrative Verse* (Cambridge, MA: Harvard University Press, 1968), 318.

3 For instance, Glaucus refers to 'proofs' (A2r). While the notion of proof goes back to classical legal rhetoric, since the poem takes place in Oxford, the activity of offering a 'proof' here is likely associated with university education.

4 One explanation for this incongruity could lie in the volume's composition, since Lodge possibly composed all or part of while he was a student at Oxford (Donno, 6). Even if he composed most of the volume at Oxford, the prefaces repeatedly suggest that readers relate him and his collection to the Inns.

5 Thomas Lodge, *Alarum Against Usurers Containing tried Experiences against Worldly Abuses* (London, 1584), STC 16653.

6 See Ellis, *Sexuality and Citizenship*, Weaver, *Untutored Lines*, and Enterline, 'Elizabethan Minor Epics', 253–71.

7 John Marston, *The Metamorphosis of Pigmalions Image and Certaine Satyres* (London, 1598), A5r, STC 17482. On Marston's poem in relation to the Inns of Court, see Enterline, *The Rhetoric of the Body*, 125–51.

8 See J.H. Baker, 'The Third University 1450–1540: Law School or Finishing School?', in *The Intellectual and Cultural World of the Early Modern Inns of Court*, eds Jayne Elisabeth Archer, Elizaeth Goldring and Sarah Knight (Manchester: Manchester University Press, 2011), 8–24.

9 Wilfrid Prest, *Rise of the Barristers: A Social History of the English Bar, 1500–1640* (Oxford: Oxford University Press, 1986), 193.

10 Mark Eccles, 'Francis Beaumont's Grammar Lecture', *Review of English Studies* 16.64 (1940): 406.

11 Wilfrid Prest, *The Inns of Court under Elizabeth I and the Early Stuarts, 1590–1640* (Totowa, NJ: Prentice-Hall Press, 1972), 40–1.

12 Lodge complains about 'prodigall' pamphleteers who plaster their title pages on posts as soon as the legal term begins (*v). Lodge's complaint suggests an audience familiar with the lively trade in the bookstalls of Paul's Churchyard and elsewhere.

13 [*A Reply to Stephen Gosson's School of Abuse*] *Protogenes Can Know Apelles* (London, 1579?), STC 16663.

14 See Alexandra Halasz, 'Lodge, Thomas (1558–1625)', *Oxford Dictionary of National Biography* (Oxford: Oxford University Press, 2004); online edn Jan 2008 [accessed 9 July 2017].

15 Wesley Rae, *Thomas Lodge* (New York: Twayne English Authors Series, 1967), 15–16.

16 Philip J. Finkelpearl, *John Marston of the Middle Temple: An Elizabethan Dramatist in His Social Setting* (Cambridge, MA: Harvard University Press, 1969), 10.

17 See Jessica Winston, *Lawyers at Play: Literature, Law, and Politics at the Early Modern Inns of Court, 1558–1581* (Oxford: Oxford University Press, 2016).

18 *The Poems of Sir John Davies*, ed. Robert Kreuger (Oxford: Oxford University Press, 1975), 130, 148.

19 Christopher W. Brooks, *Lawyers, Litigation and English Society since 1450* (London: Bloomsbury, 2003), 66.

20 After 1594, this growth was sometimes interrupted by the plague. See Louis Knafla, 'The Matriculation Revolution and Education at the Inns of Court in Renaissance England', in *Tudor Men and Institutions: Studies in Law and Government*, ed. A.J. Slavin (Baton Rouge: Louisiana State University Press, 1972), 237.

21 John Ferne, *The Blazon of Gentrie* (London, 1586), 92, STC 10825.

22 *The Thirde Universitie of England* (London, 1615), 969, STC 23338.

23 On the expansion of buildings, see Prest, *Inns of Court*, 18–19.

24 Prest, *Inns of Court*, 139–41

25 *The Poems of Sir John Davies*, 148–9.

26 Peter Lake, 'From Troynouvant to Heliogabulus' Rome and Back: "Order" and its Others in the London of John Stow', in *Imagining Early Modern London: Perceptions & Portrayals of the City from Stow to Strype 1598–1720*, ed. J.F. Merritt (Cambridge: Cambridge University Press, 2001), 247.

27 See Lawrence Manley, *Literature and Culture in Early Modern London* (Cambridge: Cambridge University Press, 1995), 141.

28 *The Tragedie of Tancred and Gismund compiled by the Gentlemen of the Inner Temple* (London, 1591), D3v, STC 25764.

29 Thomas Nashe, *Pierce Penilesse His Supplication to the Divell* (London, 1592), H3v, STC 18372.

30 Thomas Dekker, *The Seven Deadly Sins of London* (London, 1606), A2v, STC 6522.

31 Thomas Dekker, The *Dead Tearme. Or, Westminsters Complaint for Long Vacations and Short Termes* (London, 1608), B3r, STC 6496.

32 See Brent E. Whitted, 'Transforming the (Common)place: The Performance of William Browne's *Ulysses and Circe* in the Inner Temple Hall', *Theatre History Studies* 19 (1999), 160–3.

33 For a discussion of Glaucus as schoolmaster, see Enterline, 'Elizabethan Minor Epics', 257.

34 Ellis, 64.

35 Rae suggests that the 'Glaucus Complaint' may not have fit into the narrative of *Glaucus and Scilla* (*Thomas Lodge*, 52–3).

36 See Sarah Knight, 'Fantastical Distempers: The Psychopathology of Early Modern Scholars', in *Early Modern Academic Drama*, eds Jonathan Walker and Paul D. Streufert (Aldershot: Routledge, 2008), 129–52. Glaucus reinforces the narrator's position as a scholar by referring to 'thy bookes' (A2r) and 'schoolemens cunning notes' (A3r).

37 R.W. Maslen, 'Lodge's *Glaucus and Scilla* and the Conditions of Catholic Authorship in Elizabethan England', *EnterText: An Interactive Interdisciplinary E-Journal for Cultural and Historical Studies and Creative Work* 3.1 (2003): 59–100.

38 *Metamorphic Verse*, 36. See also William Keach, 'Glaucus and Scilla', in *Thomas Lodge*, ed. Charles Whitney (New York: Routledge, 2011), 380.

39 Enterline, 'Elizabethan Minor Epics'.

40 In *Untutored Lines*, Weaver does not discuss *Glaucus and Scilla*.

41 Charles J. Sisson, *Thomas Lodge and Other Elizabethans* (Cambridge, MA: Harvard University Press, 2014), 160.

42 Ellis, 80.

7

Love will tear us apart

Campion's *Umbra* and Shakespeare's *Venus and Adonis*

John S. Garrison

At the heart of the epyllia is the notion of transformation, in the sense that their frequently Ovidian narratives involve the metamorphoses of central characters and in the sense that these poems so often adapt classical narratives for early modern audiences. Because the genre was so closely tied to the schoolroom, we might think of minor epics as transformative in yet another way: they reflect the ways that their writers and readers were changed as they transitioned into adulthood in the humanist tradition. The erotic component so common in the tales that epyllia tell can be difficult to disaggregate from these diverse forms of transformation. Leonard Barkan notes that metamorphosis functions as 'a figure for all the fears and necessities of exogamy, and so stories of metamorphosis are stories of pursuit, of travel, of unfamiliar and *alien loves*'.[1] This claim can be applied not only to the events of Ovidian narratives but to the experience of reading them. Certainly *Venus and Adonis*, which depicts an attempt at sexual relations between a mortal and a god, invites readers to consider simultaneously a time, place and mode of sexual relations that are alien to them. For the reader, imagining this erotic otherness is tied to new understanding and to the pleasures of the text. As Elizabeth Freeman observes, 'contact with historical materials can be precipitated by particularly bodily dispositions, and that these connections may elicit bodily responses, even pleasurable ones, that are themselves a form of understanding'.[2]

This essay begins by tracing these interconnected elements – transformation, literary learning, sexual desire – in Shakespeare's *Venus and Adonis* (1593) before placing the poem in conversation with Thomas Campion's *Umbra* (1595/1619). Both minor epics depict erotic encounters between a mortal and a god, and both poems end with a dramatic shattering of the mortal protagonist's self. Resistance to sexual advances from a deity ultimately leads to Adonis' distillation into a flower and Melampus' dissipating into a shadow, thus emblematizing love's capacity to render the subject fragile and non-human. While Shakespeare's lush *Venus and Adonis* dances around explicit eroticism, Campion's Latin poem is striking for its frank depiction of same-sex erotics that are largely absent from epyllia written in English during the Renaissance. Campion, trained in the same type of humanist schoolroom that produced Marlowe and Shakespeare, and a resident of the Inns of Court that housed many of the writers of epyllia, seizes upon the classical language to revivify the homoerotic pleasures of the past. Yet he, like Shakespeare, innovates source material from Ovid's *Metamorphoses* in order to represent an even darker depiction of failed romance than his classical predecessor does. Such a reading of *Umbra* throws into relief the ways that *Venus and Adonis* meditates on not only the self-shattering effects of desire but also the weight of literary history itself. Both poems render visible how early modern writers of epyllia must at times increase the stakes of their re-tellings in order to escape the shadow of the tradition upon which they draw, often showcasing the profoundly negative effects of an erotic encounter.

More than simply adapting an episode from Ovid's *Metamorphoses*, *Venus and Adonis* is involved in a complex project that reflects upon the humanist pedagogy and literary tradition into which the poem enters. M.L. Stapleton argues that multiple classical texts function as important intertexts for Shakespeare's poem, including Ovid's guide to love, the *Ars amatoria*. Noting the poem's 'manifold allusions to the *Ars* as a text and genre', Stapleton identifies Venus as a teacher and Adonis as a student who finds himself under the duress of a 'tormentor's didacticism'.[3] This interpretation aligns with that of Tita French Baumlin, who posits that we see Shakespeare seeking to 'outdo his poetic forefather, to "out-Ovid" Ovid'.[4] The poem as a scene of pedagogy finds expression when Venus forces Adonis to sit early on ('So soon was she along as he was down, / Each leaning on their elbows and their hips' [43–4]) as Shakespeare mirrors the same moment in the *Metamorphoses* ('*libet hac requiescere tecum*' / *(et requievit)* '*humo*' *pressitque et gramen et ipsum*' [10.556–7]).[5] While this pose emphasizes the goddess' ability to compel her student to listen, this moment underscores the limits of Venus' ability to influence Adonis. Over the course of the poem, he will endure the full force of her persuasion but not aquiesce to it by giving in to desire. The goddess' failure is foreshadowed here by the statement that she 'governed him in strength though not in lust' (42). The term 'governed' here reminds us of the power differential between Venus and Adonis, especially as the word offers a homonymn for 'governess'. Although the *OED* suggests that this term did not take on the explicit meaning of 'a female teacher or instructor' until 1673, we can still see elements of such a role in the meaning that was in use since 1500: 'a woman responsible for the care, supervision, or direction of a person, typically a child'.[6] By deploying tactics articulated in Ovid's guide to love, Venus engages in a time-defying strategy of seduction. She is simultaneously the ancient Greek embodiment of love and a skilled orator who has studied the work of an ancient Latin writer.

The epyllia constituted a component of the rhetorical training that linked eloquence to the fashioning of gentlemen in early modern England, connecting exposure to ancient literature to masculinity. William Weaver describes the minor epic as the genre through which 'poets depicted *rites de passage* from boyhood to adolescence as enacted in the institutional context of the humanist grammar school'.[7] In turn, study of the epyllia inspired these young men to continue study and to compose new additions to the genre. Indeed, Georgia Brown describes the epyllion as 'born in and for the Inns of Court'.[8] Yet these texts also functioned to make visible the faults of humanist training. Lynn Enterline suggests that we might find within epyllia 'an institutional critique with important consequences for how we understand early modern masculinity and the passions'.[9] Such a claim holds true for *Venus and Adonis* (and, as we will see below, for *Umbra* as well), which alludes to the perils of linking schoolroom rhetoric with erotic desire.

The notion that Venus deploys a knowledge of literary texts is compounded when she demonstrates a knowledge of the Renaissance love poet's techniques. The goddess alters her appearance to appeal to Adonis, and she does so in a way that acknowledges the power of literary device. To make herself more desirable,

> She feedeth on the stream, as on a prey,
> And calls it heavenly moisture, air of grace,
> > Wishing her cheeks were gardens full of flowers,
> > So they were dewed with such distilling showers.
>
> (63–6)

It is the stuff of Petrarchan blazon; she wishes and then transforms her cheeks to appear like flowers.[10] Indeed, Shakespeare offers a well-known critique of this common trope when he remarks of his beloved in Sonnet 130, 'no such roses see I in her cheeks' (line 6). So, perhaps we should not be surprised when Venus' strategy does not influence Adonis. Still, she does not relent. When she cannot inspire the young man to compose a blazon about her, she herself conducts an inventory of her features as she praises her smooth brow, bright eyes, soft flesh, burning marrow, and moist hand (139–43). Richard Rambuss suggests that Venus 'is constrained to enact all the amorous roles [...] to be both lover and would-be beloved, both blazoner and blazoned beauty'.[11] Operating as a composite of multiple figures, she adds excess to an already powerful body that is capable of lifting the boy from his horse at the opening of the poem. This goddess, who Pauline Kiernan aptly describes as a 'figure of physical and rhetorical excess', threatens to overwhelm Adonis.[12]

Venus alludes to myth and uses anecdote as part of her efforts at persuasion. She invokes the example of Narcissus to urge Adonis to redirect self-love – love of one's own 'shadow', as she puts it – towards love-of-the-other (161–2).[13] Choosing this example risks sabotaging her endeavour because, as Jim Ellis puts it, 'Narcissus offers us the negative exemplum of a youth seduced by Petrarchan rhetoric'.[14] However, her use of 'shadow' also emphasizes her status as an object of substantive excess. The term 'shadow' appears nine times in Shakespeare's poem, polysemously used to describe at times Adonis and at other times the ways that Venus overshadows him or the spaces in which their encounter takes place. In the way that the shadow presages the instance where Adonis will be annihilated in an ambiguous scene of uncontrolled desire, we see an expression here of the 'Renaissance impulse to negate selfhood' that Cynthia Marshall has traced in narratives where pleasure and violence collide.[15] Indeed, Venus' description of Narcissus as one who 'died to kiss his shadow in the brook' is at once an admonition about self-love and also the promise of the thrill of pursuing the alien forms of love that she will offer Adonis and Shakespeare offers his reader.

Venus turns to personal recollection as she depicts how she once overcame the embodiment of war. In the three-stanza anecdote, she uses the figure of Mars to explain why Adonis should accede to her advances. This tale of an encounter where the god of war succumbed to the advances of the goddess of love embellishes brief descriptions in Lucretius' *De rerum natura* (1.29–40) and in Ovid's *Metamorphoses* (4.167–89).[16] Lucretius' version emphasizes the excess of Venus' love, where Mars is

> O'ermastered by the eternal wound of love-
> And there, with eyes and full throat backward thrown,
> Gazing, my Goddess, open-mouthed at thee,
> Pastures on love his greedy sight, his breath
> Hanging upon thy lips. Him thus reclined
> Fill with thy holy body, round, above!
>
> [*reiicit aeterno devictus vulnere amoris,
> atque ita suspiciens tereti cervice reposta
> pascit amore avidos inhians in te, dea, visus
> eque tuo pendet resupini spiritus ore.
> hunc tu, diva, tuo recubantem corpore sancto
> circum fusa super, suavis ex ore loquellas*]
>
> (1.34–42)[17]

This impressive display of power – characterized by Mars 'o'ermastered', suffering an 'eternal wound' and able to 'fill' her entire body – emphasizes the promise of how an all-encompassing encounter with her might feel while also signalling the threat of such an encounter. In Shakespeare's version, Venus threatens to overpower even her immortal partner. Mars is made her 'captive' and 'slave', with the goddess '[l]eading him prisoner in a red-rose chain' (101, 110). We can imagine how Venus, who has encountered Adonis in the midst of hunting, might think the martial analogy might persuade him. Wouldn't a violent hunter want to emulate the paradigm of martial masculinity: the god of war himself? If human eroticism is 'assenting to life up to the point of death', then the tale of a Mars' experience of sexual pleasure that renders his body and will completely subjugated could sound like an experience no mortal could survive.[18] That is, the tale of Mars might sound to Adonis more like a cautionary tale than a compelling argument. Venus uses allegory and storytelling, layering several ancient narratives on top of each other to seduce Adonis, yet her rhetorical choices may only compound the impression of her as a figure of dangerous excess.[19]

The attempted seduction (with mortal consequences) of a human by a god parallels events in Marlowe's epyllion, *Hero and Leander* (1598). Both Venus and Neptune use storytelling about previous encounters in their efforts to seduce present objects of desire. When Leander attempts to deter Neptune by announcing that 'You are deceived, I am no woman, I' (II.192), the sea god 'then told a tale' about a shepherd, who:

> Playd with a boy so faire and kind,
> As for his love, both earth and heaven pyn'd;
> That of the cooling river durst not drinke,
> Lest water-nymphs should pull him from the brinke.
> And when hee sported in the fragrant lawnes,
> Gote-footed Satyrs, and up-staring Fawnes
> Would steale him thence.
>
> (II.195–201)

Neptune seems to recount this tale of love towards several ends: to attest to his level of desire, to excite the young man by relating a story of lust, to justify attempts by mythical beings to steal away humans and to educate the young man about the availability of same-sex relationships. By being unspecific about the identity of the boy in his tale, Neptune invokes a wide literary canon of stories that depict young men beloved by other men in pastoral poetry and in myth. Yet the allusion to pastoral couplings undermines his attempted seduction. Male love here is positioned to save a young lover from being drowned by water-nymphs (alluding perhaps to Hylas, who is drowned by nymphs when he is lured away from his lover Hercules). However, Neptune does in fact almost drown Leander when he pulls him under the water in a fit of lust.

Venus' exhaustive use of literary techniques fails to seduce Adonis but does offer a substitute for bodily erotic experience. As Stephen Guy-Bray argues, 'the style is not an instrument to convey the reality (or "reality") of the narrative but rather the thing itself: the language of the poem is the only fulfillment we or Venus get'.[20] At one point in her appeal, Venus suggests the limitless promise of erotic coupling with her:

> A thousand kisses buys my heart from me;
> And pay them at thy leisure, one by one.
> What is ten hundred touches unto thee?
> Are they not quickly told and quickly gone?
> Say, for non-payment that the debt should double,
> Is twenty hundred kisses such a trouble?
>
> (517–22)

In six lines, she promises what seems would take years to deliver. The lines once more betray her and the poem's literary lineage, as they echo a popular fragment of Catullus' poetry:

> Give me a thousand kisses, then a hundred.
> Then, another thousand, and a second hundred.
> Then, yet another thousand, and a hundred.
> Then, when we have counted up many thousands,
> Let us shake the abacus, so that no one may know the number,
> And become jealous when they see
> How many kisses we have shared.
>
> [*da mi basia mille, deinde centum,*
> *dein mille altera, dein secunda centum,*
> *deinde usque altera mille, deinde centum*
> *dein, cum milia multa fecerimus,*
> *conturbabimus illa, ne sciamus,*
> *aut nequis malus invidere possit,*
> *cum tantum sciat esse basiorum.*][21]

In both Venus' and Catullus' versions, the description is exhaustive and exhausting. While intended to be romantic, they both depict a version of desire subtended by threat. Do these lines describe the promise of sating even the most rapacious of desires or do they remind us that desire itself, left unchecked, only breeds insatiability? The negative consequences of insatiable desire will drive the tragic endings of both *Umbra* and *Venus and Adonis*, a poem whose disastrous final coupling is foreshadowed by the early statement about the goddess: 'she murders with a kiss' (54).

Even when Adonis finally flees the perilous site of rhetorical seduction, he ends up annihilated in a scene that conflates sexual and martial excess. Shakespeare's version of Adonis' death scene significantly diverges from Ovid's. Goran Stanivukovic notes that while both poets describe the young man being killed by a boar, Shakespeare's Venus 'project[s] her own erotic desire onto the boar' associating the boar's 'kiss' with previous kisses that the goddess had bestowed upon Adonis.[22] Noting Shakespeare's use of the pronoun 'he' to describe the boar, Stanivukovic argues that 'the semantic shift from the man-animal to the man-man dynamic turns the death scene into an allegory of violent union between two men'.[23] As we have seen, however, the promise of heterosexual union entailed the same risks of self-annihilation, a hint already latent in the description of Adonis as a shadow or overshadowed by Venus. Lisa Starks-Estes finds that 'the boar's ravishment of Adonis' offers the ultimate expression of 'the sadomasochism underlying Petrarchan rhetoric and early modern notions of sexuality (orgasm as death), particularly the death drive, the desire to shatter the self'.[24] Indeed, when we hear that at his death the boy 'melted like a vapour from her sight', we can understand this as a physical manifestation of the catastrophic effects of a being rendered an object of the crushing affection of an immortal subject.

In order to throw into relief the complexity of the sexual situations depicted in Shakespeare's poem, we can turn our attention to a little-studied minor epic: Thomas Campion's *Umbra*.[25] Campion's epyllion not only innovates the classical tradition but also meditates on how authors' and readers' engagements with literary history amplify erotic experience. *Umbra*, an early version of which was published in 1595 and a later version in 1619, helps us chart elements of *Venus and Adonis*. Setting aside the question of how one poem may have influenced the other, I am interested in their shared thematic territory, as they engage Ovid, literary history, eroticism and self-shattering in similar and divergent ways. Indeed, Campion does so in much more explicit terms and so offers a framework to see the elements at work more implicitly in Shakespeare's minor epic. Campion's epyllion depicts Morpheus, the god of dreams, as he attempts to seduce a sleeping youth named Melampus. The god of dreams is intrigued by this young man, mistaking him at first for Venus' child but then finding himself perplexed by his dark skin.[26]

The encounter places us once again in the territory of *Hero and Leander*, as Morpheus believes the boy to be a fellow deity just as Neptune at first mistook his beloved for Ganymede. The dynamics of Campion's poem similarly echo the moment when Marlowe's Neptune tempts Leander but focus on mistaken identity as he thinks the young man is the cupbearer of the gods: 'The lustie god imbrast him, cald him love, / And swore he never should returne to Jove' (II.167–8). Though the sea god soon discovers that the youth is not Ganymede, he first calls him 'love', making it ambiguous whether he thinks of him first as Cupid or simply as an object of romantic desire. Realizing that he at first had misidentified the youth, Neptune does not relent; he 'clapt his plumpe cheekes, with his tresses playd, / And smiling wantonly, his love bewrayd' (II.181–2). Morpheus and Neptune experience lust in a similar way. Although mistakenly identifying the beloved and subsequently being rejected by him, the god desires his newfound beloved all the more.

In order to set the stage for his poem's strange scene of seduction, Campion relates how Morpheus enters dreams and takes different forms – sometimes a satyr, at other times even Adonis – in order to grant sleepers '*simulataque gaudia amoris*' ('pretended delights of love') (224).[27] The poem emphasizes that dreamers long for sexual partners unavailable to them in waking life, especially those that they would have encountered only in literary texts. By invoking the object of Venus' desire as an idealized sexual partner for any sleeper (or reader), Campion places his poem in the same symbolic arena as Shakespeare's. The possibility of a sexual encounter between Morpheus and the sleeping Melampus becomes the possibility of an encounter between Adonis and the young man, who might even imagine himself to experience the pleasures of Venus. In order for Morpheus to determine what might excite his beloved, '*Induit ex illo facies sibi mille decoras; / Versat et aetates sexumque, cuilibet aptans / Ornatus varios*' ('He assumed thereafter a thousand shapely guises; he changed his age and sex, suiting varied adornments to whatever role he wished', 249–52). We see dramatized here the dynamic where erotic love is transformative and also self-shattering as 'all identities are called into question by the landscape of Ovidian figures'.[28] Both Morpheus and Melampus undergo the protean effects of fantasy because the dream renders uncertain the validity of the appearance of whom Melampus desires and as whom Morpheus desires. Despite the god's initial efforts, the boy, like Adonis in Shakespeare's poem, is unresponsive to his advances. Like Shakespeare's Venus and Marlowe's Neptune, Morpheus begins to believe that his beloved requires more excessive wooing and deploys literary history for inspiration.

While Venus' tale of conquering Mars and Neptune's tale of the shepherds fail to persuade their objects of affection, Morpheus conflates classical and early modern literature within a more complex strategy to achieve sexual congress with his male beloved. He first surveys an array of beauties from classical antiquity that includes Antiope, Helen, Procne and Argia. Then he considers '*formis* [. . .] *Britannis*' ('the beauties of Britain' [305]) including Penelope Rich (Sidney's 'Stella') and Lucy Russell, Countess of Bedford (about whom both Donne and Jonson wrote poems).[29] Georgia Brown observes that 'When the epyllion writers reflect on authorship, they do not present the author as a solitary individual, but as a member of a poetic community', and Morpheus' systematic approach to seduction dramatizes Campion's own writing process as a consideration of predecessors.[30] Morpheus functions as an author who defies time by drawing upon literary figures from both his own classical present and Campion's early modern present. In doing so, the god of dreams dwells in the same conceptual framework within which Carolyn Dinshaw casts the Rip Van Winkle figure: 'he is the very somatization of temporal asynchrony, his flesh in one temporal framework and his mind in another.'[31]

Like Venus, Morpheus embodies forms of excess as he acts as a seducer. Rather than assuming the appearance of just one of the women he has surveyed, he transforms into a hybrid of all of the women. He returns in the form of '*congesta sed unam / Aptat in effigiem*' ('massed loveliness [. . .] fashioned all into one image') (346–7). According to the *Oxford Latin Dictionary*, '*congesta*' denotes 'in verbal senses, esp. crowded together, piled up'. The beloved offered to Melampus is an amalgamation of women's bodies and also something akin to humanist *copia* or the commonplace book, which collects a selection of the most appealing snippets of texts that might appeal to a reader. Campion's poem here embraces what Elizabeth Freeman calls 'erotohistoriography', where an encounter with a desirable object 'treat[s] the present itself as a hybrid' and 'uses the body as a tool to effect, figure and perform that encounter'.[32] The composite body delivers a lesson in literary history, as it presents a long line of authors and figures that defines female beauty both to Campion's reader and to the sleeping youth. It is also a lesson in sexual pleasures, as we see a young man encountering beauties from literature in his mind and subsequently becoming aroused. Campion's depicted student learns about great authors and literary figures, implicitly, during a sexual encounter with those very characters.

Morpheus' new guise overwhelms the young man and also seems to fuel the god's excitement about the coupling:

Sic redit ornatus, tenero metuendus amico,
Cuius in amplexus ruit, haud renuente puello.
Quo non insignis trahis exuperantia formae
Humanum genus? hac fruitur; Iunonis ut umbra
Ixion, falso delusus amore Melampus.

[Thus adorned he returned, a thing of awe to his innocent friend Melampus, into whose arms he rushed without the boy's refusal. Where has not this excess of remarkable beauty led the human race? Morpheus enjoyed him; as Ixion by the shade of Juno, Melampus was deceived by this false love.]

(348–52)

Campion plays with both the Latin and the gendered expectations here in this scene. Depictions in the tradition of pederastic poetry usually do not include the younger man experiencing pleasure from the coupling. To enjoy the sex would be to lose his *virtus*, his manliness or virtue, which drives the older man's desire for him. As one reads Campion's poem in the classical tradition, one would be inclined to accept a reading where Morpheus is the partner who enjoys the encounter. Morpheus's state of being '*ornatus*' ('adorned') points to the fact that Melampus will have sex with a cross-dressed god, rather than some sort of illusion that he creates. While Davis translates one of the final lines here as 'Morpheus enjoyed him', Dana Sutton translates the phrase as 'Melampus enjoyed her'.[33] Both interpretations are possible.[34] The poem, while showcasing multiplicity at the heart of Morpheus' depiction of himself, also allows the reader a form of multiplicity. We witness a coupling that is simultaneously heterosexual and homosexual, at once an intimate dyadic union and a scene of group sex when Melampus enjoys the delights of many women in the body of one man.

Umbra grapples with the physicality of the same-sex encounter in a way that many epyllia written in English do not.[35] The most frequently anthologized epyllia showcase the genre's predominantly heterosexual underpinnings, even if some poems flirt with or encode homoeroticism in their narratives as *Hero and Leander* and *Venus and Adonis* do. In the case of Shakespeare's poem, Starks-Estes observes that this encoding ties to Venus' role as a desiring poet-figure: 'desires are coded as heteroerotic in the surface narrative, but the conflation of Venus with male poet, male speaker of the elegies and lyrics, opens the possibility for homoerotic readings of Venus as male poet/lover and Adonis as male beloved.'[36] In another English-language example, R.B.'s epyllion entitled *Orpheus, His Journey to Hell* (1595) omits the detail that Orpheus teaches the Thracian men of the love of boys (as Ovid's version of the tale notes only in passing) and simply states that he rejects the love of women and motivates other men to reject their wives.

It is possible that the Latin epyllion has more freedom to express a certain frankness. Classical literature granted early modern readers access to diverse forms of sexuality, and classical languages provided a means to express diverse desires in a way that writers might not have been able to do in English. In his study of the reception of Ganymede in Renaissance literature and art, for example, Leonard Barkan observes that ancient myth offered 'a charged arena of symbolization, an arena in which the taboos concerning homosexuality confront the individual exercises of desire as well as the mores of a particular society, which may permit or even glorify certain homosexual practices while confirming the taboos in respect to ordinary, quotidian behaviour'.[37] Stephen Guy-Bray's insightful study of the reception of classical genres in early modern writing traces a pattern which illuminates 'sodomy as something that can be discussed by people who are not Christians and even Christians as long as they do so in Latin'.[38] Bruce Smith reminds us that for 'Renaissance schoolboys like Marlowe and Shakespeare, Latin was the public language of male power and the private language of male sexual desire – of homosexual desire in particular'.[39] Campion seizes upon the classical language to revivify the homoerotic pleasures of the past. Georgia Brown argues that the 'epyllion identifies itself with, and is identified with, the more questionable elements of classical culture', and Campion's Latin epyllion depicts not only a same-sex encounter but also a deeply disturbing scene of sexual violation as well.[40]

Umbra celebrates literary learning by dramatizing how one can marshal the work of previous authors towards desired ends, but it also warns that an over-indulgence in passion-filled literary depictions can be harmful. Walter Ong describes early modern Latin training as a 'puberty rite', part of a schooling project 'to initiate the boy into extrafamilial, adult experience', and we similarly see in Campion's poem an encounter with literature coinciding with sexual awakening.[41] Melampus' experience with Morpheus, like the reader's exposure to that depicted experience, is indeed an encounter with the 'alien love' that Barkan describes at the heart of metamorphosis in the Ovidian tradition. With startling explicitness, Campion places at the centre of his epyllion the 'critique' that Enterline argues subtends the minor epic.[42] As Alan Stewart has shown, anecdotes of schoolmasters beating boys were quite common in the early modern period. The ways in which these anecdotes are often erotic in nature, combining the habits of room- and bed-sharing among students and tutors, underscore that violence and eroticism were integral to the humanist learning tradition and could sometimes not be disaggregated from each other.[43] The desires stimulated by sexual awakening prove extremely damaging both for Melampus, who is only aroused by that which ultimately will drive him mad, and for Adonis, who says 'I know not love [. . .] nor will I know it / Unless it be a boar, and then I chase it' (409–10). Both young men seek that which will annihilate them.

In his study of young men in the epyllia, William Weaver identifies 'a basic trajectory: the cultivation of a provisional discursive abundance followed by the submission to a corrective violence'.[44] We can interpolate Melampus into the group that Weaver examines, which includes Adonis as well as Leander. The specific trajectory of Melampus' rite of passage, however, is not only violent but also self-shattering. There are at least two levels of 'discursive abundance' and 'corrective violence' depicted in *Umbra*. On one level, Morpheus exposes himself to a markedly literary abundance within the long taxonomy of figures but must obliterate any sense of his singular identity in order to seduce his beloved. Whatever hopes he had of a one-on-one sexual encounter with the boy collapse into the crowded, excessive experience he authors for the young man. On another level, Melampus is overwhelmed by the force of so many beauties combined into one body and then experiences the violence of being driven insane and subsequently transformed into a shadow. When he wakes and realizes that his sexual partner is nowhere to be found in the physical world, he pines away until he dies. His self-annihilation is made literal when he loses his corporeal form: Apollo finally turns Melampus into a shadow that '*fugit aspectum solis*' ('fled the sight of the sun', 403). This metamorphosis is already formulated, though, in his experience of the unearthly encounter with compounded desire. Campion relates how '*igne liquescit / Totus, et ardenti cedit vis victa dolori*' ('he was completely wasted away with passion, and conquered strength yielded to burning grief', 389–90). Like so many Ovidian transformations, his ultimate physical metamorphosis actualizes an internal state of being. Campion describes his desire to recapture his previous sexual experience in such a way as to remind us that longing for the past is to pursue a shadow and renders the pursuer a shadow: '*Mente sed ereptam vigili dum quaeritat umbram, / Umbrae fit similis*' ('But while he kept searching for the purloined shade, with wakeful mind, he became like a shade', 391–2). The frequent use of 'shade' in classical literature to describe a ghost underscores that this form of desire, which dwells upon a past that cannot be recaptured, is a longing for death.

Both *Venus and Adonis* and *Umbra* describe sexual experiences that resist neat classification. Jim Ellis has argued that poems in the epyllia genre 'through their reimagining of Ovid invent a kind of heterosexuality'.[45] *Umbra* departs from a genealogy that Ellis attempts to draw, where 'writers of the epyllia [...] participated in a shift that occurred over the course of the early modern period in England when more recognizable (from our modern perspective) forms of masculinity, heterosexuality, subjectivity and selfhood came into being'.[46] Instead, the poem suggests ways in which these same operations might yet maintain same-sex desire and coupling just beneath a visibly heterosexual surface. Shakespeare's poem, too, troubles normative expectations with its protagonist who resists an explicitly harmful form of heterosexuality in favour of a sexually charged, equally harmful encounter that is simultaneously homoerotic and bestial. Madhavi Menon argues that *Venus and Adonis* resists a teleology where normative heterosexuality is celebrated as a goal or even recognizable in the poem. Indeed, she notes that the end of Shakespeare's poem diverges from Ovid's version as the latter poet's Adonis is 'transformed into a flower that withers away almost immediately, with no promise of renewal'.[47] With the parallel dynamics of Shakespeare's and Campion's poems in mind, I would include *Umbra* among those '[f]ew texts' that Lynn Enterline has suggested 'call as insistently as *Venus and Adonis* for an approach that accounts both for the tenacity and the fragility of gender categories'.[48] While texts such as the epyllia that revived classical figures were central to humanist training and self-fashioning, the model that lies at the heart of Shakespeare's and Campion's poems seems to emphasize self-shattering.

Both these minor epics reveal how, as Lauren Berlant and Lee Edelman recently have put it, 'enjoyment itself [. . .] can be unbearable'.[49] The poems also help us formulate questions about *what desire wants* more generally. Rambuss asks, 'might not *Venus and Adonis* be about, among other things, desire's propensity to fashion its love-object *as it would have it*, that is according to the desirer's own desire'?[50] My analysis here suggests that we can answer 'yes' for Shakespeare's poem and for Campion's poem, while also productively complicating the implications of the question that Rambuss poses. Both epyllia reveal a dynamic interaction: both the love object and the desiring subject transform themselves to become more desirable and are at the same time transformed by being desired. Even further, both epyllia showcase the crucial role literary history plays in shaping one's expectations and experiences, sometimes with quite negative consequences. Those who desire and those who are desired in these texts undergo metamorphoses, just as the reader might, when exposed to forms of sexuality recognizable from previous encounters in literature yet remarkably strange in relation to sexual relations one might encounter in the world outside of literary representation. Seeing how acutely *Umbra* brings this evocative dynamic into focus, we can begin to explore not only the ways that minor epics revivify forms of sexual relation imagined in classical antiquity but also how the genre might use sexual situations to relate cautionary tales about literary reception – exposing the twin dangers of transforming texts and how we might be transformed by them.

Notes

1 Leonard Baskan, *The Gods Made Flesh: Metamorphosis and the Pursuit of Paganism* (New Haven: Yale University Press, 1986), 14. Emphasis mine.

2 Elizabeth Freeman, *Time Binds: Queer Temporalities, Queer Histories* (Durham, NC: Duke University Press, 2010), 95–6.

3 M.L. Stapleton, 'Venus as *Praeceptor*', 310 and 311.

4 Stapleton cites these lines from Baumlin on page 310. Tita French Baumlin, 'The Birth of the Bard: *Venus and Adonis* and Poetic Apotheosis', *Papers on Language and Literature* 26 (1990): 207.

5 The Latin and English for *Metamorphoses* are drawn from the Perseus Project version: Ovid, *Metamorphoses*, ed. Hugo Magnus (Gotha: Friedr. Andr. Perthes, 1892). www.perseus.tufts.edu/hopper/text?doc=Perseus%3Atext%3A1999.02.0029%3Abook%3D10%3Acard%3D519

6 *Oxford English Dictionary*, www.oed.com, accessed 30 June 2018.

7 Weaver, *Untutored Lines*, 3.

8 Brown, *Redefining Elizabethan Poetry*, 105. See also Jennifer Ingleheart, 'The Invention of (Thracian) Homosexuality: The Ovidian Orpheus in the English Renaissance', in *Ancient Rome and the Construction of Modern Homosexual Identities,* ed. Jennifer Ingleheart (Oxford: Oxford University Press, 2015), 60.

9 Enterline, 'Elizabethan Minor Epics', 263.

10 This rhetorical commonplace is found in poems such as Campion's 'There is a Garden in her Face'.

11 Richard Rambuss, 'What It Feels Like For a Boy', 247.

12 Pauline Kiernan, '*Venus and Adonis* and Ovidian Indecorous Wit', in *Shakespeare's Ovid:* The Metamorphoses *in the Plays and Poems,* ed. A.B. Taylor (Cambridge: Cambridge University Press, 2006), 81.

13 Venus' use of the term 'shadow' has intriguing connections to the use of the same term by Ovid's narrator when he describes the image in Narcissus' pool as an 'umbra': 'Ista repercussae, quam cernis, imaginis *umbra est*' (4.432, my emphasis).

14 Ellis, *Sexuality and Citizenship*, 118.

15 Cynthia Marshall, *The Shattering of the Self: Violence, Subjectivity, and Early Modern Texts* (Baltimore: Johns Hopkins University Press, 2002), 5.

16 As if to emphasize the ways that his epyllion transforms multiple texts into a single text, Shakespeare draws the encounter between Mars and Venus from a section of Ovid's *Metamorphoses* that is wholly separate from the story of Venus and Adonis. The story of Venus and Mars is mentioned in passing as Ovid largely focuses on Venus' husband capturing the two in a net as revenge (*Metamorphoses* 4.167–89).

17 The Latin text and English translation for *De Rerum Natura* are drawn from the Perseus Project version: Lucretius, *De Rerum Natura*, ed. William Ellery Leonard.

18 Georges Bataille, *Erotism: Death and Sexuality*, trans. Mary Dalwood (San Francisco: City Lights Publishers, 1996), 23.

19 This helps explain also why Venus turns to the analogy of a park over which the young man might roam as a deer. This does make the youth smile, though 'in disdain' (241).

20 Stephen Guy-Bray, 'Nondramatic Style', in *Shakespeare in Our Time: A Shakespeare Association of America Collection*, eds

Dympna Callaghan and Suzanne Gossett (London and New York: Bloomsbury Arden Shakespeare, 2016), 304.

21 Campion adapts Catullus' poem as 'My Sweetest Lesbia' (1601).

22 Goran Stanivukovic, 'Kissing the Boar: Queer Adonis and Critical Practice', in *Straight with a Twist: Queer Theory and the Subject of Heterosexuality*, ed. Calvin Thomas (Urbana and Chicago: University of Illinois Press, 2000), 88.

23 Ibid.

24 Lisa Starks-Estes, *Violence, Trauma, and* Virtus *in Shakespeare's Roman Poems and Plays: Transforming Ovid* (New York: Palgrave Macmillan, 2014), 80.

25 For a longer discussion of the poem under the lens applied here, see my 'Seduced by Literary History: Thomas Campion's *Umbra* and the Epyllia Tradition', *Journal of Early Modern Culture Studies (JEMCS)* 17.4 (Fall 2017). The present essay draws some content from that article and extrapolates earlier thinking articulated there. Although his Latin poems comprise approximately one third of his published work, Campion is most often recognized as the author of several English poems and songs commonly anthologized in modern collections. All quotations are drawn from Walter Davis' edition of Campion's works, which is the first collection of works published since Percival Vivian's 1909 edition and offers an excellent selection of songs and treatises, poems in Latin and English and extensive notes. *The Works of Thomas Campion*, ed. Walter R. Davis (New York: W.W. Norton and Co., 1970).

26 As Sujata Iyengar observes, his skin is black because he was conceived in the dark and the bright, sun-shaped mark beneath his breast is a birthmark signalling the identity of his father, Apollo. Morpheus does not seem to notice the mark. See *Shades of Difference: Mythologies of Skin Color in Early Modern England* (Philadelphia: University of Pennsylvania Press, 2013), 73.

27 As Garrett Sullivan has shown, early modern writers understood sleep as closely tied to the passions: slumber could be both 'a *binding* of the senses' that leaves one unaware and 'an *overindulgence* of the senses' that induces the sleeper 'to give oneself over to indulgence and "the enticements of lust"'. See

Sleep, Romance, and Human Embodiment: Vitality from Spenser to Milton (Cambridge: Cambridge University Press, 2012), 17–18.

28 Cora Fox, *Ovid and the Politics of Emotion in Elizabethan England* (New York: Palgrave Macmillan, 2009), 40.

29 For a complete list of the figures to whom the poem alludes, see Davis, 395n.15–20 to 297n.21–7.

30 Brown, *Redefining Elizabethan Poetry*, 109.

31 Carolyn Dinshaw, *How Soon is Now? Medieval Texts, Amateur Readers, and the Queerness of Time* (Durham, NC: Duke University Press, 2012), 135.

32 Freeman, *Time Binds,* 95.

33 Thomas Campion, 'Umbra', in *The Latin Poetry of Thomas Campion (1567–1620): A Hypertext Critical Edition*, Section 55.

34 For an extended discussion of the Latin in this section, see my article in *JEMCS*.

35 Campion is perhaps the most well-known English poet to have written a Latin epyllion. For a helpful overview of the known body of work, as well as the challenges in identifying a discrete canon of early modern epyllia written in Latin, see Martin Korenjak, 'Short Mythological Epic in Neo-Latin Literature', *Brill's Companion to Greek and Latin Epyllion and its Reception* (Leiden and Boston: Brill, 2012), 519–36.

36 Starks-Estes, 79.

37 Barkan, *Transuming Passion*, 24.

38 Stephen Guy-Bray, *Homoerotic Space: The Poetics of Loss in Renaissance Literature* (Toronto: University of Toronto Press, 2002), 4.

39 Bruce Smith, *Homosexual Desire in Shakespeare's England: A Cultural Poetics* (Chicago: University of Chicago Press, 1994), 84.

40 Brown, *Redefining Elizabethan Poetry*, 127.

41 Walter Ong, *Rhetoric, Romance, and Technology: Studies in the Interaction of Expression and Culture* (Ithaca: Cornell University Press, 2012), 138 and 300. For a discussion of cross-dressing and

gender fluidity in the early modern schoolroom, see Enterline, *Shakespeare's Schoolroom*, 17–18 and 71–3.

42 'Elizabethan Minor Epics'.
43 *Stewart*, 84–121. See also Enterline, *Shakespeare's Schoolroom*, 33–61.
44 Weaver, *Untutored Lines*, 2.
45 Jim Ellis, 'Imagining Heterosexuality in the Epyllia', in *Ovid and the Renaissance Body,* ed. Goran Stanivukovic (Toronto: University of Toronto Press, 2001), 38.
46 Ellis, 'Imagining Heterosexuality', 14.
47 Madhavi Menon, 'Spurning Teleology in *Venus and Adonis*', *GLQ: A Journal of Lesbian and Gay Studies* 11.4 (2005): 499.
48 Lynn Enterline, 'Reading Venus and Adonis', in *Shakespeare: An Oxford Guide*, eds Stanley Wells and Lena Cowen Orlin (Oxford: Oxford University Press, 2003), 464.
49 Lauren Berlant and Lee Edelman, *Sex, or the Unbearable* (Durham, NC and London: Duke University Press, 2014), vi.
50 'What it Feels Like for a Boy', 644.

8

Love loves

Venus and Adonis, Venus and Anchises

Stephen Guy-Bray

At the end of John Lyly's *Gallathea*, Venus descends from heaven to solve the central romantic problem of the play and grandly asks 'What is to Loue or the Mistrisse of Loue vnpossible'?[1] In that play, her confidence is justified: Venus is able to turn one of the two girls disguised as boys who have fallen in love with each other into a real boy so that a marriage can occur (although of course we never learn which girl becomes a boy and although the marriage itself takes place beyond the play). Venus' transformation of a same-sex couple into a mixed-sex couple here is an especially useful illustration of the power of the goddess of love to ensure that young people grow up and form socially legible bonds. But other Renaissance texts demonstrate that Venus' power is not absolute. In *Venus and Adonis*, for instance, the goddess is famously, comically, repeatedly unable to get the man she wants. As Shakespeare puts it in the line that provides the title for this essay, 'She's Love, she loves, and yet she is not loved' (610). The confusing and dazzling polyptoton in this line, the way in which the word 'love' changes from noun to verb and is repeated twice without being exactly repeated once, perfectly captures the way Venus and Adonis fail either to separate or to come together for most of the poem: thus, while expressing a certain sympathy for Venus, Shakespeare also underlines her failure.

While literature amply demonstrates the ability of love to change people forever, in a sense – to return to the terms I used above – in these cases love is a verb rather than a noun: a force, an emotion, a madness, or even, as in Lyly's play, a *dea ex machina*. In *Venus and Adonis* and Phineas Fletcher's *Venus and Anchises*, the two poems I discuss in this essay, however, love is not primarily a force or even a personification: instead, she is a person, a character in a poem and, as it turns out, not always a successful character. The epyllion has often been understood as a kind of narrative in which a young man learns how to become an adult, something typically achieved through love.[2] In the poems I discuss here, love has become Love, which is to say Venus, and the poems are chiefly about her and her attempts to educate two young men in the ways of love or, to put it another way, into a form of heterosexuality that is seen as one of the prerequisites of adult male life. The two poems are mirror images of each other: in *Venus and Adonis*, Venus is an unsuccessful lover; in *Venus and Anchises*, a successful one. What unites the poems is that in each Venus is unsuccessful as an educator: neither young man can really learn the lessons either of love or of Love.

Almost nothing has been written on Fletcher's *Venus and Anchises* or, to give it its full title, *Venus and Anchises: Brittain's Ida*, although his long allegorical poem *The Purple Island* has become increasingly popular in recent years. *Venus and Anchises* was published (under Edmund Spenser's name) in 1628, well after the period in which the most famous epyllia had appeared and thirty years after Spenser's death.[3] The attribution to Spenser, whether meant sincerely or merely to sell copies, is certainly not implausible. The published poem is divided into very short cantos and is composed of eight-line stanzas rhyming ABABBCCC, a variation of the rhyme scheme Spenser used in the *Faerie Queene* (and one that was also used by Phineas' younger brother Giles). The fact that the manuscript version is not divided into cantos could support the argument that the publisher imposed this structure to lend more credibility to his attribution of the poem to Spenser. That the final line of each stanza is an alexandrine further increases the resemblance, as does the fact that many scenes in the poem seem like versions of scenes in the *Faerie Queene*. In his book on the Fletchers, which was published almost forty years ago, Frank S. Kastor spends several pages describing the poem and its publication history, concluding that, 'In terms of consistency and unity this poem may be Phineas Fletcher's finest work'.[4] *Venus and Anchises* may not be a great poem, but I hope to show that it is an interesting one and that the comparison between it and *Venus and Adonis* can be illuminating.

In contrast, *Venus and Adonis* has been written about frequently, and many critics have looked at the Venus of the poem as a teacher. For instance, in his very technical analysis of the poem, William P. Weaver refers to 'Shakespeare's representation of the goddess as a pedagogue' and states that many of her speeches are constructed 'according to the humanist discourse of boyhood exercise'.[5] This aspect of the story is only latent in Ovid; what makes Shakespeare's presentation of the story so pedagogical is partly due to the fact that Shakespeare turns Adonis, who was a man in Ovid, into a boy.[6] Of course, to make this a story about pedagogy is also to make this a story about pederasty, and in Venus, Shakespeare gives us a powerful picture of predatory heterosexuality. Like the speaker of Frank O'Hara's 'Meditations in an Emergency', Shakespeare's Adonis could exclaim 'Heterosexuality! you are inexorably approaching. (How discourage her?)'.[7] A considerable amount of time has been spent on figuring out exactly what Adonis' sexuality is, since he is not attracted to the most beautiful woman in the world – would he prefer another woman? a man? hunting itself? – but this is not my concern here. I shall assume that he is asexual and look instead at some of those moments in the poem that specialists in pedagogy might call 'teachable moments'.

The first of these is Venus' reference to her triumph over the god of war: 'I have been wooed, as I entreat thee now, / Even by the stern and direful god of war' (97–8). The moral of the story is soon given: 'O, be not proud, nor brag not of thy might, / For mast'ring her that foiled the god of fight!' (113–14). Even apart from the fact that Adonis is simply uninterested, however, Venus is a poor teacher. For one thing, she goes on and on, eventually resorting to the argument of use, an argument that requires her to attempt to persuade Adonis that he should have children. Not only is this not an especially high-yield strategy, but Venus herself has no apparent interest in having children with Adonis and the idea is incongruous here. What is more, her reference to Mars is undermined by a comparison Shakespeare makes shortly before the speech: 'Look how a bird lies tangled in a net, / So fastened in her arms Adonis lies' (67–8). I would argue that this reference to a net reminds the reader of the famous story that Vulcan entangled Mars and Venus in a net and exposed them to the mockery of the gods. Thus, the reference to Mars is doomed to fail, and the very elaboration of the rhetoric Venus uses here and throughout the poem is beside the point, as is often the case in the seduction scenes of Renaissance literature.[8]

The next scene of instruction occurs in a long section (approximately 150 lines – it is difficult to say when the section ends) and concerns Adonis' horse, which forsakes Adonis in order to pursue a female horse.[9] After providing a lubricious recap of the events that led to the stallion's flight – a recap in which the equine situation quickly gives way to a human one, as Venus incongruously compares the horse to a man 'Who sees his true-love in her naked bed, / Teaching the sheets a whiter hue than white' (397–8) – she gives the moral:

> Let me excuse thy courser, gentle boy;
> And learn of him, I heartily beseech thee,
> To take advantage on presented joy.
>
> (403–5)

The moral is obvious indeed, at least to Venus, and probably to us as well, but the presentation of the episode in the poem has been quite different than Venus' paraphrase of it. Initially, Shakespeare describes the arrival of the mare and the stallion's excitement in terms quite similar to the ones Venus uses, but he also does two significant things that change our sense of how this episode fits into the poem and precisely what lesson is being learned.

The first occurs in the scene's opening, when the narrator describes the movements of the horse and imagines it as saying 'this I do to captivate the eye / Of the fair breeder that is standing by' (281–2). In referring to the horse as a breeder, Shakespeare reminds us that while horses may be used as symbols for passionate desire, they are also subject to human use in a number of ways. As well, his word choice presents even this (literally) unbridled animal sexuality as leading to reproduction and he thus alludes to Venus' own use of the argument of reproduction as the motivation for sexual activity just over a hundred lines earlier (163–74). Curiously, although Venus thinks the problem is that humans are not like horses, Shakespeare shows us in his description of the mare when the stallion approaches her that horses are like humans:

> Being proud, as females are, to see him woo her,
> She puts on outward strangeness, seems unkind,
> Spurns at his love and, scorns the heat he feels.
>
> (309–11)

In using real-life examples to make her point, Venus uses a pedagogically sound technique, one recommended by writers on education for centuries; the problem is that real life is actually different from what she thinks.

What follows the reference to the mare as a 'breeder' is even stranger. To describe the stallion, Shakespeare compares it to a painting of a stallion: 'Look when a painter would surpass the life / In limning out a well-proportioned steed' (289–90). Shakespeare wants to make the point that Adonis' horse is better than any horse the reader might have seen and in order to do so he writes an equine blazon ending in this (metaphorically) revealing couplet: 'Look what a horse should have he did not lack, / Save a proud rider on so proud a back' (299–300). While the description has seemed to be heading towards the genitals – like most blazons – it leads us instead to the missing figure of Adonis. The substitution refutes much of what Venus has said up to this point in the poem: while she has employed the argument of use to persuade Adonis to have sex with her, and while the description of the mare as a 'breeder' has seemed to support her to a certain extent, it appears that the real use of horses is as a means of transport. This description looks forward to the moment at the centre of the poem when Venus falls on her back and Adonis falls on top of her and he still does not have sex with her: 'All is imaginary she doth prove: / He will not manage her, although he mount her' (597–8).[10] Adonis is only interested in literal riding, rather than in the metaphorical riding Venus desires.

Much of the poem is similarly taken up with these moments in which Venus tries and fails to persuade Adonis to have sex with her. But if she fails as a teacher in this respect, we could say that she succeeds in another. Just after Venus' attempt to persuade Adonis to imitate his horse's lust, he answers her. In this speech he rejects love, justifying his refusal by stating that he is too young and, in a manner familiar to us from Venus' own pedagogy, supports his view with example (409–26). The last of these is especially noteworthy: 'The colt that's backed and burdened being young / Loseth his pride, and never waxeth strong' (419–20). It is clearly significant that Adonis returns to the image of the horse but uses it in a manner that is diametrically opposed to the way in which Venus has used it. His mode of refusing her here, as well as in his later and longer refusal (769–810; his final speech in the poem), shows that Adonis has been paying attention to Venus, and if he has not given into her desires, he has at least learnt something about rhetoric. As M.L. Stapleton points out, 'To Venus' treatise, Adonis offers his own "text" in refutation'.[11] Venus has taught

Adonis the techniques of argumentation, and his profit on it is that he knows how to refuse.

In her discussion of the poem, Enterline argues that in refusing Venus, Adonis 'Is turning his back on more than sex. He also turns it on the language, lessons, and practices, that sixteenth-century pedagogy indelibly associated, in the experience of its initiators, with eroticism and violence'.[12] The question then remains of what, exactly, he is turning towards. I would go even further than Enterline and argue that he also turns his back on the ceaseless becoming of human life, one salient form of which is pedagogy. Madhavi Menon reads the poem as a movement against teleology, against, among other things, the idea that having a body should lead to sex or that language – highly ordered, ornate, poetical language – should have a result in the real world. Menon has suggested that we can see the poem's epigram from Ovid – '*Vilia miretur vulgus: mihi flavus Apollo / Pocula Castalia plena ministret aqua*' ('let the crowd marvel at base things: let golden Apollo give me full cups of the Castalian fount') – not as an opposition between the vulgar mob and the cultivated few, but as a narrative.[13] In this view, the passage from one side of the colon to the other would then be a teleology made possible by pedagogy and it could even be a successful one if we as readers are in any way edified by the poem. Venus is unchanged, however, and although Adonis is obviously changed, in becoming a flower he has remained beautiful and has left behind the world of doing and learning. Education has failed, but beauty remains.

The education that is one of the themes of *Venus and Adonis* is explicitly referenced at the beginning of *Venus and Anchises*, as Fletcher begins by telling the reader about 'Thirsil (poore ladd) whose Muse yet scarcely fledge' (I.1.1.) and goes on to place the poem's composition by 'lovelie Came' (I.1.6; Fletcher was himself a student at Cambridge from 1600 until 1608).[14] We are told that the poem was written 'to trye his downie Muses wing, / For soe the fayre Eliza deign'd desire' (I.2.3–4) and that Thirsil 'thought with song his raging fire to tame, / Fond boye that fewell sought to hide soe great a flame' (I.2.7–8). The poem thus begins by presenting us with two kinds of education: Thirsil must learn how to be a poet, but he must also learn that words have power. Writing love poetry is not, as young Thirsil foolishly thinks, a way to control love by subjecting it to rhetorical expression, but is rather a way to increase the power of love. In a way that differs considerably from what I see as Shakespeare's point in *Venus and Adonis* about rhetoric's failure (specifically, of course, Venus' failure to persuade Adonis to have sex with her), Fletcher presents love poetry as all too effective – not indeed as something that has an effect on either the characters in the poem or even the readers of the poem but rather as something that affects the poet himself.

The poem's main character is Anchises, like Thirsil an immature boy and like Adonis a very beautiful one. Although the poem tells the well-known story of Venus' love for Anchises, there is no hint in the poem that this Anchises is also a Trojan prince – here, he is only one of 'A hundred Shepheards' (I.3.3) – nor is there any reference to their child, Aeneas. Anchises also resembles Adonis in being interested in hunting and uninterested in love.[15] Interestingly, in *Venus and Adonis*, Venus at one point suggests that Adonis' refusal to have sex with her is motivated by his love for himself and mentions Narcissus (161–2); in Fletcher's poem, Anchises' indifference to love is described thus:

> Thousand boyes for him, thousand maidens dy'de,
> Dye they that list, for such his rigorous pride,
> He thousand boyes (ah foole) and thousand maids deni'd
> (I.7.6–68)

As any educated reader in seventeenth-century England would have seen, this is very close to (almost a translation of) Ovid's description of Narcissus in the *Metamorphoses*:

> *multi illum iuuenes, multae cupiere pullae;*
> *sed (fuit in tenera tam dura superbia forma)*
> *nulli illum iuuenes, nullae tetigere puellae*

[Many boys, many girls desired him, but such was the pride in that delicate beauty that no boys, no girls moved him].[16]
(III.353–5)

The most important change that Fletcher makes is the parenthetical 'ah foole', an addition that indicates that one way to read the poem that follows is as the story of Anchises as someone who needs to be educated. What is more, as 'foole' could also mean child in the period, Fletcher emphasizes Anchises' immaturity.

In the second canto, Anchises enters Venus' grove (closely modelled on Spenser's Bower of Bliss), which provides him with a disorienting surfeit of pleasure. Initially entranced by the beauty of the flowers, his attention is then taken by the music he hears:

But soone the eyes rendred the eares their sight;
For such strange harmony he seem'd to heare,
That all his senses flockt into his eare,
And every faculty wisht to be seated there

(II.4.5–8)

The music comes from a bower within the garden that is within the grove. Fletcher describes the beautiful flowers and the beautiful music as competing over 'Which the distracted sense should most delight; / That, raps the melted eare; this, both the smel and sight' (II.5.7–8). One of the main issues in Spenser's Bower of Bliss is the conflict between art and nature, but here they appear to be working as one. While we would normally think of the song as art and the flowers as nature, Fletcher describes the bower as 'appareld' (II.5.2) with roses. Just as the senses are merged by what they perceive in Venus' grove, so too art and nature can no longer be distinguished.

The missing senses in the couplet I quoted above are taste and touch, which we would typically describe as the most obviously sexual of the senses. I think that in *Venus and*

Anchises, however, it is hearing that is the most sexual of the senses and that this is because it is through hearing that language is first understood. When the two first speak, their conversation is introduced through notably sexual language: Fletcher tells us that Anchises 'stood with eares arected' (IV.5.2) when he hears Venus speak; when he answers, her ears are described in similarly sexualized terms: 'each word bold would venter / And strive the first, that dainty labyrinth to enter' (IV.5.7–8). Interestingly, the garden itself was initially described as a 'sweete Labyrinth' (II.4.1). We are all familiar with the trope of the enclosed garden as symbolizing female genitalia and Fletcher's description of the grove of Venus certainly relies on our knowledge of this metaphor. But here the sexual organ for both the male and the female appears to be primarily the ear. I would argue that one reason to make the ear an erogenous zone is that it makes poetry not only something that can lead to sex (which seems to be Thirsil's goal in writing the poem as well) but also something that is itself sex. That is, both speaking and listening to poetry are perhaps themselves sex acts rather than merely activities that might lead to sex acts.

Up to the moment at which the two eponymous characters meet the poem has concentrated on Anchises and on his ignorance and lack of experience, but at this point there is a crucial – if temporary – shift to presenting Thirsil as someone who is in the process of being educated. The change occurs as an interruption in the long blazon of Venus that takes up most of Canto III. As the description passes between Venus' breasts towards 'the sweet dwelling, / Where best delight all joyes sits freely dealing' (III.10.4–5), Fletcher says 'But stay bold shepheard, here thy footing stay, / Nor trust too much unto thy new-borne quill' (III.11.1–2). In the next stanza, Fletcher cites the example of a painter in ancient Greece who stopped his portrait at the same point at which the blazon stops because, despite his great artistry, 'Yet would these lively parts his hand of skill deprive' (III.12.8). Here, however, the issue is one of decorum and reputation rather than skill:

> But were thy Verse and Song as finely fram'd,
> As are those parts, yet should it soone be blam'd,
> For now the shameles world of best things is asham'd
>
> (III.11.6–8)

Fletcher thus identifies three potential problems for the young poet: lack of skill, a subject that is so magnificent that it cannot adequately be portrayed, and the poor taste of the public. Almost all of the rest of *Venus and Anchises* is taken up with Anchises' story, but these stanzas serve to remind us that the poem as a whole tells the story of Thirsil's education as well as of that of Anchises.

As the story returns to Anchises, Fletcher emphasizes the pedagogical aspect of the poem when Venus takes Anchises into her service: 'And like another Love, with Bow and quiver fits him' (IV.8.8). In the next stanza, Fletcher stresses the closeness between Anchises and 'Cupids selfe' (IV.9.2). It is Cupid who first undertakes Anchises' education and teaches him the ways of love until Anchises 'with such grace and cunning arte did move him, / That all the pritty loves, and all the Graces love him' (IV.9.7–8). Anchises has learnt a good deal, but it is clear that his new knowledge of love is applied to the loves of others and that he makes no progress in his own. At this point Anchises sings a song that brings together the themes of learning to love and learning to write poetry:

> Whoe ever Could by learning learne forgetting?
> Cann'st thow forget a song by often singing
> Or dittie canst unlearn by oft repeating?
>
> (V.3.2–4)

Anchises' sexual problems will be solved – temporarily, at least – within the narrative, but the implications of these lines for Thirsil, whose vocation as a love poet requires him to sing about love, will survive the poem's ending. In this presentation of the subject, writing love poetry can never be cathartic; the possibility that *Venus and Anchises* could lead to seduction is not even mentioned.

It is Venus herself who breaks the impasse here by asking Anchises to describe the woman he loves (V.6.8). In answering, Anchises attempts to be subtle but Venus easily sees through his plans. The fact that despite learning much about love he has not learnt how to woo actually helps him:

> No tongue was ever yet so sweetely skil'd,
> Nor greatest Orator so highly stil'd;
> Though helpt with all the choisest artes direction,
> But when he durst describe her heav'ns perfection,
> By his imperfect praise, disprais'd her imperfection
> (V.9.4–8)

While for much of the poem Anchises and Thirsil have seemed alike in that they are both learning about love, the one through wooing and the other through writing poetry, at this point their narratives diverge. In lines that I have already quoted from the beginning of the poem, Fletcher tells us that Thirsil 'thought with song his raging fire to tame, / Fond boye that fewell sought to hide soe great a flame' (I.2.7–8). For Thirsil, then, writing poetry, however good the poetry itself may be, will only serve to increase his love and his frustration; for Anchises, in contrast, his imperfect speech will actually help to end his frustration.

As we might have assumed, Venus ultimately has to do everything, and she does so in a way that emphasizes their unequal positions, presenting him as her servant: 'But if to me thy true love is presented, / What wages for thy service must I owe thee' (VI.1.5–6). In return, Anchises asks only for a kiss – the modesty of this request reveals what a poor student of love he is, and Venus mocks his modesty (VI.3.1–2) – but when he takes the kiss he cannot restrain himself and takes many more. Fletcher describes Anchises' greediness with a simile that emphasizes Anchises' continuing adolescence:

> Looke as a Ward, long from his Lands detain'd,
> And subject to his Guardians cruel lore,

Now spends the more, the more he was restrain'd,
So he . . .

(VI.5.1–4)

Paradoxically, in presenting Anchises as a young man who is now technically an adult and free of supervision, Fletcher stresses that Anchises is still immature. The verb 'spends' is used in several senses here, including to make an outlay, to consume, to waste, and, foreshadowing the 'liquid joyes' (VI.10.3) that Anchises later enjoys, to ejaculate.[17] Despite his education in love in the grove of Venus, Anchises lacks the discipline to profit from the favour that he has won.

Predictably, Venus encourages his greediness: she and Anchises have sex, an experience that translates the young man into a state of bliss in which he lives 'Free from sad care, and fickle worlds annoy' (VI.10.2). In a fatal demonstration of his callowness, however, Anchises ruins everything:

he (ah foolish Boy!)
Too proud, and to impatient of his joy,
To woods, and heav'n, and earth his blisse imparted;
That Jove upon him downe his thunders darted,
Blasting his splendent face, all his beauty swarted

(VI.10.4–8)

This is the penultimate stanza of the poem, and until this point Anchises' narrative has gone very well indeed. Fletcher's epyllion has come much closer to a happy ending than is customary in epyllia. Anchises' sad fate is not strange in the context of the genre, but what is strange is that he apparently survives: after we learn that his beauty has been destroyed we hear no more about him. What is important to Fletcher, I think, is not that Anchises die but rather that he serve as an example – to lovers and to poets – of the importance of managing language correctly.

In the final stanza Fletcher makes his hero's disastrous fate into a general lesson – 'He is not fit for love, that is not fit to hold it' (VI.11.8) – and hopes that he will have better success. Fletcher thus returns the poem to its beginning, when it was the story of a young poet (whether Fletcher himself or Thirsil is unclear). This is not a surprising conclusion, but what should be surprising is that the story does not end with the birth of Aeneas, the son of Venus and Anchises and arguably the most important hero of the classical tradition in Renaissance England. Indeed, it is noteworthy that while *Venus and Adonis* and *Venus and Anchises* both tell the story of a young man being educated in love, neither ends in reproduction, which was after all seen as one of the chief duties of a young man. What we are left with instead of progeny are a flower, in the case of Shakespeare's poem, and, in the case of Fletcher's, a poem that can serve at once as a guide on how to love and as a beginning in a poetic career. As well, in both poems the rhetoric in which Renaissance students were so carefully trained and which is intended to produce real world results can only be an end in itself. Unlike the epic, which narrates decisive moments in the history of entire peoples and often, as in the *Aeneid*, the beginning of a new empire, the epyllion, that minor genre, can only lead to more art. Poetic beauty (which arguably for Shakespeare ultimately takes the form of a flower) is all that the epyllion can give us. But perhaps that is enough.

Notes

1 *Gallathea*, V.iii.142. From John Lyly, *Complete Works*, Vol. II, ed. R. Warwick Bond (Oxford: Clarendon Press, 1902).

2 A good discussion is Jim Ellis, *Sexuality and Citizenship: Metamorphosis in Elizabethan Erotic Fiction* (Toronto: University of Toronto Press, 2003), especially the introduction, 3–16. See also Jeffrey Masten, *Queer Philologies: Sex, Language, and Affect in Shakespeare's Time* (Philadelphia: University of Pennsylvania Press, 2016), 166–70 for a brief discussion of what we could call the intersection of pederasty and pedagogy in the Renaissance.

3   In 1923, Ethel Seaton discovered a manuscript copy, differing somewhat from the printed version. For a discussion of the two versions, see Elizabeth Story's Donno's 'A Note on the Text', in *Elizabethan Minor Epics*, 305–7. Donno incorporates some elements from the manuscript version, but chiefly uses the printed version.

4   Frank S. Kastor, *Giles and Phineas Fletcher* (Boston: Twayne Press, 1978), 95. His discussion of the poem is on pages 90–5.

5   *Untutored Lines*, 73, 72. See 77–80 for Weaver's discussion of the three features of classical rhetoric and the role they play in the poem.

6   Richard Rambuss, 'What It Feels Like For a Boy'. Another good analysis of Shakespeare's transformation of Ovid is Laetitia Sansonetti, 'Out-Oviding Ovid in Shakespeare's *Venus and Adonis*', in *The Circulation of Knowledge in Early Modern English Literature*, ed. Sophie Chiari (London and New York) 175–87.

7   'Meditations in an Emergency', in Frank O'Hara, *The Collected Poems of Frank O'Hara*, ed. Donald Allen (Berkeley: University of California Press, 1995), 197. This reference is to a page number, as the edition does not give line numbers.

8   For my earlier discussion of another seduction scene that employs elaborate and ultimately pointless rhetoric (in Marlowe's *Hero and Leander*), see *Against Reproduction: Where Renaissance Texts Come From* (Toronto: University of Toronto Press, 2009), 110–27.

9   There have been numerous analyses of this scene. See, for instance, Enterline, *Shakespeare's Schoolroom*, 73–4; Meek *Narrating the Visual in Shakespeare* (Farnham: Ashgate, 2009), 32–4; and Miriam Jacobson, *Barbarous Antiquity: Reorienting the Past in the Poetry of Early Modern England* (Philadelphia: University of Pennsylvania Press, 2014), 114–45, especially 120–6. Jacobson points out that the horse is another of Shakespeare's additions to Ovid's story.

10 As the poem has 1,194 lines, the exact halfway point is between the two lines I have just quoted.

11 Stapleton, 'Venus as *Praeceptor*', 312.

12 Enterline, *Shakespeare's Schoolroom*, 91.

13 Menon, 'Spurning Teleology in *Venus and Adonis*'.
14 My parenthetical references give canto, stanza and line numbers, the first in Roman numerals.
15 In fact, when Venus first sees Anchises as he faints in his amazement over her beauty, 'She thinks that there her faire Adonis dyes, / And more she thinks the more the Boy she eyes' (IV.1.4–5).
16 *Metamorphoses*, ed. R.J. Tarrant (Oxford: Oxford University Press, 2004).
17 According to the *Oxford English Dictionary* the first use of 'spend' in the sense of 'ejaculate' comes from 1662 (see spend, *v.1* 15.c; perhaps unsurprisingly, the first example is from Pepys' diary), but it is not unlikely that it was in use when Fletcher wrote his poem not quite forty years earlier. In any case, the metaphor is hardly obscure.

PART FOUR

Classicism and mercantile capital

9

Crossing the Hellespont

The erotics of the everyday in Marlowe's *Hero and Leander*

Jane Raisch

At the end of Ben Jonson's *Bartholomew Fair*, the main characters attend an unusual dramatic adaptation of Christopher Marlowe's *Hero and Leander*. Entitled 'The ancient modern history of Hero and Leander', the production is performed by puppets and relocated from the banks of the Hellespont to the banks of the Thames (5.3.7).[1] The aptly named organizer of the production, Lantern Leatherhead (a lantern figures prominently in the original Greek epyllion), explains to Bartholomew Cokes that Marlowe's book in its original form is 'too learned and poetical for our audience' (5.103). Quoting the famous opening lines of Marlowe's poem, Leatherhead elaborates: 'What do they know what Hellespont is, "guilty of true love's blood"? Or what Abydos is? Or "the other Sestos hight?"' (5.3.104–5). To 'reduce it to a more familiar strain for [the] people' (5.3.109), Leatherhead reimagines the Thames as the Hellespont, recasts Leander as a dyer's son from Puddle Wharf and Hero as a wench from Bankside. What follows is a parodic reimagining of the famous story of love at first sight: Hero is first impressed by a view of Leander's 'naked leg and goodly calf' (5.4.122) and Cupid 'strikes Hero in love' not with arrows but with a pint of sherry (5.3.119). Alas, the puppet show is cut short by the objections of the Puritan Zeal-of-the-land Busy, who is scandalized by the cross-dressing in the performance and is only pacified after the puppets lift their clothing and reveal themselves to be genderless (5.5).

Jonson's choice to relocate *Hero and Leander* from the symbolically significant shores of the Hellespont to the humble, even tawdry, shores of the Thames is predicated on a humourous contrast; the move is funny because of how *unlike* Sestos and Abydos Puddle Wharf and Bankside are. Indeed, the burlesques and satires that enjoyed popularity during the seventeenth and eighteenth centuries are frequently predicated on this kind of mismatch, of irreverently mixing high and low styles or applying classical *gravitas* and grandeur to the mundane or familiar. Yet Jonson's satirical 'updating' of Marlowe's poem also reveals certain affinities between the setting of the story and early seventeenth-century London. As Roy Booth proposed, 'Jonson's naturalization – with the Hero and Leander story relocated to London and the River Thames – was felt to be so apt that it helped to make the narrative a settled favourite' in seventeenth-century England.[2] This 'aptness' tells us something crucial about not only Marlowe's poem but also its Greek minor epic model: the fifth-century CE poem of Musaeus Grammaticus. This poem, and other Greek epyllia like it, offered early modern readers an image of an already 'updated' ancient world, one that became increasingly resonant for turn-of-the-seventeenth-century London as it confronted its own shifting urban and cosmopolitan identity.[3]

In Musaeus' Greek original and in Christopher Marlowe's late-sixteenth-century retelling, the occasion of the two lovers meeting is an annual, urban festival where the residents of Abydos visit Sestos to mingle and meet a future spouse, an occasion not unlike the annual festival of Bartholomew Fair during which the events of Jonson's play take place. By Jonson's time, the fair was an event that brought visitors together from across England and in the play it functions as an occasion for several romantic matches to be made. While Leander's secretive, nightly swim to see Hero might seem to be a far cry from the typical conditions of a liaison in early seventeenth-century London, taking small boats across the Thames was evidently the preferred mode of transport for men looking to frequent South Bank brothels incognito, and Jonson's Leander fittingly 'swims' across the Thames in a small sculler.[4]

Even Leander's new profession as a dyer evokes the commercial trade associated with the Hellespont in both the ancient and early modern worlds. As Miriam Jacobson recently demonstrated, the Hellespont was an important channel for a burgeoning seventeenth-century trade market of precious metals, jewels and dyes between England and the Ottoman Turks; and early sixteenth-century images of the story of *Hero and Leander* nicely capture this sense of commercial hustle-and-bustle and military activity.[5] An early sixteenth-century plate pictures Leander's swim as one occurrence amidst many in the channel's routine daily traffic (even depicting a canon in the background of Sestos (see Figure 9.1).[6]

Another mid-sixteenth engraving depicts Leander's swim amidst a busy commercial backdrop (see Figure 9.2). Though the first phase of Leander's swim is foregrounded, the viewer's eye is also drawn to the urban centre of the image. Hero's climactic discovery of Leander's death has receded into the background and margins of the image (in the back, right side) threatened to be subsumed by other pictorial elements.

Jonson's 'naturalization' of the story onto the Thames represents less an act of violence to the story's literary tradition than a continuation of its erotic exploration of the everyday. I thus propose something of a paradox: that it is precisely the story's inextricability from the conditions of its topographic

FIGURE 9.1 *Unknown*, Plate with Hero and Leander, *about 1525, tin-glazed earthenware, 3.8 cm × 44 cm, J. Paul Getty Museum, Los Angeles*

FIGURE 9.2 *Philips Galle, after Maarten van Heemskerck,* Hero en Leander, *1569, engraving, 17.2 cm × 32.2 cm, Rijksmuseum, Amsterdam*

locality – the Hellespont – that makes its transposition to the Thames in Jonson so satisfying. In maintaining the narrative's anchor in a central, semi-civic commercial waterway, and in finding semi-analogous topographical correspondents, Jonson's burlesque throws into relief crucial elements of the story's construction. That this topographic transposition necessarily involves a temporal transposition – relocating the story to 'modern' London – reflects the way in which *Hero and Leander*'s emphasis on civic life *already* situates the story in a more modern ancient world. Jonson's burlesque was, after all, called 'the ancient *modern* history of Hero and Leander'. Not so unlike turn-of-the-seventeenth-century London, fifth-century Egypt (the world in which Musaeus would have most likely been active) experienced an intensification of civic life, as cities like Alexandria became vibrant urban centres in the shifting political, economic and religious landscape of late antiquity.[7]

One consequence of Musaeus' emphasis on civic life is a move away from the epic world of heroism and myth. *Hero and Leander* presents a Greek antiquity in which the gods are commemorated in festivals but rarely encountered and in which the everyday logistics of movement between two metropolitan areas replaces the sweeping odysseys of epic. I therefore locate the poem's appeal to the early modern world *not* in its 'violent, and even bombastic ... writing', as Gordon Braden does in his influential comparison of Musaeus and Marlowe's 'baroque style', but rather in its cultivation of a kind of proto-realism grounded in the representation of everyday life.[8] Indeed, while Marlowe's poem has often been understood as almost hysterically 'mythological' – overburdened with anecdotes, comparisons and ekphrases – I see Marlowe's emphasis on the mythic and divine prehistory of Hero and Leander's world as a way to illustrate its irrelevance.[9] Musaeus and Marlowe's Hero and Leander happily navigate their brave new world of sexual awakening and cross-channel swimming without the need for, or use of, the mythological exempla and divine figures that intermittently appear. At crucial moments throughout both poems they figuratively – and literally – turn their backs on the world of the divine, constructing a new fictional space of antiquity animated not by the whims of gods, the call of heroic duty, or the perils of fantastic adventure, but by the negotiations of youthful sexual desire amidst the routines and habits of everyday life.

Musaeus and Greek minor epic between the ancient and (early) modern

The status of minor epic, or epyllion, as a recognizable genre in antiquity (and even early modernity) is famously fraught. Since the term 'epyllion' was not coined until the nineteenth century, what counts and what does not count as 'minor epic' is a question that has plagued classicists and early modernists alike as the canon of texts that comprise the form seems ever shifting. Perhaps the only universally unifying quality these poems share is their status as *not epic*, or to put it another way, their status as evoking, engaging in and playing with the epic form while at the same time ostentatiously and defiantly rejecting it. As its Greek and English monikers make clear, minor epic or eyllion is defined relationally, less a form on its own terms than one adjacent to or in distinction from another.

This adjacent-to-epic quality fittingly characterizes the only known ancient attestation of the word (at least in a sense similar to its use today) which occurs in Athenaeus: 'The short epic poem attributed to Homer and entitled *Epikichlides* ('For Thrushes') got this name, according to Menaechmus in his *On Artists*, because when Homer sang it to the children, they would give him thrushes'.[10] Here, while Homer's name and supposed authorship function as a touchstone, this Homer is not the venerated bard of the *Iliad* and *Odyssey*, but rather the playful (and often irreverent) character out of Homeric pseudo-biography.[11] Not only is the text in question itself not-quite-epic (literally, 'little epic') but the context of its performance domesticated. Homer-the-children's-entertainer replaces the sage and serious poet of epic; from its first articulation, 'epyllion' as a concept inhabits the space of the quotidian.

While the exact origin of the ancient epyllion remains debated, the form seems to have risen to new prominence in the Hellenistic period. Like epyllion itself, the Hellenistic period was defined by, on the one hand, the dedicated study and codification of Homer's epic, and, on the other, the outspoken rejection of epic as a poetic form (most famously championed by Callimachus) – all of which took place within a world of increasing urban growth and cultural mobility.[12] It was the poet Theocritus who perhaps most influentially combined this turn towards smaller, non-epic poetic forms with a newfound preoccupation with the realism of everyday life both bucolic and urban.[13] Three of Theocritus' poems (2, 14 and 15) are categorized as 'urban mimes' and tend to relocate the same problems of unrequited love that dominate Theocritus' more famous bucolic poems to cosmopolitan and urban contexts.[14] In Theocritus 14, for instance, a young man, Aeschinas, complains that he's hopelessly in love with a young woman, a situation shared by many of Theocritus' lovelorn shepherds. The love tryst between Aeschinas and his girlfriend, however, unfolds during a rowdy drinking party and Aeschinas ends the poem deciding to join the military, rather than compose bucolic songs, as a strategy for managing his affections. The pragmatism of civic life in an expanding empire inflects the representation of erotic love. War and exploration, moreover, the conventional subjects of epic, become similarly suffused with the pragmatic: a far cry from Achilles' feats of heroic valour, Aeschinas seems to most look forward to being on Ptolemy II's payroll.[15]

Despite the Greek origins of minor epic, scholars of Elizabethan England have tended to conceptualize its minor epics as fundamentally Ovidian.[16] Ovid, far more than Theocritus or even Musaeus, would have been the familiar – and accessible – ancient authority for sixteenth- and seventeenth-century English writers: Ovid's representations of gods, heroes and star-crossed lovers in both the *Metamorphoses* and the

Heroides are clear sources for the narratives of many minor epics in the period.[17] The influence of Ovid is indisputable. Nonetheless, the form of the minor epic is rather conspicuously absent from Ovid's corpus; Ovid, in other words, offers no true examples for early modern authors of this particular narrative mode. Despite the fact that the *Metamorphoses* can feel like a collection of minor epics woven together into a longer narrative, its sweeping mytho-historical narrative from creation to Augustan Rome remains firmly epic in scope. The *Heroides*, though shorter in form and more intimate in story, are exclusively narrated in the first person (unlike the third person narrative voice that frames almost every early modern minor epic) and are composed not in the epic hexameters of Theocritean narrative poetry, but elegiac couplets associated with lyric. Moreover, the emphasis on the civic everyday is, by-and-large, not a central feature in Ovid's representation of the story. While the epistolary exchanges between Hero and Leander in the *Heroides* often display a loving attention to elements of everyday romance, the construction of a *civic* space of exchange and routine is largely absent. Indeed, the letters capture a kind of erotic claustrophobia or vacuum. In turning away from the world of myth (so deeply associated with Ovid in the early modern period) and in asserting the narrative potential of everyday life, *Hero and Leander* conjures a particularly Greek minor epic tradition that culminates in Musaeus.[18]

Although produced centuries after the Hellenistic world of Theocritus, Musaeus' *Hero and Leander* (quite probably composed in fifth-century Egypt, maybe even in Alexandria itself) is similarly marked by a self-conscious negotiation of the legacy of epic through a reorientation towards the civic. Like Theocritus' poetry, Musaeus' *Hero and Leander* is filled with allusions to Homeric epic, as the aquatic wanderings of Odysseus are domesticated and rewritten via Leander's nightly swims.[19] Seventeenth-century English readers evidently connected Musaeus and Theocritus, with London editions that paired Musaeus with Theocritus, Moschus and Bion (the conventional bucolic trio).[20] A very small number of Theocritus' poems were also printed in an English translation as early as 1588.[21]

But it was Musaeus, not Theocritus, who enjoyed perhaps the greatest popularity of any Greek poet during the sixteenth century. One of the earliest works of Greek literature ever printed, Musaeus appeared in numerous editions and translations well into the seventeenth century and every European vernacular tradition produced its own version of the poem during the sixteenth century, a testament to its status as barometer of cultural prestige.[22] Short and with relatively accessible Greek, *Hero and Leander* was one of the first Greek texts printed with a facing Latin translation and would have thus been, for many burgeoning early modern Hellenophiles, their first encounter with Greek literature.[23]

A deep-rooted 'Greekness' would have thus infused Musaeus' minor epic, one intensified by an historical mix-up that coloured its reception. In what is now a familiar story, there was a confusion surrounding Musaeus' dating and identity throughout the sixteenth and seventeenth centuries: it was believed that the author of *Hero and Leander* was in fact a different Musaeus, the mythological student of Orpheus, primeval singer and pre-Homeric poet who was understood to herald the beginning of poetry.[24] For the early modern imagination, *Hero and Leander* was the first extant example of poetry ever created, a testament *not* to the belated, civic dynamics of postclassical minor epic, but a precursor to Homer himself. The cache of Musaeus' supposed primeval origins animated the poem's first printed edition. Aldus Manutius, the famous Renaissance printer and Hellenist, justified his choice to make the poem the inaugural literary text of his own print enterprise by appealing to its status in literary history: 'I wanted the most ancient of poets, Musaeus, to be the first precursor of Aristotle and the other great geniuses I am about to publish.'[25] In this way, Aldus reimagined an ur-text of poetry as an ur-text of print itself.

And yet, even in the Aldine edition (the edition that forms the foundation for the poem's printing and dissemination through the sixteenth century), the story is more complicated.

In the 1497 Aldine edition, directly facing Aldus' confident declaration of poetic primacy, is a caveat admitting that the *Suda*, a Byzantine encyclopaedia widely consulted in the early modern period, mentions four different poets all named Musaeus, and it's not entirely clear which one wrote *Hero and Leander*.[26] This sense of historical indeterminacy, of *Hero and Leander* evoking multiple historical registers, persisted during the sixteenth century. The Italian classical scholar Julius Caesar Scaliger, famously preferred Musaeus to Homer and indeed regarded Musaeus (alongside Virgil) as one of the great models for poetics. While he did locate Musaeus at the origin-point of Greek literature, he remarked in his *Poetics* (1561) that there was something distinctly un-primeval about Musaeus' style: 'if it were not for the histories', he observed, 'you would think Mousaios more recent than Homer'.[27] By 1566, the scholar and editor Henri Estienne definitively stated that the author of *Hero and Leander* could not possibly be pre-Homeric, pointing to the inclusion of the name 'Musaeus Grammaticus' on certain manuscripts containing the poem.[28] The Hebraist and classicist, Isaac Casaubon, citing stylistic and historical problems, came to the same conclusion as Estienne in a note in his 1593 edition of Diogenes Laertius.[29]

This tradition of ruminating on Musaeus' identity reaches a kind of culmination in Robert Stapylton's 1647 English translation of the poem, which opens by listing every known identity attached to Musaeus, including the four listed in the *Suda* and Musaeus the Grammarian identified by Causabon. Not particularly troubled by this multiplicity, Stapylton declares:

> For my part, I dare not affirme any of them to be the Musaeus that writ Hero and Leander: but this I dare boldly say, whosoever writ it had the gifts and endowments of them all. For his language might have become Musaeus the Grammarian, his knowledge in passions and affections, Musaeus the Philosopher: and the divinity of his verses, the First and Great Musaeus, that dedicated his Hymne Περὶ Θεῶ of God to Orpheus.[30]

Musaeus thus resided in the early modern imagination at the border between the shadowy world of myth and the increasingly more visible world of later literary production. And so Musaeus was at the centre of questions about the nature of literary history and the role of the literary scholar in producing tenable chronologies. While Estienne and Causabon note the title 'Grammaticus' as a crucial piece of evidence in their dating of the poem, they also respond to the stylistic and representational qualities of the poem itself.[31] Both scholars, in other words, implicitly respond to the poem's own demarcation of its fictional boundaries, its multilayered presentation of a Greek society where the primeval, mythic world of the ancient Musaeus is already past.

The memorialization of this mythic past provides the occasion for Musaeus' poem: the annual festival of Aphrodite and Adonis, which the narrator describes as a happening local destination for the surrounding area's youths. Walking us through the area's major cities and regions, the narrator emphasizes the festival's status as a site of youthful convergence:

> For it was time to celebrate the festival of the Cyprian goddess (a festival they hold in Sestos in honour of Adonis and Cytheraia). Anyone who lived on the edges of those islands crowned by the sea rushed in crowds to attend the sacred day: there were some from Haemonia, some from Cyprus in the sea. Not one woman stuck around in the cities of Cythera, and not a single dancer stayed behind in the mountain of sweet-smelling Lebanon. None of the neighbors missed the festival: no one who lived in Phrygia, no citizen of nearby Abydos, and certainly no one who was single and looking for a young maiden. Indeed, wherever there was talk of a festival, this young crowd gathered with enthusiasm, not so much to offer a sacrifice to the immortals then to get together to honour the beauty of young women.[32]

What motivates at least some part of this influx of hopeful young people from nearby environs is not, as we learn, a sense of genuine religious devotion. Festivals function as opportunities for intermingling and, most importantly, for meeting a potential spouse. Musaeus then sidelines devotion to the immortals not only as a motive for the youths' enthusiastic travel but also for the poem's own *raison d'etre*: 'honouring the beauty of young women' replaces religious sacrifice. As soon as the immortals are dispensed with as the prime motivators for the poem's actions, the poet dutifully turns to honouring the beauty of mortal women, offering an extended description of Hero's exceptional beauty (55–85). One smitten youth captivated by Hero's appearance goes so far as to remark: 'I wouldn't desire to be a god in Olympus / If I had Hero as a wife in my house' (80–1). The world of everyday youthful desire is more appealing than the world of the gods.

Mocking the gods in Marlowe

When we turn to Christopher Marlowe, over a thousand years and twenty printed editions of Musaeus' poem later, we see that he also sets his poem in a world of civic festival, local travel and youthful eroticism. He even gestures toward the socio-economic structure of Sestos, making sure to remark that the festival is funded and organized by the city's upper-class:

> The men of wealthie Sestos, everie yeare,
> (For his sake whom their goddesse held so deare,
> Rose-cheekt Adonis) kept a solemne feast:
> Thither resorted many a wandring guest,
> To meet their loves; such as had none at all,
> Came lovers home, from this great festivall.
>
> (1.91–6)

Here, the festival is even further detached from the context of religious observation. By going out of his way to characterize it as an event bankrolled by the city's wealthy, Marlowe deeply entrenches the festival in a world of civic hierarchy. The cause of celebration – Venus' love for Adonis – is bracketed as a kind of footnote, secondary to its status as a municipal attraction and a meet-and-greet event for the hopelessly single.

Marlowe's overall diminishment of myth takes an even more explicit form than Musaeus'. While in Musaeus the world of the immortals slips unceremoniously into the poem's background, in Marlowe, that slip becomes a visible act of rupture. The gods, in other words, do not go quietly. This difference is clear in the poem's opening lines, which dispense with Musaeus' encomiastic invocation to a lamp in favour of a geographic declaration centrally concerned with poem's urban and littoral locations:

> On Hellespont guiltie of True-loves blood,
> In view and opposit two citties stood,
> Seaborderers, disjoin'd by Neptunes might:
> The one Abydos, the other Sestos hight.
>
> (1.1–4)

Here, Marlowe gives 'Neptune's might' a prominent place in the poem's opening, although this place is proleptically tinged with the 'guilt' associated with the Hellespont. Given the way in which Neptune's power is underscored, we might expect Neptune to appear in the poem a force to be reckoned with – perhaps as the force responsible for keeping the lovers apart. However, when we do encounter the god, during Leander's first and only swim across the Hellespont, he is everything *but* an imposing presence. In fact, Neptune comes across as rather ridiculous: susceptible to the same erotic desires as the lovers, he is unable to secure Leander's reciprocal affection.

Though mortal and immortal interact, the encounter becomes a study in misrecognition and miscommunication. The two speak past each other, each operating, it would seem, in different narrative registers governed by incompatible priorities. The scene unfolds thus: diving naked into the water, Leander catches the eye of Neptune, who mistakes Leander for the beautiful youth Ganymede, a companion of Jupiter who was made immortal for his beauty and resided in Olympus. Thanking his lucky stars, Neptune snatches Leander and takes him down to his underwater palace. However, things quickly deteriorate when Neptune realizes that Leander cannot possibly be the immortal Ganymede, 'For under water [Leander] was almost dead' (2.170). Realizing his mistake, and choosing not to enact the actual drowning of Leander the reader expects, Neptune quickly parts the waves to allow Leander to breathe and resumes his seduction. In a seeming act of contrition, 'the god put Helles bracelet on [Leander's] arme/ And swore the sea should never doe him harme' (179–80). However, Helle, as we learned earlier, was a young maiden who drowned in the Hellespont and gave the channel its name, making the gift of her bracelet a distinctly alarming assurance of underwater safety. The bracelet, Marlowe's invention, further encodes deception and unreliability into the material traces of the story's mythic past.

During Neptune's extended seduction, Leander, in turn, becomes confused, dutifully informing Neptune: 'You are deceav'd, I am no woman I' (192). Unfazed, Neptune merely smiles and begins to tell Leander a story about a shepherd and his beautiful boy love. But Leander could not be less interested. Boldly cutting the god off mid-tale, Leander reveals that he is entirely preoccupied with the time:

Aye me, Leander cryde, th'enamoured sunne,
That now should shine on Thetis glassie bower,
Descends upon my radiant Heroes tower.
O that these tardie armes of mine were wings.

(2.202–5)

Leander has places to be and seems either unaware of or uninterested in Neptune's divine status. Indeed, Leander seems to know nothing about the Greek mythic tradition, where male gods frequently fall in love with beautiful male youths. Conversely, Neptune seems not to understand what kind of world in which he lives, one where young boys are not plucked from earth and turned into immortal companions and where indulging the erotic whims of the gods is not, in fact, obligatory. Neptune comes across as rather out of step with the times, blunderingly old-fashioned in his seduction techniques. Even after Leander rebuffs Neptune's advances and continues on his way, Neptune still convinces himself that Leander cares. Believing Leander pities him for cutting open his own hand (when it seems Leander was simply made queasy by the sight of blood), Neptune departs the scene in search for gifts to give him (2.224–6). The fact that Neptune's attempted seduction is entirely Marlowe's invention solidifies his narrative investment in actively rejecting the world of myth. Neptune appears in the poem's story only to be ignored and abandoned.[33] Indeed, given that Marlowe's version ends where it does, it's hard not to read this scene of failed seduction as also a scene of failed or aborted drowning. Any reader with knowledge of Musaeus' poem or the story would be anxiously waiting for the expected drowning that never comes. Moreover, Neptune fails to seduce Leander and, perhaps more importantly (given Judith Haber and James Bromley's argument that the poem valorizes non-teleological sexuality) to communicate with him.[34]

Neptune is not the only god to suffer a small humiliation at Marlowe's hands. Like Musaeus, Marlowe too singles out Aphrodite (in Marlowe, called Venus) for a downgrade. No longer relegating her to the poem's background, Marlowe presents the very events which Sestos' festival is commemorating – Venus' love for Adonis – as the stuff not of religious solemnity but of fetching outfit design:

> The outside of [Hero's] garments were of lawne,
> The lining, purple silke, with guilt starres drawne,
> Her wide sleeves greene, and bordered with a grove,
> Where Venus in her naked glory strove,
> To please the carelesse and disdainfull eies
> Of proud Adonis that before her lies.

(1.9–14)

Marlowe reimagines Venus' desire for Adonis as essentially ornamental, as important primarily for its contributing to Hero's beauty. But at the same time he captures Venus in a less-than-flattering scenario, desperately hoping for Adonis' attention. In a different way, Shakespeare would also 'immortalize' Venus in the same situation. Adorned with images of Venus' sexual exploits, Hero seems to become a replacement for Venus herself:

> But this is true, so like was one the other,
> As [Cupid] imagyn'd Hero was his mother.
> And oftentimes into her bosome flew,
> About her naked necke his bare armes threw,
> And laid his childish head upon her brest,
> And with still panting rockt, there tooke his rest.
>
> (1.39–44)

Going beyond the conventional ancient and Renaissance trope, in which it is not uncommon to liken mortal female beauty to that of Venus, the similarity described here practically nullifies Venus' maternal – and, secondarily, her sexual and physical – identity.[35] Venus' own son, the one person who should intuitively recognize her, confuses her with Hero, going so far as to take a nap on Hero's chest.

The ornamentality of mythic desire becomes a defining feature of Venus' presence in the poem. In what's called Venus' 'church', where we see Hero performing her priestly duties, is a looking glass in which 'you see the gods in sundrie shapes, / committing headdie ryots, incest, rapes' (143–4). The narrator lists several of these scenes (Danae, Ganymede, Europa, Iris, etc.), all famous moments of rape that recall Ovid's *Metamorphoses*. The scene also recalls – and collapses – two separate moments of ekphrastic spectatorship experienced by Britomart, the female protagonist of Edmund Spenser's *Faerie Queene* Book III. The first is a direct reference to 'Venus looking glass' that occurs at the beginning of the book (3.1.8): we learn that this magic glass produced an image of Britomart's future love and that this vision is the catalyst for her current wanderings. The other moment occurs at the end of the book in the house of Busirane, when Britomart finds herself staring at elaborate tapestries graphically depicting Ovidian rapes that decorate his walls (3.11). The extensive description of these tapestries, taking up almost an entire canto, forms one of the *Faerie Queene*'s most important ekphrases. Like the image on Hero's outfit, these images represent the gods in compromising and often unflattering erotic scenes.

Most important for my argument is the difference between the centrality of female spectatorship in both moments in Spenser and the absence of female spectatorship in Marlowe's reworking. By contrast to Britomart, Hero is not looking: 'And in the midst a silver altar stood; / There Hero sacrificing turtles blood, / Vaild to the ground, vailing her eie-lids close' (157–9). Focusing on the sacrifice at hand, Hero does not seem interested in viewing the images and when she does look up, it is (momentously) to see Leander for the first time. Thus, Hero's looking departs from and even undoes the moments of spectatorship in Spenser it evokes. For Britomart, 'Venus looking glass' allows her to see her lover; it is an essential mediator of erotic desire. Hero, in contrast, sees her lover in the flesh while ignoring Venus' glass altogether. In addition, Britomart does not simply stare at the Ovidian tapestries of rape, but is problematically transfixed by them: 'The wondrous sight faire Britomart amazd, / Ne seeing could her wonder satisfie, / But evermore and more upon it gazd' (3.11.49).[36] In fact, the insatiability that characterized Britomart's spectatorship of the tapestries ('evermore and more') is transferred, in Marlowe, to Leander's insatiable desire to look at Hero when their eyes meet for the first time: 'Stone still [Leander] stood, and evermore he gazed' (163). In rewriting these famous moments of erotic ekphrasis, therefore, Marlowe is going out of his way to present Hero (and later, even Leander) as spectators of a different kind, focused not on images from mythology but engaged simply in beholding the physical presence of a mortal lover.

Marlowe also exploits the contradiction of being a virgin priestess to the goddess of sexual desire. He makes this point a key part of Leander's seduction speech: he calls Hero 'Venus' Nun', a phrase that was used in the sixteenth century to describe London prostitutes.[37] The phrase thus takes us back to Jonson's burlesque – indeed, Jonson was probably at least in part inspired by this very *double entendre* to transpose the story as he did, one in which the wench, Hero, seems to be a prostitute. While Marlowe is capitalizing on the phrase's currency in English, he is also letting the story's mythic scenario subvert itself and expose its own absurdity: being a prostitute would be a more fitting form of reverence to Venus than a promise of life-long chastity.

In the depictions of Neptune and Venus, then, Marlowe links his subversion of mythic authority to a subversion of mythic eroticism: alongside the rejection of divinities themselves is a rejection of their hierarchical and largely rapacious erotic conduct. In its place, Marlowe offers the eroticism of two more or less equal young lovers, Hero and Leander, without censure (indeed, it is also presented essentially without censure in Musaeus too).[38] This post-mythic eroticism is thus explicitly presented as rejecting or ignoring the divine erotics of rape: Leander is able to deflect Neptune's unwanted and almost lethal advances to make it to Hero's bed, and Hero falls in love with the sight of Leander while ignoring the mythological images of rape that surround her.

Marlowe's invented 'myth of Mercury', an extended narrative tangent that purports to 'explain' (among other things) why scholars are poor, offers a further example of the poem's censure of divine eroticism. Unlike the civic world of festival in which Hero and Leander meet, the world evoked in this tangent is agrarian with little or no sense of place. It opens with Mercury 'spie[ing] a countrie mayd' (388), an event introduced without any indication of when, where, or how, only that he 'made her stay / The while upon a hillocke downe he lay' (399–400). In this barely perceptible, vaguely pastoral space of myth, only the actions of Mercury and the country maid feel truly visible. Those actions, in turn, feel almost painfully delineated by the violence of their erotic encounter:

> Till in his twining armes [Mercury] lockt her fast,
> And then he woo'd with kisses, and at last,
> As sheap-heards do, her on the ground hee layd,
> And tumbling in the grasse, he often strayd
> Beyond the bounds of shame ...
>   but she,
> Whose only dower was her chastitie,
> Having striv'ne in vaine, was now about to crie,
> And crave the helpe of sheap-heards that were nie.

(1.403–14)

This scene of near-rape sets in motion a circuitous series of mythic events that negatively depict eroticism, desire and the world of the divine. So desperate is Mercury to sleep with the maid that once he realizes rape will not work, he agrees to steal some of Jupiter's ambrosia. Unsurprisingly, Jupiter is none too pleased and thrusts Mercury down from heaven. Mercury convinces Cupid to enlist the help of the Fates in overthrowing Jupiter, but this Olympian revolution is short-lived because the Fates quickly realize that Mercury's affections are easily changeable. The episode ends with Jupiter restored to power and the Fates arbitrarily punishing humanity: scholarship and learning (traits associated with the god Mercury) are doomed to be unremunerated professions with little worldly influence.

Many readers of *Hero and Leander* have seen the myth of Mercury as an extension – one, albeit, of excessive and almost manifest superfluity – of the poem's larger erotic concerns. But I contend that the mythic eroticism in this episode stands in contrast to the eroticism of the poem's protagonists. While Hero and Leander's sexual dynamics often play with violence and troublingly toy with the question of Hero's consent, the sheer directness of Mercury's physical overpowering of the maid ('lock't') contrasts starkly with the misunderstandings and *double entendres* that define the erotic inexperience of the two lovers.[39] Indeed, their desire is at times described as almost comically equal, as they variously confuse and titillate each other in their unsophisticated flirtations:

> He askt, she gave, and nothing was denied,
> Both to each other quickly were affied.
> Looke how their hands, so were their hearts united,
> And what he did, she willingly requited.
> (Sweet are the kisses, the imbracements sweet,
> When like desires and affections meet).
>
> (2.25–30)

The setting in which their sexual encounters tend to take place – Hero's tower and bedroom – underscores this ideal of a mutual erotic charge. A far cry from the placeless meadow in which Mercury nearly rapes the maid, this setting is saturated with the logistics of day-to-day life. The tower's unremarkable structural features crucially play into the scene's humourous subversion of outlandish romance tropes:

> And therefore to [Hero's] tower [Leander] got by stealth.
> Wide open stood the doore, hee need not clime,
> And she her selfe before the pointed time,
> Had spread the boord, with roses strowed the roome,
> And oft look't out, and mus'd he did not come.
>
> (2.18–22)

Here, the small pragmatic detail that Hero leaves the door open for Leander prevents the scene from becoming a heroic spectacle of Leander's climbing abilities. Leander seems to expect that some kind heroic feat will be required of him and thus approaches the tower 'by stealth'. He is, however, greeted not by insurmountable obstacles but by Hero's pragmatic forethought and by her touchingly adolescent preparation of the room with rose petals as she anxiously waits for Leander to arrive a bit earlier than arranged. Unlike Mercury's seduction of the maid, which happens in the vacuum of myth, the erotic encounter of Hero and Leander unfolds amidst the boundaries of familiar structures and familiar daily routines.

Hero, Leander and Nashe's red herring

It is fitting that Marlowe's poem ends not at the tragic conclusion of Musaeus' original, but rather in the midst of the lovers' awkward erotic play. They remain preserved for posterity not as doomed embodiments of ill-fated love, but as living – slightly absurd – markers of everyday sexuality. While Marlowe's conclusion constitutes a departure from the narrative arc of Musaeus, then, it is in keeping with both poems' celebration of youthful eroticism. Marlowe's poem represents a natural next step, presenting the youth's sexual exploits without censure (essentially like Musaeus) and sparing them the 'punishment' that their drowning potentially suggests. If Marlowe's abrupt conclusion was indeed intentional, in orchestrating this evasion he also surpasses the power of Cupid: Cupid's fruitless pleas to the Fates to spare Hero and Leander sparked the recounting of the myth of Mercury. Cupid's asks that 'Both might enjoy ech other, and be blest' (380) and Marlowe delivers that conclusion by ending the poem where he does.[40]

For some, most notably George Chapman, Marlowe's untimely death and the apparently unfinished nature of the poem presented an occasion for writing a proper conclusion. In Chapman's case, this meant extending the narrative so it aligned with Musaeus' tragic conclusion. Chapman's reverence for Musaeus' original, and conversely for the originality of Musaeus, is a defining quality of his ongoing engagement with this narrative. Chapman titled his 1616 translation *The Divine Poem of Musaeus: First of All Bookes*, emphasizing the primacy and almost primordial divinity of Musaeus' authorship (and, more pragmatically, avoiding confusion after Marlowe's version, titled simply *Hero and Leander*, became quite popular).

In many ways, Chapman's so-called 'continuation' is less an extension of Marlowe's vision than a reorientation, one signalled by Chapman's opening line: 'New light gives new directions' (1).[41] As Marion Campbell aptly remarks, to attend to the differences between Marlowe and Chapman's visions is not to dismiss Chapman's appreciation of Marlowe's poem, but rather to acknowledge 'that he understood Marlowe's poem very well indeed, but set out deliberately to redirect and to appropriate it to his own ends'.[42] As Campbell also points out, one intervention on Chapman's part is the division of the poem into 'Sestiads', an invented term derived from the city, Sestos, that is clearly meant to resonate with Homer's *Iliad* and thus make the poem less minor and more epic.[43]

Making *Hero and Leander* more epic, Chapman reintegrates numerous divinities – mostly of his own invention – into the narrative, manifestly reintroducing the significance of divine guidance.[44] These divinities often function as the voice of censure, critiquing not only the lovers' sexual choices but also, implicitly, Marlowe's poetic judgements. The newfound role of divine wisdom suggests that the lovers' ill-advised erotic choices in Marlowe's poem were the direct consequence of divine absence. A mere hundred lines into the continuation, for instance, the lustful Leander finds himself suddenly 'ravished' by 'music so divine' (107–8) and is greeted by a vision of 'the goddess Ceremony' accompanied by an extensive retinue of other deities, including Religion, Devotion, Order and Reverence (112–20). They engage in a kind of allegorical pageant, after which Ceremony chastises Leander for 'his violent love' and Leander begins to regret trying to sleep with Hero without marrying her (146).

While Chapman ostentatiously puts the divine back on display, classical divinities remain conspicuously absent. It would seem that Marlowe too soundly humiliated them in his opening and that Chapman must now find new, less tarnished gods, to re-energize the power and value of divinity.[45] This predicament becomes most apparent when Chapman includes the god Neptune at the end of the poem, largely, it would seem, to kill Leander by accident. While Chapman assigns Neptune some sort of power by making him responsible for Leander's demise – precisely the role he was denied by Marlowe – it remains a slightly embarrassing episode: Neptune is not the god he used to be. Chapman, for his part, cannot seem to escape Marlowe's depiction of Neptune as the doddering lover: Neptune's foolish attempt to prevent the Fates from killing Leander – by hurling his 'marble mace' at one of them – causes his death because the injured Fate accidentally drops the thread of Leander's life (225–34).

We might say that a 'truer' inheritor of Marlowe's vision, then, is not Chapman or Henry Petowe (the poem's other literal continuator) but rather Thomas Nashe, who seems to have collaborated with Marlowe years earlier on *Dido, Queen of Carthage* (422) and who irreverently 'epitomizes' the story of Hero and Leander in his sprawling mock encomium to red herring, *Lenten Stuff*.[46] Nashe introduces his epitome of Hero and Leander by explicitly hailing Marlowe's legacy, offering himself as a kind of disciple of Musaeus and Marlowe, bringing their story from the book-stalls of London to the port town of Yarmouth (where *Lenten Stuff* is set and where Nashe was currently living in exile). 'Hath anybody in Yarmouth heard of Leander and Hero', asks Nashe's narrator, 'of whom divine Musaeus sung, and a diviner muse than him, Kit Marlowe? Two faithful lovers they were, as every apprentice in Paul's churchyard will tell you for your love, and sell you for your money' (242). Expressing the story's popularity in terms of the commercial success of the booksellers at St Paul's, Nashe implicitly connects the production of narrative in London with the production of fish in Yarmouth. *Hero and Leander* thus becomes another English export. Nashe too is acknowledging the story's strong connections to the print market, something that would have resonated with Nashe's own authorial obsessions with print technology and the mechanics of preproduction.[47]

Nashe is in many ways a natural inheritor of Marlowe's fictional experiments with the urban everyday; his fictions are profoundly concerned with and coloured by city-life and the cultivation of an urban sensibility. As Georgia Brown puts it, 'Nashe not only writes about the city, he also incorporates the city into his own identity'.[48] An important part of this urban and urbane identity was an interest in travel and its educating, and mis-educating, potential – a topic Nashe explored in perhaps his most famous work, *The Unfortunate Traveller*. But *Lenten Stuff* also exhibits Nashe's fascination with travel and the gritty day-to-day activity of urban commerce. Indeed, *Lenten Stuff* is essentially an extended parody of civic chorography, in which Nashe playfully and exhaustively describes and celebrates the humble port town of Yarmouth. Taking up their primary export, red herring, as an occasion for recapitulating various aspects of the classical tradition, Nashe connects the town's status as a major trade port linking England and the North Sea to the strategic location of Abydos and Sestos on the Hellespont. He even changes the story slightly to emphasize the chorographic and cultural affinities between the two locations, proposing that Sestos and Abydos were rival cities 'like Yarmouth and Leystoffe [Lowestoft] ... still at a wrig-wrag ... suck[ing] from their mothers' teats serpentine hatred against one another'. And he soon compares Hero's tower to 'one of our Irish castles' (425). Indeed, the playful connections Nashe draws between England and the Hellespont may have inspired the similar transposition in Jonson's *Bartholomew Fair* with which this essay opened. As W. Scott Blanchard notes, the sculler's remark to Leander in Jonson's puppet show that 'Hero ... is come over into Fish Street to eat some fresh herring' would certainly seem to be a winking reference to Nashe's retelling (5.4.143–5).[49]

But beyond establishing civic affinities between Sestos and Abydos and the Yarmouth metropolitan area, Nashe directly embeds the story of Hero and Leander within Yarmouth's economy and local history. Here, Nashe travesties the classical gods, thereby expanding Marlowe's irreverent depictions while offering a parody of Chapman's slightly heavy-handed continuation. These gods, like Marlowe's Neptune, are all absurdly invested in Hero and Leander's fate: they end up so devastated by the lovers' deaths that 'they began to abhor all moisture for the sea's sake' (428). Capitalizing on the cluelessness of Marlowe's Neptune and extending it to other gods, Nashe reports that 'Jupiter could not endure Ganymede, his cup-bearer, to come in his presence ... [for] he was so like to Leander' (428). While 'the dint of destiny could not be repealed in the reviving of Hero and Leander', the gods decree and (with a subtle nod to the language of Marlowe's third line) that 'for they were either of them sea-borderers and drowned in the sea, still to the sea they must belong' and transform each of them into fish: Leander is turned into a ling while Hero becomes none other than a red herring (429). Attentive to the details of the story, Nashe even has the gods take pity on Hero's chambermaid (mentioned only briefly in Musaeus), transforming her into a mustard-seed. Together, then, the three of them form a typical meal, fittingly metamorphosed into day-to-day sustenance, permanently integrated into the everyday, civic life of sixteenth- and seventeenth-century Yarmouth.

Notes

1   All references to *Bartholomew Fair* from Ben Jonson, *Volpone and Other Plays*, ed. Michael Jamieson (New York: Penguin Classics, 2004).

2   Roy Booth, 'Hero's Afterlife: *Hero and Leander* and "lewd unmannerly verse" in the late Seventeenth Century', *Early Modern Literary Studies* 12.3 (2007): 4.1–24.

3   Susanne L. Wofford similarly identifies the ways in which Shakespeare turned to literary models from the Hellenistic empire to understand England's growing imperial ambitions and global imagination. See 'Against Our Own Ignorance', in *Shakespeare in Our Time: A Shakespeare Association of America Collection*, eds Dympna Callaghan and Suzanne Gossett (New York: Bloomsbury Arden Shakespeare, 2016), 159–67.

4   Booth, 'Hero's Afterlife', 7.

5   Miriam Jacobson, *Barbarous Antiquity: Reorienting the Past in the Poetry of Early Modern England* (Philadelphia: University of Pennsylvania Press, 2014), 149–87.

6 I am indebted to Jacobson for her reference to this plate (*Barbarous Antiquity*, 154–5).

7 For a discussion of cities in Late Antique Hellenism as spaces that fused 'classical' Greek culture with local, civic traditions and beliefs, see Glen Bowerstock, *Hellenism in Late Antiquity* (Ann Arbor: University of Michigan Press, 1990), 1–13.

8 Gordon Braden, *The Classics and English Renaissance Poetry: Three Case Studies* (New Haven: Yale University Press, 1978), 55–100.

9 For examples of this mythological view of the poem see Ellis, *Sexuality and Citizenship*; Keach, *Elizabethan Erotic Narratives*; Paul Miller, 'A Function of Myth in Marlowe's *Hero and Leander*', *Studies in Philology*, 50 (1953): 158–67; and Weaver, *Untutored Lines*, 47–69.

10 Athenaeus, *The Learned Banqueters, Volume I: Books 1–3.106e*, ed. and trans. S. Douglas Olson, Loeb Classical Library 204, (Cambridge, MA: Harvard University Press, 2007), 365 (65b).

11 For Homeric biography's colourful tradition, see Barbara Graziosi, *Inventing Homer: The Early Reception of Epic* (Cambridge: Cambridge University Press, 2002).

12 See Joan Burton, *Theocritus' Urban Mimes: Mobility, Gender, and Patronage* (Berkeley: University of California Press, 1995), 1–40.

13 For Theocritus' investment in realism both urban and bucolic, see Marco Fantuzzi and Richard Hunter, *Tradition and Innovation in Hellenistic Poetry* (Cambridge: Cambridge University Press, 2012), 133–7.

14 The definitive study is Burton, *Theocritus' Urban Mimes*.

15 A.S.F. Gow, ed. and trans. *Theocritus* (Cambridge: Cambridge University Press, 1952), 14.58.

16 See, for example: Donno, *Elizabethan Minor Epics*, 1–20; Enterline, 'Elizabethan Minor Epics'; Hulse, *Metamorphic Verse*; and Keach, *Elizabethan Erotic Narratives*.

17 See Enterline, 'Elizabethan Minor Epics', especially 253–4, for a discussion of Ovidian influences, particularly via the Tudor schoolroom, and an overview of the form in the 1590s.

18 This is not to claim that Ovid was completely disconnected from the civic world, but an interest in urban life colours the *Amores* and the *Ars amatoria* rather than the *Heroides* or the *Metamorphoses*. For the influence of Ovid's 'urbanity' on early modern English authors, see Georgia Brown, 'Sex and the City: Nashe, Ovid, and the Problems of Urbanity', in *The Age of Thomas Nashe: Text, Bodies and Trespasses of Authorship in Early Modern England*, eds Stephen Guy-Bray, Joan Pong Linton and Steve Mentz (Burlington, VT: Ashgate, 2013), 11–26. For an argument that Ovid and Musaeus would have been fused for early modern readers as an 'Ovidian Musaeus', see Warren Boutcher, '"Who Taught Thee Rhetoricke to Deceive a Maid?": Christopher Marlowe's *Hero and Leander*, Juan Boscán's *Leandro*, and Renaissance Vernacular Humanism', *Comparative Literature* 52 (2000): 11–52. For recent views on the significance of Greek antiquity to Shakespeare, see *Shakespeare and Greece*, eds Alison Findlay and Vassiliki Markidou (London: Bloomsbury, 2017).

19 The poem opens with an invocation that takes a humble lamp rather a hero's deeds as its topic. See Musaeus, *Hero and Leander*, in *Callimachus: Aetia, Iambi, Hecale and Other Fragments; Musaeus:* Hero and Leander, trans. C.A. Trypanis, T. Gelzer and Cedric H. Whitman, Loeb Classical Library 421 (Cambridge, MA: Harvard University Press, 1973). Leander later compares the lamp, which Hero lights to guide his way at night, to the stars that Odysseus used to navigate. See Musaeus, *Hero and Leander*, line 212 and Gelzer, 372na.

20 For instance: *Musæi, Moschi & Bionis, quæ extant omnia: quibus accssere quædam selectiora Theocriti Eidyllia*, trans. David Whitford (London: Typis Thomæ Roycroftij, impensis autoris, [1655] and *Musæi, Moschi & Bionis, quæ extant Omnia: quibus accessere quædam selectiora Theocriti Eidyllia . . .*, trans. David Whitford (London: Typis Thomæ Roycroftij, impensis Jo. Martin, Jac. Allestrye, & Tho. Dicas [1659]).

21 *Sixe idillia that is, sixe small, or petty poems, or aeglogues, chosen out of the right famous Sicilian poet Theocritus, and translated into English verse* (Oxford: Joseph Barnes, 1588).

22 There were two first editions of the poem: a 1494(?) edition printed by Aldus Manutius and a 1494(?) edition printed by

Lorenzo de Alopa and Janus Lascaris. Weaver offers a useful overview of the poem's print and translation history (*Untutored Lines*, 47–69). For a detailed account of the poem's print and translation history on the continent see Braden, *The Classics and English Renaissance Poetry*, 55–100 and Boutcher, '"Who Taught Thee Rhetoricke to Deceive a Maid?"', 2–25.

23 See Musaeus, *Hero and Leander* (Venice: Aldus Manutius [1497?]).

24 Braden offers a good account of the stylistic implications of the confusion (*The Classics and English Renaissance Poetry*, 57, 81–94).

25 Aldus Manutius, *The Greek Classics*, ed. and trans. N.G. Wilson (Cambridge, MA: Harvard University Press, 2016), 9.

26 See Musaeus, *Hero and Leander*, A1.

27 Quoted in Braden, *The Classics,* 82.

28 Henri Estienne, ed., *Poetae Graeci* (Paris: Estienne, 1566), 487.

29 Isaac Casaubon, 'Isaaci Casauboni notae ad Diogenis . . .' in Diogenes Laertius, *Diogenous Laertiou Peri biōn* (Geneva: Estienne, 1593), 8.

30 Robert Stapylton, *Musaeus on the Loves of Hero and Leander: with Annotations upon the Originall* (London: F.B. Humphrey Mosley, 1647), A9v.

31 Estienne claims that the title 'Grammaticus' on certain manuscripts confirmed that the poem was not extremely ancient. See Anthony Grafton's discussion of Causabon's marginalia in Estienne's *Poetae Graeci* in Grafton and Joanna Weinberg, '*I have always loved the holy tongue*': *Isaac Casaubon, the Jews, and a Forgotten Chapter in Renaissance Scholarship* (Cambridge, MA: Harvard University Press, 2011), 33.

32 Lines 42–54. All translations of Musaeus are mine and cited by line number. The best edition of the poem (and only complete English translation) is Gelzer's.

33 For a reading that takes the encounter with Neptune as the erotic centerpiece of the poem, see James Bromley, '"Let it Suffice": Sexual Acts and Narrative Structure in *Hero and Leander*', in *Queer Renaissance Historiography: Backward Gaze*, eds Vincent Joseph Nardizzi, Stephen Guy-Bray and Will

Stockton (Burlington, VT: Ashgate, 2009), 67–84. Unlike Bromley, I see the power dynamics of Neptune's attempts to possess Leander (god controlling mortal) as a problematic epic component that the poem ultimately rejects.

34 See Bromley, '"Let it Suffice"', and Judith Haber, *Desire and Dramatic Form*, 39–49.

35 For a discussion of this trope in the ancient novel, see Froma Zeitlin, 'Religion', in *The Cambridge Companion to the Greek and Roman Novel*, ed. Tim Whitmarsh (Cambridge: Cambridge University Press, 2008), 91–108.

36 Edmund Spenser, *The Faerie Queene*, ed. A.C. Hamilton (New York: Pearson Education Group, 2007).

37 See Patrick Cheney and Brian J. Striar, eds, *The Collected Poems of Christopher Marlowe* (Oxford: Oxford University Press, 2006), 196, note 45.

38 Musaeus refers to their sexual consummation as a kind of wedding [ὑμέναιος], thus mitigating the problem (221–5).

39 For the semantic confusion that defines Hero and Leander's sexual play, especially the readerly confusion in ascertaining if and when consummation occurs, see Haber, *Desire and Dramatic Form*.

40 Marion Campbell argues that Marlowe intended to end the poem where he did – a view with which many agree – and fully discusses the differences between Marlowe's poem and Chapman's continuation ('"*Desunt Nonnulla*": The Construction of Marlowe's *Hero and Leander* as an Unfinished Poem', *English Literary History* 51 [1984]: 241–68).

41 All references to Chapman's continuation are from Cheney and Striar, eds, *The Collected Poems of Christopher Marlowe*, 220–68.

42 Campbell, '"*Desunt Nonnulla*"', 249.

43 Ibid., 250–1.

44 W. Scott Blanchard discusses Chapman's interest in mythography (*Scholars' Bedlam: Menippean Satire in the Renaissance* [Lewisburg: Bucknell University Press, 1995]), 127–8.

45 I am grateful to David Landreth for this suggestion.

46 All references to *Lenten Stuff* come from Thomas Nashe, *The Unfortunate Traveller and Other Works*, ed. J.B. Steane (New

York: Penguin, 1972). While the extent of Nashe's collaboration remains debated, the title page of the 1594 copy reads, 'The tragedie of Dido Queene of Carthage: played by the Children of her Maiesties Chappell. Written by Christopher Marlowe, and Thomas Nash. Gent.'.

47 Much has been written on this subject, but see for instance Jonathan Crewe, *Unredeemed Rhetoric: Thomas Nashe and the Scandal of Authorship* (Baltimore: Johns Hopkins University Press, 1982).

48 Brown, 'Sex and the City', 12.

49 Blanchard, *Scholar's Bedlam*, 125.

10

'Unthriftie waste'

Epyllia, idleness and general economy

Barbara Correll

A lengthy essay on leisure, idleness and *otium* in the Renaissance by Brian Vickers reviews a wide range of texts, classical, English and European, concluding that authors from Cicero and Virgil to Spenser, Milton and Marvell distinguish between the virtues of contemplative leisure as a model for productive thought, and the negative effects of mere wasteful idleness.[1] His selection of texts from English and Continental sources, ancient, medieval, early modern, does not, however, include what we now call the epyllion, perhaps because Vickers' judgement is challenged by texts in which idleness is not so marginalized and thought is productive in other ways.[2] The erotic epyllion that is my focus here opens up the question of a general economy of idleness and waste; its influence on other genres such as Shakespeare's drama, which incorporates significant elements from the epyllion, underscores the significance of the topic of waste and idleness in early modern literature and culture and its critical potential for current economic criticism.

In the late sixteenth century, at a time when Protestant values of thrift, discipline and productivity, along with the humanist ideal of the *vita activa* were officially dominant, three writers taken on the problem of idleness and the epyllion. Marlowe's *Hero and Leander* poses a challenge to an emerging capitalist society and culture. This epyllion celebrates idleness and waste, not only in his characters' actions but in the writing itself and its strategic display of narrative purposelessness, digression and incompletion.[3] Spenser's complex reaction to the Ovidian fashion that Marlowe embraces can be found not only in his own *Muiopotmos* and amatory verse but in Book 2 of *The Faerie Queene* where, while negatively representing wastefulness and unproductive inactivity, he also struggles with the narrative errancy and excesses of his own text. Shakespeare's *Venus and Adonis* echoes the genre's attachment to unproductive idleness and gives us an adaptation of Ovid in which an obstreperous Venus pursues, assaults and lengthily debates a resistant Adonis, only to brush off his rebuffs, walk away from his gory death and disappear into the heavens.[4] But importantly, Shakespeare later revisits the epyllion's valorization of idleness in *Antony and Cleopatra* (1606–7) when, against Plutarch and conventional humanist criticism of the play, he presents Antony's epic failure, his vacillation between the idle sport of Egypt and the political demands and opportunities of Roman values, as something other than failure.

This essay examines Marlowe's *Hero and Leander*, episodes in Spenser's *Fairie Queene* Book 2 and Shakespeare's *Antony and Cleopatra* as texts, despite differences, united in their investments in the topic of idleness and waste. While Spenser condemns waste, undisciplined and unproductive inactivity in the figure of Phaedria, in Maleger's battle with Arthur and in the Bowre of Blisse, Marlowe celebrates profitless pleasure and narrative titillation and frustration as another economy, and Shakespeare constructs a character who moves between the idle pleasures of Egypt and the disciplinary demands of Rome in an interrogation of literary and cultural productivity reminiscent of that undertaken in any number of Tudor minor epics.

A recent study on Renaissance drama argues that it presents economic models that offer alternatives to contemporary economic writing's preoccupation with the balance of trade and the stabilization of currency (Malynes, Mun, Misselden), writings that anticipate the development of classical political economy.[5] In *Performing Economic Thought*, Bradley Ryner offers an appealing way to read drama as actively addressing its context, an appealing argument because it goes against and points beyond current economic criticism that sees literature as simply reflecting its historical-economic setting and adequately explained by it.[6] While such criticism has produced remarkable work that adds significantly to our knowledge of early modern political economy, of the place and importance of economic treatises, and while it also produces readings of texts that have overlapping concerns with affective and social-economic structures, such circumscription tends to be explanatory and under-theorized.[7] In approaching the early modern past as a structure that can be exposed and explained, it remains a kind of structuralist-functionalism that does a disservice to early modern literary work that could resist such containment – work, that is, that leans towards another 'economic' reading.

The argument can be made that another genre, the epyllion, may also contribute to less deterministic modes of economic thinking in the early modern period, that it can not only reflect but actively challenge early modern economic thought on profit, scarcity and exchange. Looking at Marlowe's, Spenser's and Shakespeare's complex reaction to the Ovidian fashion suggests ways in which some important early modern texts are concerned with general economy as theorized by Georges Bataille.

For those unfamiliar with the two notions of economy, restricted economy – the dominant model – assumes an all-encompassing structure of limits and scarcity in which values of individual acquisition and gain prevail against ever threatening loss, the dearth that haunts early modern culture. General economy, on the other hand, is based on Bataille's theory that unproductive expenditure, waste and loss, characterize human life and even, from the most 'general' perspective, the natural or cosmic order.[8] Bataille argues for the unacknowledged, but ubiquitous presence of 'unconditional expenditure', set against the balanced books and economic gains and losses of restricted economy.[9]

While Bataille sees the relationship between the two economies as intertwined, rather than binary oppositions – 'Real life ... knows nothing of purely productive expenditure ... it knows nothing of purely non-productive expenditure either'[10] – his insistence on the persistence of the general economic in human history distinguishes him from nearly all the historicists writing about early modern literature and economy whose selective perspective recognizes only restricted economy and who interpret events and texts in that containing frame. For Bataille, general economy is the ever elusive 'accursed share' in questions of gift, sacrifice, exorbitant expenditure, irrecuperable and unreserved loss. Attending to the interest in unproductive waste in Marlowe, Spenser and Shakespeare gives a less deterministic view of the past. It opens a space for reading at least part of what I would call, after utopian philosopher Ernst Bloch, the incomplete agenda of the past.[11]

The issue of writing and sexuality, of sexual and gender relations, is clearly central to these writers with very different representations, but closely related to it is another key point of departure for Marlowe, Shakespeare and Spenser: their attitudes toward idleness. The 'slacke muse' of Marlowe's translation of Ovid's *Amores* reappears in *Hero and Leander*, and Shakespeare turns away from epic privilege towards the allure of the epyllion, while Spenser's epic muse is immersed in a project of 'endlesse worke'.

Published in 1595, Spenser's *Amoretti and Epithalamion*, with its emphasis on reproductive sex in marriage, constitutes a response to the developing vogue for writing epyllia, to the epyllion's Ovidian sources, to Marlowe himself in his close association with Ovid's *Amores* and, if Spenser knew it, to *Hero and Leander*. Critics routinely contrast Marlowe and Spenser in terms of their classical sources and their opposing views of sexuality and reproductivity: Marlowe's Ovid, erotic license, pleasure and indulgence, are set against Spenser's Virgil, temperance and proper marital relations. The contrast, however overly simplified, is posed in generic terms: Spenser's *Epithalamium* effectively rebukes Marlowe's epyllion and its indifference to conventional unions. Their differences, too, include contrasting notions of literary culture: Spenser's adherence to the Horatian dictum *dulce et utile* against what we could call Marlowe's *dulce et dulce* or, better, *dulce et inutile*.

Spenser might have known Lodge's *Scillaes Metamorphosis* of 1589, which initiated the genre of the epyllion, and he may well have had access to Marlowe's as yet unpublished translation of Ovid's *Amores*, a model for the narrative epyllion as a lyric promoter of sensual indulgence and erotic recreation. It is a text that tacitly mocks early modern poet haters like Gosson, not by supporting Sidney's defence of poetry's edifying qualities but rather by defying their criticism of poetry as idle, self-indulgent, amoral, frivolous and composing poetry that valorizes idleness, the amoral, indulgence itself. One could surely hear Marlowe's voice in Ovid's self-declaration: 'I, Ovid, poet of my wantonness...'[12]

In his own metamorphic *Muiopotmos*, Spenser would certainly be reacting to the fashion of revivifying the erotic Ovid in the epyllia vogue of the 1590s.[13] His *Amoretti* and *Epithalamion* counter erotic pleasure with socially directed marriage and reproduction. But Spenser's *Faerie Queene* sharply addresses the epyllion's valorization of idleness and idle sensuality in Book 2, certainly and conclusively in canto 12, when Guyon encounters Verdant and Acrasia in amorous and emasculating dalliance in the Bowre of Blisse.[14] There are, however, adumbrating and thematically interrelated episodes. One is the directionless boater and mistress of drivel, that great time waster, Phaedria. The other is the skull-helmeted Maleger, captain of the forces that assault the castle of Alma in cantos 9 and 11. Aside from their perversely intemperate actions, what is the relationship between the unpiloted boater and the skull-helmeted captain? Together they represent the allure and the threat of the epyllion for Spenser. Guyon's encounter with Phaedria in canto 6 and Arthur's battle with Maleger in canto 11 are prologue to canto 12 and the epyllion's threat to epic realization for Spenser.

Phaedria ferries Guyon across the river that feeds her territory, Idle Lake. Her loud laughter at her own merriment, her self-pleasuring 'Making sweete solace to herself alone' (6.3.2) and her forward behaviour show her markedly uninterested in the feminine precepts of chastity, silence and obedience and markedly invested in trivial pursuits.[15] In service to Acrasia, she dallies with Cymocles as Acrasia will take her pleasure with Verdant in canto 12, and her song in praise of pleasure, as carefully crafted by Spenser as Despair's mesmerizing appeal to Redcrosse in Book 1, extols a pre-lapsarian version of nature that flourishes without 'toilesome paines', 'fruitlesse labors', the 'needlesse paine' of knightly endeavours, both labour and adventure (15.1, 16.3, 17.4). It is, we could say, less about pleasure than disdain for labour of any type, much like the way she navigates her vessel.

In canto 9 Guyon and Arthur approach Alma's castle, under siege by Maleger's troops, and scatter them to gain entrance. In canto 11 Arthur defends the castle of Alma against Maleger's renewed assault with those legions: the seven deadly sins and the five troops who batter each of the five bulwark-senses supporting the castle. As a kind of rehearsal of canto 12, canto 11 presents an excoriating interrogation of a civil war, an attack against the disciplined senses who fortify the castle by forces that seem a perverted version of them. Spenser describes the 'foolish delights' that attack Smell (2.11.11), the painful 'stinges of carnall lust' and 'dartes of sensuall delight' (11.13) that attack Touch, but especially the 'luxury', the 'unthriftie waste' and the 'ydle superfluity' that go after Taste (11.12.8).

Ungoverned, excessive, wasteful, they are a rude and obstreperous retort to and a 'restlesse siege' upon canto 9's harmoniously orchestrated architecture of the castle (2.11.14). Maleger is roused when Arthur disperses the 'raskell routs' and his steed Spumador tramples the 'monstrous rabblement' (11.8.1). Just as Phaedria exposes his revulsion with undirected pleasure, Spenser's horror of idleness and waste as the incubator of evil is unfurled in Maleger's struggle with Arthur.

Arthur's bafflement in his laborious struggle with Maleger – literature's first zombie, who gains strength with every deadly blow from Arthur's weapons, even from the bare-handed wrestling to which Arthur resorts – ends with his realization that this elemental figure birthed by Mother Earth can only be overcome by removing him from that material element and, let us say, 'wasting' him in another, as, 'having scruzd out of his carrion corse / The lothfull life' (46.2–3), he carries him 'Untill he came unto a standing lake' and delivers Maleger to a watery demise (46.6).

Spenser's labour to condemn idleness and waste in *The Faerie Queene* would align the poem with the epic identity Spenser claimed for himself, and his lyric poems reinforce his judgement on idle and unproductive sexuality on display in so many epyllia. But another way of looking at the epithalamium-epyllion debate as a debate about amoral leisure and virtuous reproductive activity is to look away from the *Epithalamion* and, more fruitfully, to speculate on Marlowe's tacitly polemical response to the 1590 *Faerie Queene*, which, if we accept 1593 as the date of composition for *Hero and Leander*, follows Spenser's epic. Marlowe's poem takes up and exploits the allure that Spenser and his heroes struggle to resist.

In an approach that reveals the limits of economic criticism, Aaron Kitch claims that Marlowe 'uses economic language in *Hero and Leander* to describe sexuality as a form of money to put to "use" in exchange for interest', and that 'Hero, like a golden treasure, has value only in circulation'.[16] Epyllion writers 'employed an economic language to *frame* their erotic subject-matter'; 'Marlowe and other authors of English epyllia *blend* sexuality and economy in order to produce a counter-national genre that regards trade as an agent of peace'.[17]

Against Kitch's restrictive economic reading, Helga Duncan's essay on *Hero and Leander* examines the setting of the text in the Temple of Venus and its careful description of Hero's religious rites and argues that Marlowe's *Hero and Leander* presents a 'libertine' theology and a 'poetics of degeneration' as a specifically heretical alternative to English Reformation and Calvinist doctrines. She links this epyllion's domestic (un)reproductive economy to Bataille's theory of general economy and sees its 'unconventional aesthetics of religion' connected to Bataille on religious experience as constitutively involving ecstasy, self-sacrifice, transgression.[18] To this I would suggest that Marlowe's *Hero and Leander*, like his *Tamburlaine*, *Dido* and *Edward II*, is more than willing to counter contemporary economic understanding of exchange, to defy the restriction Kitch imposes and to entertain a general economy of non-productive expenditure.

Marlowe's epyllion begins in the setting of the Adonia in Sestos, a striking urban location described (although 'wealthy') not as a bustling and industrious city with shops, markets and sites of economic activity but rather as a civic sex club; the Adonia is an unabashed celebration of idleness and voluptuousness. As Helga Duncan puts it, 'The Adonia is put on and financed by the unrestricted spending of resources that have no origin, no purpose even, beyond expenditure itself . . . the city turns out lovers rather than spouses'.[19] Citizens dedicate themselves to nothing more or less than erotic pleasure, and the only work being done seems to be hooking up:

> The men of wealthy Sestos, every year,
> . . .
> kept a solemn feast.
> Thither resorted many a wand'ring guest
> To meet their loves; such as had none at all
> Came lovers home from this great festival.
>
> (91, 92–6)[20]

Sestos' church, the Venus temple, provides inspiration for such idling sensuality in its very foundation: the Venus glasse on the floor illustrates 'the gods in sundrie shapes, / Committing headdie ryots, incest, rapes' (143–4). As Duncan suggests, 'what is most freely expended in Sestos, as the temple images confirm, are bodies'.[21]

Leander, introduced as 'made for amorous play' (88), visits Sestos for no purpose other than that contrived by Marlowe and Musaeus. Marlowe circumscribes the description of Leander with his source Musaeus' tragic trajectory, in which Leander is doomed to drown in swimming the Hellespont:

Amorous *Leander*, beautifull and yoong,
(Whose tragedie divine *Musaeus* soong)
Dwelt at *Abidus*, since him, dwelt there none,
For whom succeeding times make greater mone.

(51–4)

But as Stephen Orgel argues, Marlowe's ending is strategically aborted; he 'deals with the necessary tragic conclusion by omitting it ... This is a work designed to be a fragment'.[22] Chapman's attempts in his continuation to domesticate the work to perform moralizing labours only underscore the role of pleasure, diversion and seduction in Marlowe's poem that he labours to contain. That containment takes the form of dividing the work into sestiads that would dilute or undercut Marlowe's text by incorporating it into Chapman's 'continuation'. Even in the narrative of seduction Marlowe remains committed to expending time. If we think of seduction as a trajectory with sexual consummation as the concrete outcome, Marlowe's characters are deployed to do all they can to frustrate that expectation.[23] Leander's very lengthy rhetorical performance of about 120 lines (199–294, 299–310, 315–28), offering a catalogue of arguments against chastity, is less proleptic (Hero and Leander will have sex) than comically anti-climactic and self-defeating: 'The arguments he us'de, and many more, / Wherewith she yeelded, that was woon before'

(329–30). And Hero, as the founder, president and sole member of Virgins for Venus, wears the signifiers of the erotic – the sleeves her gown bear an image 'Where Venus in her naked glory strove, / To please the careless and disdainfull eies, / Of proud *Adonis*' and a petticoat (kirtle) stained 'with the blood of wretched Lovers slaine' (12–14, 16) – in ways that make over-determination seem a risible understatement.

Marlowe's narrator refers to his 'slacke muse' (72) in introducing and blazoning Leander, revoicing the opening of his earlier translation of Ovid's *Amores* in which both source and translator disingenuously apologize for not writing epic, for writing in elegiac meter and for being 'obliged' to write about love and leisurely sexual pursuits: 'Love slacked my muse and made my numbers soft.'[24] Although it does the work of dislocating any notion of aligning sexuality and gender, Neptune's playful and frivolous hitting on Leander as he swims for his assignation with Hero is a digression that, like Leander's impatient interruption of Neptune's attempt to tell a story about a shepherd, leads nowhere in the seduction narrative. The poem itself ends without concluding, and the printer's added *dessunt nonulla* is one attempt to explain it away, to contain it, or (for Chapman) to invite a continuation; others, like Orgel, find its frustration of readers' expectations intentional and appropriate.

For Georgia Brown, *Hero and Leander* 'self-consciously constructs itself as disorderly: Marlowe's epyllion is a deliberately self-marginalizing text which pursues all kinds of contamination', including genre mixing and the ekphrases which 'get in the way of the narrative . . . and enter the realm of dilation, of leisurely expansion and time-wasting, which is a specifically aesthetic space'.[25] Phaedria's idle pleasure presents an episodic conflict for Spenser; Marlowe's sustained focus on idleness, time-wasting and narrative digression enters social space by refusing labour, effort, profit-making, (restricted) economic value. The 'production' of pleasure is an unacknowledged value that is neither measurable gain nor the profit of an exchange transaction, but immeasurable expenditure and extravagant waste. Brown argues that both in its indebtedness to Ovid and in its self-conscious triviality, the epyllion stands in an oppositional relation to the heroic epic, even as it plays with epic conventions such as digression and ekphrasis. Its authors repeatedly insist on the fluidity of the genders, 'embrac[ing] femininity to construct a hermaphroditic model of literary prowess'. It is also for her a social genre, not only in the sense of creating a literary community against orthodox humanist morality but 'a community defined by the quality of its emotional and aesthetic responses'.[26]

The artifice of the Bowre that Spenser so carefully constructs, condemns and has Guyon obliterate – the allure that Spenser would resist – is embraced by Marlowe. The investment in artifice and allure is Marlowe's achievement, but Spenser's epic work, too, has more than mere moments of compromising narrative and moral errancy that complicate the reading of the text – the chief example being when a fabliau hijacks the epic (Book 3, cantos 9 and 10) and Hellenore abandons the parsimonious Malbecco to dance with the satyrs. If *Hero and Leander* 'is devalued by a critical paradigm which attempts to keep things clean', contamination, generic mixture, instability also characterize *The Faerie Queene* and the less than disciplined pleasures of reading it.[27]

Cutting through Marlowe's debate with Spenser vis-à-vis the epyllion is Shakespeare's *Antony and Cleopatra*. The play is staged and plotted through the perspective of Roman values, even as, like other Shakespearean Roman plays, it scrutinizes that perspective. In *Antony and Cleopatra* that scrutiny comes about through a generic conflict. Epic and epyllion collide fruitfully in the drama as Shakespeare effectively addresses Spenser through Plutarch as problematic moral arbiter and draws elements of the epyllion into the play in disruptive ways. For Plutarch, in North's translation, Antony's life is an exemplary moral tale of a great man undone by a woman's seductive wiles and his own childish passion. He condemns Antony's wasted life in Egypt, 'where he spent and lost in childish sports . . . and idle pastimes the most precious thing a man can spend . . . that is, time'. He harshly describes Antony's corruption: 'the last and extremest mischief of all other (to wit, the love of Cleopatra) lighted on him, who did waken and stir up many vices yet hidden in him . . . and, if any spark of goodness or hope of rising were left him, Cleopatra quenched it straight and made it worse than before'.[28] Much traditional criticism of the play affirms this judgement, including, to refer back to the beginning of this discussion, Vickers' comments in his essay on *otium*: he denounces Antony's vacillation between stern Roman values and Egyptian 'dotage' and broadly claims that 'For Shakespeare as for the Roman and medieval moralists, a stagnant pool summed up the evils of inactivity'.[29]

Philo ventriloquizes Plutarch's comments on Antony's degeneration to time-wasting in Egypt, opening the play when he describes the Roman general's 'turn' from martial pursuits of a 'plated Mars' only intemperately to 'become the bellows and the fan / To cool a gipsy's lust' (1.1.4, 9–10).[30] Antony himself extravagantly fantasizes the fall of the Rome he has, as its general, defended: 'Let Rome in Tiber melt, and the wide arch / Of the ranged empire fall! Here is my space!' (1.1.34–5). This is no frivolous remark and, as when Antony declares himself and the queen nonpareils ('We stand up peerless' [1.1.41]), it invites viewers to imagine a radical loss of what should give ethical-political structure to the play. As for idleness, that important topic for debate in Spenser and Marlowe, Octavius makes it the theme of Antony's Roman report card, seeing him emasculated as he 'wastes / The lamps of night in revel', willing 'To give a kingdom for a mirth' (1.4.4–5, 18) and, leaving Caesar idling, endangering Octavius' political projects: 'Pompey', he states of his chief enemy, 'Thrives in our idleness' (1.4.76). In an apostrophe he urges Antony to 'Leave thy lascivious wassails' (1.4.57). And Antony, sobered by 'a Roman thought' in Act 1, sees 'Ten thousand harms, more than the ills I know, / My idleness doth hatch' (1.2.135–7), and reproaches Cleopatra 'that your royalty / Holds idleness your subject', that she could be 'idleness itself' (1.3.93–5). That reproach, of course, is not Antony's final word.

Shakespeare's critical response to Plutarch also involves matters of the market and economic exchange. Octavius' attachment to market values and political gain is countered by Antony and Cleopatra's idling, their attachment to an unrestricted economy of sporting and self-destructive pursuits. In Act 3, Octavius is scandalized by Antony and Cleopatra's public and extravagant display of their 'unlawful issue': 'I'th' market-place, on a tribunal silvered, / Cleopatra and himself in chairs of gold / Were publicly enthroned' (3.6.3–5). Their regal and openly transgressive display defies his commodifying judgement: their public performance announces their peerlessness and aggressive defiance of the Roman Gaze of Octavius ('I have eyes upon him / And his affairs come to me on the wind' [3.6.62–3]) and of the Rome that Antony would surrender to the Tiber. The conflict between the two economies becomes even clearer when Octavia quietly arrives at Rome in a spectacularly unsuccessful attempt to reconcile Antony and her brother. It lays bare her naiveté and betrayal in the political marriage; the humiliation extends to Octavius, whose intimate attachment to his sister is well noted, as well. He bristles that Octavia has been denied the 'augmented greeting' befitting 'The wife of Antony' (3.6.55, 44): 'But you are come / A market maid to Rome' (3.6.51–2). Octavia, to her brother, is debased by the market but when, in Act 5, Octavius wants to parade Cleopatra in the market as his triumphant product, he disingenuously promises that 'Caesar's no merchant to make prize with you / Of things that merchants sold' (5.2.182–3).

Antony resembles what Spenserian figures like Guyon are empowered to resist. But as many have noted, Shakespeare turns away from Plutarch's moralizing, putting that judgement in the mouths of characters like Octavius who have determining political and military power, who determine the structural outcome of the play, as Caesar defeats Antony and takes control of Cleopatra's kingdom. But that officially recuperated power structure is also thematically emptied out in the drama's conclusion when Cleopatra's suicide eludes Octavius' control. If, as Antony ponders, 'authority melts from me' in his defeat at the battle of Actium (3.13.95), and he and Cleopatra commit suicide, it also melts from congealed classical authority: Antony's putative loss, necessarily tragic, also suggests another realm, another subject economy in which, like the cross-dressing play in which Cleopatra and Antony engage, it does not matter if, as Canidius says of Antony, 'we are women's men' (3.7.69). This other economy is not exactly equipment for living in Rome, but it marks a powerful refusal. Insofar as that other realm becomes a generic matter, the epyllion enters the play's imaginary and collides with epic: Antony's ship, the Antoniad, stands in as an aborted epic, a text that will never be written.

Criticism of the play takes note of the play's ambivalence toward its hero, an ambivalence also at times seen in its ancient source. Plutarch extols Antony's military talent and his 'liberality, who gave all to the soldiers and kept nothing for himself' while, on the other hand, he reproaches him 'for his naughty life; for they (common, noble) did abhor his banquets and drunken feasts he made at unseasonable times, and his extreme wasteful expenses upon vain light huswives'.[31] Of course, that seeming distinction between magnanimity and extravagance is resolved for Plutarch once Cleopatra undermines Antony's better angel. In his introduction to the Arden edition, John Wilders notes the consequences of Shakespeare's transposition of Plutarch's moral judgement to Roman characters: 'As a result of this transposition the unfavourable comments on Antony become distinctively Roman and lose something of the authoritative force and objectivity they had when delivered by Plutarch himself. They become only one of several ways in which he can be assessed'.[32] Janet Adelman also appreciates the inability of the drama to come to rest in an evaluative stance: 'the play insists that we see all the perspectives at once.'[33]

Michael Neill calls for a dialectical reading of *Antony and Cleopatra* in which restricted economy plays a determining role. He notes the opposition between a '"Roman" ideology of identity as a species of property' and an '"Egyptian" ethos of spontaneity and bounty in which consuming, spending, giving and largesse of all kinds are celebrated'.[34] The Roman 'expresses only self-devouring contradiction', while the Egyptian 'figures the inalienable doubleness of things, by which opposites flourish in mysterious complementarity'. In the end, for Neill, 'self-loss, through an erotic version of a familiar Christian paradox, can finally appear as a more profound kind of self-realization'.[35]

Although Neill is clearly attuned to the nuances and complexities of the play, another reading, attentive to Bataille, might read loss and self-loss more radically. In constructing the opposition as dialectical tension, Neill thus re-contains what could be read as a deliberate echo of the epyllion in Shakespeare's play. As a dramatic text that appears some years after the vogue for minor epics in the 1590s has waned, the play gestures toward a general economy of pleasure and (self) waste, strategically deviating from Aeneas' renunciation of Dido in *The Aeneid*. It recalls, instead, Marlowe's *Dido, Queen of Carthage*, where another queen's suicide also refuses a Virgilian evaluation. Marlowe and Shakespeare both revisit Virgilian epic by incorporating the leaning towards excess and waste on display in Tudor minor epics. At the same time, Shakespeare revivifies the epyllion's celebration of the inability to sustain existence in an erotic milieu not as failure but rather as provocation, potentially liberating.

Antony and Cleopatra is a tragedy of generic struggle, a drama in which the epic demands of Roman civilization – a sacrificial symbolic contract of empire – contend with Egyptian decadence, sensuality, gender-bending, the very ethos of the epyllion. Antony and Cleopatra are an Ovidian couple, pleasuring in the milieu of the minor epic, caught in a Virgilian world of stoic discipline. Confronting the haunting authorities of 'Rome', epic models of manliness, renunciation and ambition, the allure of the epyllion is not just generic allure, a turning away from epic privilege; it joins with the allure of a general economy of 'unthriftie waste' and profitless pleasure.

The reading that I offer here has two critical influences, in addition to the inspiration offered by Spenser, Marlowe and

Shakespeare. Georges Bataille's theory of general or unrestricted economy provides a necessary challenge to the limits of current economic criticism. Other interpretive limits are breached if we keep in mind utopian philosopher Ernst Bloch's answer to the question, *Is there a future in the past?* ('Gibt es eine Zukunft in der Vergangenheit?'). To this Bloch responds: Yes, but not if it is contained in the frame of teleological history, as a stream that runs from point A to a point B, predictable and predetermined. Rather, the past is figured as a stream that flows on, with discontinuities and unrealized (for Bloch, revolutionary) hopes, into a possible future, an unfinished agenda.[36] Considering this question of the future in the past, one might ask, What would it mean for economic criticism to take account of Bataille? What is gained by submitting reading to a determining contextual frame; what, in the way of another reading, is lost? In addition, the question I have tried to address: What does the erotic epyllion contribute to Bloch's other agenda, to the unfinished business of the past?

Against the scholarship that reads early modern literature as aligned with a context of proto-capitalist economic structures, we can read in Marlowe's epyllion and Shakespeare's *Antony and Cleopatra* not only the evidence of a literary vogue or a drama with a tragic trajectory but a kind of literature that offers not just subversion of what will become dominant economic structures – the hegemonic restricted economy of frugality, profit, cost and benefit calculation and their attendant social arrangements – but an alternative, a creative rebuff that has the ability to imagine or theorize other economic-social arrangements, then or now or in a future the past may, suggestively, gesture towards.

Notes

1 Brian Vickers, 'Leisure and Idleness in the Renaissance: The Ambivalence of *otium*', *Renaissance Studies: Journal of the Society for Renaissance Studies* 4.1–2 (1990): 1–37, 107–54.

2 The discussion of the word 'epyllion' is long standing. See W. Allen, 'The Epyllion: A Chapter in the History of Literary Criticism', *Transactions of the American Philological Association* 71 (1940): 1–26.

3 As Clark Hulse writes, 'They are by turns artificial, frivolous, arcane, even subversive' (*Metamorphic Verse,* 3). While my essay is concerned with idleness as a social topic in an early modern context of general economy, two recent essays discuss purposelessness and end-lessness in Marlowe's poem in relation to sexuality and rhetoric. See Judith Haber, *Desire and Dramatic Form*, chapter 3 and Lynn Enterline, 'Elizabethan Minor Epics'.

4 See Donno, *Elizabethan Minor Epics* (New York: Columbia University Press, 1963), 10: 'if the dominant tone of Marlowe's poem has insured its generic acceptance by critics, the same cannot be said for Shakespeare's contribution to the vogue ... Shakespeare offered a poem quite different in effect from that of Marlowe, with the result that *Venus and Adonis* ... became the second prototype of the erotic epyllion'.

5 Mark Blaug, *The Early Mercantilists: Thomas Mun (1571–1641), Edward Misselden (1608–1634) and Gerard de Malynes (1586–1623)* (Aldershot: E. Elgar, 1991).

6 Bradley D. Ryner, *Performing Economic Thought: English Drama and Mercantile Writing 1600–1642* (Edinburgh: Edinburgh University Press, 2014).

7 See as good examples of superb early modern scholarship that confines itself to restricted economy and never considers other models Valerie Forman's *Tragicomic Redemptions: Global Economics and the Early Modern English Stage* (Philadelphia: University of Pennsylvania Press, 2008) and Linda Woodbridge's *English Revenge Drama: Money, Resistance, Equality* (Cambridge: Cambridge University Press, 2010).

8 Georges Bataille, 'The Meaning of General Economy' and 'Laws of General Economy', in *The Accursed Share*, 1, trans. Robert Hurley (New York: Zone Books, 1991), 19–41.

9 Benjamin Noys' summary of Bataille is helpful: 'For Bataille, unproductive expenditure is about loss, loss as an end in itself ... a loss that must be as great as possible in order for that

activity to take on its true meaning' (*Georges Bataille: A Critical Introduction* [London: Pluto Press, 2000], 119).

10 Bataille, *Accursed Share*, 12, quoted in Noys, 115.

11 Ernst Bloch, 'Gibt es Zukunft in der Vergangenheit?', radio lecture (1960), in *Tendenz-Latenz-Utopie* (Frankfurt am Main: Suhrkamp Verlag, 1978).

12 *Ovid's Elegies*, II.1, 1 in *Christopher Marlowe, The Complete Poems and Translations*, ed. Stephen Orgel (London: Penguin, 1971), 137.

13 See Andrew Fleck's essay on *Muiopotmos* in this volume.

14 See my 'Guyon's Blush: Shame, Disgust, and Desire in *The Faerie Queene*, Book 2', in *Disgust in Early Modern English Literature*, eds Natalie K. Eschenbaum and Barbara Correll (New York: Routledge, 2016), 38–52.

15 All citations from Edmund Spenser, *The Faerie Queene*, ed. A.C. Hamilton (London: Longman, 2001).

16 Aaron Kitch, *Political Economy and the States of Literature in Early Modern England* (New York: Routledge, 2009), 58.

17 Kitch, 50, 51. He also claims that Shakespeare in *Venus and Adonis* 'approaches sexuality in terms of economic value ... His economic language invokes humanist discourses centred on the potential "profit" of rhetoric and literature for virtuous pursuits in the world', 66. Venus for him becomes a great bargainer and the rhetoric of persuasion is reduced to economic terms.

18 Helga Duncan, '"Headie Ryots" as Reformation: Marlowe's Libertine Poetics', *Early Modern Literary Studies* 12.2 (September, 2006): 2. paras 1–38 (para. 37): http://purl.oclc.org/emls/12-2/duncmarl.htm (accessed 26 December 2015). Her focus, centred on religion, sees Marlowe not as an atheist but as a radical religious reformer, but to claim that Marlowe was, as Bishop Parker scholar, a theology student at Cambridge (para. 8), seems weak evidence of a reform-minded Marlowe rather than someone attracted to experiential extremes. For more on Bataille and religion, less bound to reform, see essays in *Negative Ecstasies*, eds Jeremy Biles and Kent L. Brintnall (New York: Fordham University Press, 2015).

19 Duncan, para. 23.

20 All quotations from *Hero and Leander* are from *English Sixteenth-Century Verse: An Anthology*, ed. Richard S. Sylvester (New York: W.W. Norton, 1974), the only edition I know of that reproduces Marlowe's 818-line text without Chapman's divisions into sestiads or the addition of 'Arguments'.

21 Duncan, para. 24.

22 Stephen Orgel, 'Introduction' to Christopher Marlowe, *The Complete Poems and Translations*, ed. Orgel (New York: Penguin, 1980), xvii.

23 Judith Haber notes Marlowe's 'aesthetic of pointlessness', and *Hero and Leander*'s strategic 'disruption of end-directed narrative . . . equivalent to end-directed sexuality' (39, 43).

24 Elegy I, Book I, in *The Collected Poems of Christopher Marlowe*, eds Patrick Cheney and Brian J. Striar (Oxford: Oxford University Press, 2006), 34.

25 Georgia Brown, 'Marlowe's Poems and Classicism', in *The Cambridge Companion to Christopher Marlowe*, ed. Patrick Cheney (Cambridge, 2004), 117.

26 Brown, *Redefining Elizabethan Literature*, 108, 175.

27 Ibid., 173.

28 Thomas North, *Shakespeare's Plutarch*, ed. T.J.B. Spencer (London: Puffin, 1964), 203, 199.

29 Vickers, 142.

30 All citations from *Antony and Cleopatra*, ed. John Wilders (London: Bloomsbury, 1995).

31 North, 178, 183.

32 Wilders, 59.

33 Janet Adelman, *The Common Liar: An Essay on Antony and Cleopatra* (New Haven: Yale University Press, 1973), 95.

34 Michael Neill, 'Introduction' to *The Oxford Shakespeare: Anthony and Cleopatra* (Oxford: Oxford University Press, 2001), 120–1.

35 Ibid., 102–3.

36 Bloch, 'Gibt es Zukunft in der Vergangenheit?' I offer the following translation: 'The question is, is the past not only the tradition to which we relate in a purely reactionary sense, or

does it also contain utopian elements; does it offer a future in the past. The question is, does the utopian – if it must not be abstract, merely wishful thinking, empty daydreaming, just tinkering with the unlikeliest possibilities – only remain confined to a stream that flows from the past into the now, into the present, or does it rather not stop at all but rather flow on, further, into the future . . . If we could combine tradition and past, utopia and future into a definition of revolution as the turning toward something better, brighter, that definition would be this: tradition is the revolution of the departed, revolution is the tradition of the future'.

APPENDIX

Chronological list of narrative poems mentioned in this volume

Thomas Lodge, *Scillaes Metamorphosis* (1589)
Edmund Spenser, *Muiopotmos* (1590)
William Shakespeare, *Venus and Adonis* (1593)
Thomas Heywood, *Oenone and Paris* (1594)
Shakespeare, *The Rape of Lucrece* (1594)
Thomas Campion, *Umbra* (1595/1619)
Christopher Marlowe, *Hero and Leander* (1598)
John Marston, *The Metamorphosis of Pigmalions Image* (1598)
John Weever, *Faunus and Melliflora* (1600)
Francis Beaumont, *Salmacis and Hermaphroditus* (1602)
George Chapman, *The Divine Poem of Musaeus: Hero and Leander* (1616)
Phineas Fletcher, *Venus and Anchises: Brittain's Ida* (1628)

INDEX

Adelman, Janet 250
Alighieri, Dante 48, 61
Altman, Joel 6, 58, 61, 66
Ariosto, Lodovico 75–6, 86, 90
Arkin, Samuel 34
Augustine 54, 58

Barkan, Leonard 14, 167, 180, 181
Barret, J.K. 132
Barthes, Roland 25, 39
Bataille, George 13–14, 185, 239–40, 244, 251–2, 253, 254
Baumlin, Tita French 169
Beaumont, Francis 3, 7–8, 9, 10, 106, 109, 146, 164, 257
Berger, Harry Jr. 54
Berlant, Lauren 183
Blanchard, W. Scott 230
Bloch, Ernst 240, 252
Booth, Roy 208
Braden, Gordon 211
Bromley, James 221
Brown, Georgia 5, 14, 170, 177, 180, 230, 233, 246
Bruni, Leonardo 55
Burrow, Colin 15, 51, 61
Burton, William 101–2
Bush, Douglas 45, 67, 89, 137

Callimachus 213
Cambridge, University of 10, 195

Campbell, Marion 228
Campion, Thomas 10, 12, 167–88
Casaubon, Isaac 216–17
Catullus 91, 174
Chapman, George 10, 100, 227–9, 235, 245–6, 255, 257
Cheney, Patrick 15, 94, 117, 235
Cicero 26, 39, 53–5, 57, 63, 121, 237, 255
classicism, early modern 1–14
  and homosexuality 180–2
  and mercantile capitalism 207–52
  and pedagogy 1–14, 46–56, 64, 65, 84–6, 90, 91, 93, 98, 115, 117–37, 146–7, 153, 159, 164, 165, 166, 167–70, 180–1, 187, 190–202, 232
Clement, Francis 28
Clody, Michael C. 36
complaint poetry 6, 77, 79, 154–7, 159, 164, 166

Dekker, Thomas 151
Dinshaw, Carolyn 178
Dolven, Jeff 15, 56, 93, 120–1
Donaldson, Ian 67
Dubrow, Heather 64, 68, 117, 118
Duncan, Helga 244–5

Edelman, Lee 183
Ellis, James 4–5, 15, 93, 154, 159, 163, 164, 166, 171, 182, 188, 202, 232
Enterline, Lynn 34, 35, 42, 43, 44, 62, 64, 65, 86, 90, 91, 115, 116, 117, 122–3, 125, 138, 139, 159, 170, 181, 183, 187, 195, 253
epyllion, difficulty defining 6, 9, 76, 170, 253
   and civic space 12, 23, 38, 72, 159–63, 211–31
   and cosmopolitanism 207–56
   and digression 3–4, 17, 34, 87, 104, 238, 246–7
   and ekphrasis 108–14
   and gender fluidity 5, 7,–8, 177–9, 247
   and genre 6–9, 11, 16, 71–94, 136, 145, 212–15, 229–30, 237–56
   and metamorphosis 125, 182–4, 154–5, 167–8, 182–3
   and *otium* 237–8
   and poetic community 1–15, 95–118, 143–66, 177–8
   and poetic competition 97–114
   and prostitution 150, 162, 224–7
   and rape 12, 21–70, 119–42, 175–84, 226
   and same-sex erotics 117, 168, 176–84
   and social critique 5, 9, 11, 15, 55 160–3, 170, 181, 210–11
   and *translatio imperii* 86–7

Erasmus 32, 41, 57, 115, 123, 135–6
Estienne, Henri 216–17
excess, rhetorical, stylistic and sexual 4, 13, 14, 33, 46, 105, 121, 171–5, 178–9, 182, 225, 237–56

female complaint 7–8, 16, 77–9, 90, 91, 93
Fineman, Joel 34, 43, 64, 137
Fletcher, Phineas 9, 10, 12–13, 189–204
Forman, Simon 133
Freeman, Elizabeth 168, 178
Fumaroli, Marc 53–61, 65, 66

Garter, Bernard 95
Gascoigne, George 151
Gismond of Salerne 151
Gosson, Stephen 101, 241
grammar school
   humanist 2, 4–5, 54, 56–7, 123, 125–6, 159, 170,
   and *imitatio* 5, 11, 66, 71–94, 103–18
   and rhetoric 4–6, 11, 46, 48, 53–7, 90, 91, 98, 115, 119, 121, 125, 136, 170, 202
Gregerson, Linda 101
Greville, Fulke 56
Guy-Bray, Stephen 77, 116, 174, 180

Haber, Judith 17, 114, 221, 235, 253, 255
Hercules Gallicus 23, 28–31, 41

INDEX

Heywood, Thomas 7, 8–9, 10, 11, 71–94, 257
Homer 25, 108, 212–16, 228
Horace 22, 26–7, 98–100, 103, 116
Hulse, Clark 6, 76, 90, 117, 118, 159, 160, 253
Hutson, Lorna 47, 65

Inns of Court 2, 4, 12, 54, 91, 98, 143–66, 168, 170
  Gray's Inn 10, 151,
  Inner Temple 3, 151, 166
  Lincoln's Inn 3, 143, 147

Jacobson, Miriam 209
James, Heather 68, 93, 115
Jardine, Lisa 122
Jed, Stephanie 40, 42
Jonson, Ben 13, 177, 207–11, 224, 230

Kahn, Coppélia 40, 43, 137
Kahn, Victoria 56
Kastor, Frank S. 191
Keach, William 73, 115, 166, 232
Kiernan, Pauline 171
Kitch, Aaron 243–4
Keilen, Sean 125,
Kerrigan, John 16

Livy 33, 42, 120, 133
Lodge, Thomas 3, 7, 10, 12, 143–66, 241, 257
  Alarum against Usurers 144, 147–52
  Glaucus Complaint 154, 157

London 1–2, 9, 12, 13, 133, 143–66, 207–36, 229–30
  and Alexandria 211
Lucian 28–31, 41
Lucretius 172–3
Lyly, John 189–9
Lyric, female audience for 48–50

Marlowe, Christopher 3–4, 7, 9–10, 13, 14, 15, 47, 87, 96–8, 100, 104, 107–9, 113, 145, 168, 173, 176–7, 180, 207–36, 237–48, 252
Marshall, Cynthia 171, 185
Marston, John 116, 145, 164, 257
masculinity, differing views of 4–6, 12, 78–87, 153–63, 167–88, 189–206
Maslen, R.W. 156, 159
Maus, Katherine Eisaman 34, 64, 137
Meres, Francis 72, 89, 97
Menon, Madhavi 183, 195
Mirror for Magistrates, The 119–20
Musaeus 1, 13, 208–21, 227–9, 231, 233, 245, 257

Narcissus 8, 105, 171, 185, 196
Nashe, Thomas 10, 13, 151, 227–31
Neill, Michael 250–1

Ong, Walter 138, 181, 187
Orgel, Stephen 245, 246

Ovid 1–6, 10–11, 23, 33, 36–9, 42, 62, 67, 72–3, 75, 81, 85–7, 89, 93, 94, 100, 104–6, 108, 109, 112, 114, 117, 121–2, 135, 159, 160, 167–8, 176, 177, 181, 213–14, 223, 233, 238–9, 247, 251
  Amores 233, 240–1, 246
  Ars amatoria 2, 169
  Fasti 133
  Heroides 7, 75, 90, 82, 90, 92, 214, 233,
  Metamorphoses 4, 7, 25–6, 38, 87, 106, 125, 130, 134, 144–5, 168–9, 172, 175, 182–3, 185, 191, 196–7, 201, 213–14, 222, 233
Oxford, University of 3, 143, 147, 152, 155, 164

Painter, William 120
Paragone 11, 110–14
pastoral 8–9, 71–94, 97, 173
pedagogy, humanist 2–3, 11, 12, 85–6, 115, 120–3, 126, 130, 169–70, 191–9, 202
  curriculum 5, 12, 90, 173, 224–5
  and sexuality 115, 125, 167–71, 181, 191–202
  and teleology 12, 195
Petowe, Henry 229
Petrarch 7, 43, 48, 61, 64, 105, 115, 117, 159, 162, 170–1, 175
  Petrarchism 7, 105–61, 162, 159–60, 170–1, 175, 194
Plutarch 9, 114, 133, 238, 247–50

Pontano, Giovanni 56
Poole, Joshua 28
Puttenham, George 22, 27, 29, 30, 100

Quintilian 39, 51–2, 57, 67, 115

Rambuss, Rick 117, 171, 183, 203
Rebhorn, Wayne 39, 40, 41
rhetoric
  and the aesthetic 6, 11, 14, 15, 21–2, 34, 105, 121, 244, 246–7, 255
  and anthropology 6, 66
  copia 4, 14, 15, 32–3, 115, 136, 178, 181–2, 270
  ekphrasis 14, 49, 108–14, 118, 223, 247
  enargeia and *energeia* 27, 41, 100
  and erotic *suasoria* 7, 169–71
  and force 11, 21–39, 57, 100, 182
  forensic 2–3, 45, 47, 56–7
  imitatio 2, 5, 11–12, 72, 76, 84–9, 103–4, 122–37, 160
  Orpheus as figure for 11, 21–44
  and poetics 21–118, 202
  school training in 4, 9, 38, 56–7, 170
Ryner, Bradley 239

Scaliger, Julius 53, 216
Scott, William 103–4, 111
sexuality

and epyllia 4–5, 12–13, 143–206, 221, 227, 240–3, 246–7
and hearing 197–8
and pedagogy 195–206
and reading 12, 178–81, 197–202
and reproduction 13, 193, 202–3, 241
and shattering 168, 176–7, 181–3
and teleology 17, 114, 183, 221, 227, 235, 243, 253, 255
Shakespeare, William
  Antony and Cleopatra 9, 238, 247–52
  Cymbeline 131–37
  Hamlet 15, 52, 55, 65
  Love's Labour's Lost 56
  The Merchant of Venice 14, 56
  Othello 48–9, 58
  Rape of Lucrece 2, 4, 7, 8, 9, 10–11, 21–70, 109, 119–42, 257
  Taming of the Shrew 56
  Two Gentlemen of Verona 35
  Venus and Adonis 2, 4, 7–8, 11, 12, 72, 74–5, 84, 96–9, 105–8, 112–14, 146, 161–3, 167–206, 238, 257
Sherman, William 122
Sidney, Philip 27–8, 53, 56, 100–3, 136, 148, 159, 177, 241
Skinner, Quentin 56–8
Smith, Bruce 180
Spenser, Edmund
  Epithalamion 240–3
  The Faerie Queene 9, 10, 11, 54, 59–60, 73–94, 101, 190–1, 197, 222–3, 238–43, 247
  Muiopotmos 10, 104–5, 111–12, 238, 241, 257
Stanuvukovic, Goran 175
Stapylton, Robert 216–17
Starks-Estes, Lisa 175, 188
Stewart, Alan 181

teleology 12, 183, 188, 195
Theocritus 213–14, 223
Tudeau-Clayton, Margaret 16

ventriloquism 7, 42, 159, 248
Veronese, Guarino 135
Vickers, Brian 237–8, 248
Vickers, Nancy 33, 34, 43, 64, 137
Virgil 1, 5–6, 9, 13, 25–6, 71–94, 108–11, 121, 123, 216, 237, 241, 251
  Aeneid 5, 77–80, 82–5, 92, 108, 202, 251
  Eclogues 77–8, 83
  Georgics 25, 44

Walsall, John 99, 115
waste 9, 13–14, 136–7, 201, 237–56
Weaver, William 4–5, 42, 47, 84, 90, 92, 115, 125, 160, 163, 170, 181, 191, 234
Webbe, William 27
Whetstone, George 114
Whigham, Frank 39
Wilders, John 250
Wilson, Thomas 24–5, 29–30

Yarmouth 13, 229–31